GENDER AND CONVERSION NARRATIVES IN THE NINETEENTH CENTURY

Gender and Conversion Narratives in the Nineteenth Century

German Mission at Home and Abroad

KIRSTEN RÜTHER
University of Vienna, Austria

ANGELIKA SCHASER
Universität Hamburg, Germany

JACQUELINE VAN GENT
University of Western Australia

Routledge
Taylor & Francis Group
LONDON AND NEW YORK

First published 2015 by Ashgate Publishing

Published 2016 by Routledge
2 Park Square, Milton Park, Abingdon, Oxon OX14 4RN
711 Third Avenue, New York, NY 10017, USA

First issued in paperback 2017

Routledge is an imprint of the Taylor & Francis Group, an informa business

British Library Cataloguing in Publication Data
A catalogue record for this book is available from the British Library

The Library of Congress has cataloged the printed edition as follows:
Rüther, Kirsten.
Gender and Conversion Narratives in the Nineteenth Century: German Mission at Home and Abroad / by Kirsten Rüther, Angelika Schaser and Jacqueline Van Gent.
pages cm
Includes bibliographical references and index.
1. Missions – Germany – History – 19th century. 2. Missions, German – Australia – History – 19th century. 3. Missions, German – South Africa – History – 19th century. 4. Conversion – Christianity – Social aspects – History – 19th century. 5. Women – Australia – Social conditions – 19th century. 6. Women – South Africa – Social conditions – 19th century. I. Schaser, Angelika. II. Van Gent, Jacqueline. III. Title.
BV2950.R88 2015
248.2'409034 – dc23 2015005737

ISBN 13: 978-1-138-09962-3 (pbk)
ISBN 13: 978-1-4724-4923-8 (hbk)

Contents

List of Figures

Notes on the Authors

Kirsten Rüther is Professor of History and Societies in Africa at the Department of African Studies at the University of Vienna. Her main areas of research include Christianisation and colonialism, health and popular culture, and the study of family and kinship. She has published on Protestant mission activities in South Africa, African Religion and health-related topics. Currently she is working on an anthology of African life histories and on a transcontinental and transgenerational family history. Recent publications include: 'The King, the Missionary and the Missionary's Daughter', in *Journal of Southern African Studies* (jointly with P. Delius), and 'Der Streit um Englisch als Unterrichtsfach in lutherischen Missionsschulen Südafrikas (1895–1910). Impulse für eine Geschichte der Resonanzen' in R. Habermas and R. Hölzl (eds), *Mission global: Eine Verflechtungsgeschichte seit dem 19. Jahrhundert.*

Angelika Schaser is Professor for Modern History at the Universität Hamburg. From 2004 to 2010 she was a member of the DFG research group *Self-Narratives in Transcultural Perspective* at the Freie Universität Berlin. She has published on nation and gender in the history of the nineteenth and twentieth centuries as well as on religious conversions, minorities, collective memories, history of historiography, and auto/biographical research.

Jacqueline Van Gent is a historian at The University of Western Australia and Chief Investigator with the ARC Centre of Excellence for the History of Emotions (1100–1800). She has published on Protestant missions, indigenous people and gender in colonial Australia and the early modern world, as well as on emotions, gender and power in the early modern Nassau-Orange family and Scandinavian early modern cultural history. Her publications include *Magic, Body and the Self in Eighteenth-Century Sweden* and *Governing Masculinities in the Early Modern Period: Regulating Selves and Others* (edited with S. Broomhall, Ashgate Publishing). Forthcoming publications are *The Indigenous Evangelist in British Empire History 1750–1940: Questions of Authority* (co-authored with P. Brock, N. Etherington and G. Griffiths); *Gender, Power and Identity in the Early Modern Nassau Family, 1580–1814* (co-authored with S. Broomhall, Ashgate Publishing); 'Emotions and Conversion', Special Issue of *Journal of Religious History* (co-edited with S. Young) and 'Gender, objects and emotions in Scandinavian history', Special Issue of *Journal of Scandinavian History* (co-edited with R. Toivo).

Notes on the Authors

Acknowledgements

It all began in Berlin, where we met for the first time for a joint panel discussion in 2008. At the time, Kirsten Rüther held a one-year guest Professorship in Modern Global History at the Friedrich-Meinecke-Institut of the Freie Universität Berlin. Angelika Schaser, based at the Department of History of the Universität Hamburg, was a member of a research group on 'Self-Narratives in Transcultural Perspective' (2004–2010) funded by the German National Research Foundation (Deutsche Forschungsgemeinschaft, DFG). Jacqueline Van Gent, who had come all the way from the University of Western Australia, was invited to speak again at one of the research group's conferences in 2012. This conference showcased the group's methodological approach of parallel readings of self-narratives from different cultural-social contexts, a method that we further develop in this book. Over the years the research group became a vital focal point for our interactions, and indeed, our book would not have been possible without the particular engagement and support of Claudia Ulbrich (Freie Universität Berlin), the director of that research group. She helped us connect and encouraged us to work on conversions in comparative perspective.

In the following years we cooperated, juggling our various academic timetables and the geographical distances between us to keep in touch and learnt by experience what it meant to write a book not as a volume with three editors but as joint authors. IT and electronic media were critical in facilitating our conversations, but they never made up for actual meetings, which we enjoyed the most and which also facilitated the development of our arguments most effectively. We met in Berlin, Erfurt and Vienna. It was there that we advanced our manuscript to the almost final stage, weaving together the strands and paths that we had developed over the years.

In those years since 2008 each of us has learnt a lot about doing collaborative research. Not only did we benefit from additional and respective expertise, we also learnt that research really is a process. We regard what we have produced here as a beginning, an important step for our own conversations, at any rate, but a beginning rather than an end in itself. We also learnt how much sense it makes to combine our areas of specialisation – and noticed in the process of sharing, debating and parallel reading that we were often challenged to rethink the very basis of our original expertise so as make it intelligible to the others.

We would like to thank our translator and editor Pamela Selwyn in Berlin, Lesley O'Brien in Perth for her indexing work and our student assistants Carolin Knoop in Vienna and Nils Kühne in Hamburg. We are also grateful to our anonymous reviewers, who made valuable suggestions for improving the manuscript. And we were delighted to receive prompt permission from the Berliner Missionswerk and the Brüdergemeine Herrnhut to print here visual material from their archives. Last but not least, we would like to thank Erika Gaffney and Emily Yates from Ashgate Publishing, and most particularly Amanda Buxton for her support during the publication process.

Hamburg, Perth, and Vienna, August 2014

Introduction

Religious conversion occurred and continues to occur all over the world, changing the ways in which people live and interact with one another and changing the religions themselves. Conversions often had far-reaching social and especially gender-specific consequences, or reflected changes that had already taken place. Individual persons, couples, families and/or groups set themselves apart by converting, and hoped that it would help them to integrate into existing, newly emerging or changing communities – and all of this at times when major changes were in the air, frequently as yet intangible to those who experienced them – 'at home and abroad' in a mid-nineteenth-century 'world in motion'.

Conversion, which played a key role in structuring religious and societal change globally, had its own locally and regionally specific expressions and was integrated into both small and large-scale social dynamics. Conversions are thus eminently suitable for study as globally integrated and globality-producing phenomena. Proceeding from our own diverse regional research areas, this book approaches conversion processes – and their narratives – that took shape in Europe, Australia and Africa, to speak in terms of continents and greater regions.[1] We would like to explore what conversions and their narratives had in common at a time when reciprocal relationships and dependencies were becoming permanently more intensive, and how they related to one another, but also how they existed in their own right, and how in the process converts translated the alien and the new into something all their own.

As a rule, conversions were strongly embedded in society, politics, culture, kinship and the family. They involved women and men, old and young, mothers, fathers, wives and husbands, widowers, widows, orphans, sons, adopted children, uncles, aunts, sisters and brothers, but also rulers and dependants, young men, workers and patriarchs and others in social domains characterised, among other things, by the interactions between different religions or confessions. As

[1] Relevant preliminary studies include Kirsten Rüther, *The Power Beyond: Mission Strategies, African Conversion and the Development of a Christian Culture in the Transvaal* (Münster: Lit, 2001); Angelika Schaser, 'Schreiben um dazuzugehören. Konversionserzählungen im 19. Jahrhundert', in *Selbstzeugnis und Person*, ed. Claudia Ulbrich, Hans Medick and Angelika Schaser (Cologne, Weimar and Vienna: Böhlau, 2012), 381–98; and Jacqueline Van Gent, 'Changing Concepts of Embodiment and Illness among the Western Arrernte at Hermannsburg Mission', in *Indigenous Peoples, Christianity and Religious Change*, ed. P. Brock (Leiden: Brill, 2005), 227–48.

diverse as the social strata and social roles of converts may have been, both the sources and the secondary literature tend to focus on conversions by men. Upon closer scrutiny, the gender of converts proves to have been a central relational category, one that structured conversion processes as clearly as it did processes of societal change.

Religious Conversions: State of the Art

Theologians, sociologists and historians have tended to study conversions to or within Christianity mainly as individual cases for specific regions or groups. Historical research on conversion long existed in its own small niche, largely unnoticed by the rest of the profession. Recently, however, it has started to gain more attention, especially among historians of the early modern period.[2] In this instance, scholars have mainly studied conversions from Judaism to Christianity and from one Christian confession to another.[3] There has been far less research on conversions in the nineteenth century. Conversion to Islam has also met with growing interest of late.[4] Globalisation is inherent to Christianity, since the

---

[2] Ute Lotz-Heumann, Jan-Friedrich Missfelder and Matthias Pohlig (eds), *Konversion und Konfession in der Frühen Neuzeit* (Gütersloh: Gütersloher Verlagshaus, 2008); Ines Peper, *Konversionen im Umkreis des Wiener Hofes um 1700* (Cologne, Weimar and Vienna: Böhlau, 2010); Angelika Schaser, 'Inclusion et exclusion: La recherche sur les conversions religieuses en Allemagne à l'époque moderne', in *Religion ou confession: Un bilan franco-allemand sur l'époque moderne (XVI*[e]*–XVIII*[e] *siècles)*, ed. Philippe Buttgen and Christophe Duhamelle (Paris: Édition de la Maison des Sciences de l'Homme 2010), 577–94.

[3] Elisheva Carlebach, *Divided Souls: The Convert Critique and the Culture of Ashkenaz, 1750–1800* (New York: Leo Baeck Institute, 2003); Maria-Cristina Pitassi and Daniela Solfaroli Camillocci (eds), *Les Modes de la conversion confessionelle à l'Epoque moderne: Autobiographie, altérité et construction des identités religieuses* (Florence: Leo S. Olschki, 2010); Magdalena Teter, 'Jewish Conversions to Catholicism in the Polish-Lithuanian Commonwealth of the Seventeenth and Eighteenth Centuries', *Jewish History* 17, 3 (2003): 257–83. On early modern conversions, see, for example, Lance Gabriel Lazar, 'Negotiating Conversions: Catechumens and the Family in Early Modern Italy', in *Piety and Family in Early Modern Europe*, ed. Marc R. Forster and Benjamin J. Kaplan (Aldershot: Ashgate, 2005), 152–77; Marilyn J. Harran, *Luther on Conversion: The Early Years* (Ithaca: Cornell University Press, 1983), 25; James Muldoon, 'Introduction', in *Varieties of Religious Conversion in the Middle Ages*, ed. James Muldoon (Gainesville: University Press of Florida, 1997).

[4] Tijana Krstić, *Contested Conversions to Islam: Narratives of Religious Change in the Early Modern Ottoman Empire* (Stanford: Stanford University Press, 2011); Tijana Krstić, 'Illuminated by the Light of Islam and the Glory of the Ottoman Sultanate: Self-Narratives of Conversion to Islam in the Age of Confessionalization', *Comparative Studies in Society and History* 51 (2009): 35–63; Eric R. Dursteler, *Renegade Women: Gender, Identity and*

various Christian churches are convinced that they represent the 'true religion', and are thus active on an international level to persuade people to share this conviction.[5] For that reason, conversions and the ways they are narrated are especially suitable objects for the study of transnational, global developments.[6] A look at other religions suggests how strongly the Christian conversion narrative has shaped the literature, and how very much we need new definitions, since both the rules and rituals of conversion and the narratives about it differ. A more recent study that treats conversion from a global perspective over the long period from 1800 to 2000 makes this very clear.[7] That is why the large-scale Swiss research project 'Crossing Religious Borders: Studies on Conversion and Religious Belonging', which focuses on today's globalised world, dispenses with a general definition or theoretical framework in order not to distort the participating scholars' 'view of the multifarious nature of the phenomena'.[8]

Like many other scholars, we question the conventional notion of conversion as an expression of growing individualisation.[9] According to our basic understanding, conversions are the expression of religious, cultural, social, gender-specific and politico-economic interactions.[10] We can therefore

Boundaries in the Early Modern Mediterranean (Baltimore: Johns Hopkins University Press, 2011); Monika Wohlrab-Sahr, *Konversionen zum Islam in Deutschland und den USA* (Frankfurt am Main and New York: Campus 1999); Monika Wohlrab-Sahr, 'Conversion to Islam between Syncretism and Symbolic Battle', *Social Compass* 46 (1999): 351–62.

5 Kirsten Rüther, 'Christianisierung', in *Enzyklopädie der Neuzeit*, vol. 2, ed. Friedrich Jäger (Stuttgart: Metzler, 2005), 741–57.

6 Jürgen Osterhammel, 'Transnationale Gesellschaftsgeschichte: Erweiterung oder Alternative?' *Geschichte und Gesellschaft* 27 (2001): 464–79, 473; Pamela J. Stewart and Andrew Strathern, 'Reinforcing comparative dimensions', in *Religious and Ritual Change: Cosmologies and Histories*, ed. Pamela J. Stewart and Andrew Strathern (Durham: Carolina Academic Press, 2009), 329–52, 337.

7 David Lindenfeld and Miles Richardson (eds), *Beyond Conversion and Syncretism: Indigenous Encounters with Missionary Christianity, 1800–2000* (New York and Oxford: Berghahn, 2012), 2.

8 Wolfgang Lienemann, 'Einführung' to *Religiöse Grenzüberschreitungen: Studien zu Bekehrung, Konfessions- und Religionswechsel*, Studien zur Außeneuropäischen Christentumsgeschichte, vol. 20, ed. Christine Lienemann-Perrin and Wolfgang Lienemann (Wiesbaden: Harrassowitz, 2012), 3–37, here p. 14.

9 'Individualisierung durch christliche Mission?/ Individualization through Christian mission activity?' International conference, Erfurt University, April 25–28, 2012. Despite this title, the panel discussions established that Christian missions and conversions did not necessarily produce the 'individual' and that the concept of the 'individual' deserves more critical attention.

10 With this open definition, we follow the recent tendencies in conversion studies that, proceeding from the research on religious conversions, have been calling for more complex definitions (Lindenfeld and Richardson 2012) or, rather, defining the term conversion

examine conversions side-by-side that occurred from various religious milieus into various religious communities and social milieus and moreover contributed to diversifying religious landscapes as well as stabilising or transforming power relations within them. We are not primarily concerned with explaining individual motives for conversion. Even though motives have to be taken into consideration, the 'how' of the process interests us more than the 'why'. Thus on an initial level, we understand mid-nineteenth-century conversion as a social reorientation within the context of a plural range of religions that was at once voluntary and other-determined, and that kept elements of the former religion available for the new religious affiliation. On a second level, we understand conversion as a contribution to the further differentiation of religious landscapes, in which relations of power and dependency were negotiated, balanced and consolidated in the course of changes of religion. In this way we can examine various conversion scenarios that require specific explanation and, proceeding from them, abstract and conceptualise processes of conversion.

We know about changes of religion because of surviving conversion accounts in which the converts themselves or other people talked and wrote about them. In this connection conversion narratives played an important role on all three continents studied here, but they varied widely. The European conversion narrative can be traced back to the earliest days of Christianity, but assumed its particular character after the Reformation. For the first time since the Eastern Schism, intra-Christian competition took on a new dynamism when the Catholic Church and the papacy were forced to confront the emerging Protestant churches. Catholic conversion narratives in nineteenth-century Europe continued to be influenced by this tradition. Reformation-era narratives were adopted in a very particular way by the Moravians, who developed a form of autobiographical writing between the conversion narrative and the curriculum vitae as an educational example.[11] Although missionaries from

far more broadly. See, for example, Heinz-Gerhard Haupt, 'Politische Konversion in historischer Perspektive: Methodische und empirische Überlegungen', in *Zeitperspektiven. Studien zu Kultur und Gesellschaft. Beiträge aus der Geschichte, Soziologie, Philosophie und Literaturwissenschaft*, ed. Uta Gerhardt (Wiesbaden: Franz Steiner, 2003), 267–304; Lewis R. Rambo, *Understanding Religious Conversion* (New Haven: Yale University Press, 1993), 3; Todd Weir, 'Between Colonial Violence and Socialist Worldview: The Conversions of Ernst Däumig', *German History* 28 (2010): 143–66; Kenneth Mills and Anthony Grafton (eds), *Old Worlds and New* (Rochester: University of Rochester Press, 2003).

[11] Gesine Carl and Angelika Schaser, 'Konversionsberichte des 17. bis 19. Jahrhunderts als Selbstzeugnisse gelesen: Ergebnisse und Forschungsperspektiven' in Digitale Quellenedition Konversionserzählungen, http://www.geschkult.fu-berlin.de/e/konversionen/ergebnisse/beitraege/Konversionsberichte_als_Selbstzeugnisse_gelesen.pdf?1369918255 [2013]; Calvin B. Kendall et al. (eds), *Conversion to Christianity from Late Antiquity to the Modern Age: Considering the Process in Europe, Asia and the Americas*

Europe were familiar with these conversion narratives and used them in their reports on Australia and Africa, they altered the narratives by adapting them to the various local historical contexts as well as with respect to their own roles and to reader expectations.

Conversion Narratives and Gender in Europe, Australia and South Africa

The first chapter of the present volume introduces those characteristics of nineteenth-century European conversion narratives that have been noted by literary scholars in particular.[12] The narratives matter greatly for this study because they provide a common starting point, and a common theme, for the ensuing analysis. From a historian's perspective, however, and worth noting, it is the regional and temporal specificity of these narratives that is especially striking, not their stereotypical elements. The two chapters that follow use Australian and African case studies to explore the peculiarities of the genre of the conversion narrative in their respective contexts. All three chapters inquire into the significance of gender as a category that proved constitutive of the respective narratives and societies studied.

In Europe, the Christian churches had become increasingly differentiated since the sixteenth-century Reformation. Alongside Catholicism, which had dominated in central Europe up to that time, new Protestant churches arose that claimed to be the sole representatives of divine truth. The Catholic Church used this fragmentation of Protestantism to bolster its unique claim to authority and tradition. Only the institution that embodied the direct succession to Saint Peter could guarantee ecclesiastical and divine order. Despite irenicist, interdenominational and ecumenical aspirations within the various Christian churches and efforts at union among the Protestant churches, the situation in Europe was largely marked by clear efforts at disassociation as well as defamation campaigns. Even if the different confessions met in everyday life and the number of so-called mixed marriages increased in the German territories, for example,[13] the confessions tended to live parallel rather than shared lives well into the twentieth century.

(Minneapolis: CEMH, 2009); Katherine M. Faull (ed.), *Moravian Women's Memoirs. Their Related Lives 1750–1820* (Syracuse, NY: Syracuse University Press, 1997).

[12] Michael Sheringham, 'Conversion and Turning Points', in *Encyclopedia of Life Writing*, vol. 1, ed. Margaretta Jolly (London: Fitzroy-Dearborn, 2001), 233–4.

[13] Tillmann Bendikowski, '"Eine Fackel der Zwietracht": Katholisch-protestantische Mischehen im 19. und 20. Jahrhundert', in *Konfessionen im Konflikt. Deutschland zwischen 1800 und 1870: Ein zweites konfessionelles Zeitalter*, ed. Olaf Blaschke (Göttingen: Vandenhoeck & Ruprecht, 2002), 215–41.

The competition between the Christian churches was not limited to Europe. Since the fifteenth century, missionary activities had expanded to the 'New World', initially through the efforts of the Catholic Church. When Protestant congregations began their overseas missionary campaigns in the late eighteenth century and, more intensively, from the mid-nineteenth century, they were at first eager not to reproduce the confessional boundaries between the Protestant denominations in Europe. Only in the second half of the nineteenth century did they turn to confessionally conscious and ultimately also to nationally organised missionary initiatives. As a result of these long-term transformations, autonomous versions of Christianity emerged in many parts of the world.[14] While in Europe and Australia the Christian churches competed with one another, in many African mission territories the Catholic Church and the Protestant churches were at least not active on the same terrain, or at any rate tried not to get in one another's way. In some settings such as among the Yoruba in West Africa, for instance, the competition or disassociation between Islam (which came with trade across the Sahara) and Christianity (which, after a phase of failed missions in the early modern period, came with the abolition of the Atlantic slave trade, the introduction of so-called legitimate trade and with colonialism) was as strong as that between the variants of Christianity.[15] In places such as Buganda in East Africa, however, competition between the three religions of Islam, Catholicism and Protestantism was highlighted, with the effect that even today the three religions' share of Uganda's spiritual landscape reflects the proportion of the population they originally 'won over' in

[14] Klaus Koschorke (ed.), *'Christen und Gewürze': Konfrontation und Interaktion kolonialer und indigener Christentumsvarianten*, StAECG, vol. 1 (Göttingen: Vandenhoeck & Ruprecht, 1998); Hartmann Tyrell, '"Organisierte Mission": Protestantische Missionsgesellschaften des langen 19. Jahrhunderts/"Organized Missions": Protestant Missionary Societies in the Long Nineteenth Century', in *Etappen der Globalisierung in christentumsgeschichtlicher Perspektive / Phases of Globalization in the History of Christianity* (StAECG 19), ed. Klaus Koschorke (Wiesbaden: Harrassowitz, 2012), 255–72; Norman Etherington (ed.), *Missions and Empire* (Oxford: Oxford University Press, 2005); Peggy Brock (ed.), *Indigenous Peoples and Religious Change* (Leiden: Brill, 2005), and *The Many Voyages of Arthur Wellington Clah: A Tsimshian Man on the Pacific Northwest Coast* (Vancouver: UBC Press, 2011); Amanda Barry, Joanna Cruickshank, Andrew Brown-May and Patricia Grimshaw (eds), *Evangelists of Empire? Missionaries in Colonial History* (Melbourne: eScholarship Research Centre in collaboration with the School of Historical Studies, 2008); Hilde Nielssen, Inger Marie Okkenhaug and Karina Hestad Skeie (eds), *Protestant Missions and Local Encounters in the Nineteenth and Twentieth Centuries* (Leiden: Brill, 2011).

[15] J.D.Y. Peel, *Religious Encounter and the Making of the Yoruba* (Bloomington: Indiana University Press, 2003). But even here, the African Bishop Samuel Crowther, so important for advancing Christianity, chose terms from Islam rather than African religions to denote and translate central Christian and biblical vocabulary.

the nineteenth and early twentieth centuries.[16] And no Christian missions were established on the Swahili coast, for instance.[17] It was common policy to 'ignore' and not comment on each others' ventures as long as possible and as long as competition did not cause open friction.

Christianity reached Australia in the late eighteenth century in the wake of the establishment of European settler society, and was intertwined with colonial rule from the beginning.[18] Because of this late European colonisation, we do not encounter the first generation of indigenous converts in Australia until the mid-nineteenth century. Many of them had notions of the spiritual that differed sharply from the European Christian understanding of religion and conversion. Indigenous Australians held religious beliefs that were localised, interconnected and that, via songlines, could be traced across huge geographical expanses. The authority of ancestors extended to all spheres of life, and their power was evident in the natural as well as the human world. Women and men alike had spiritual responsibilities and authority that related to specific sacred sites. Access to sacred knowledge was granted in guided stages of initiation and increased with age, and there was no formal priestly caste.[19]

In Africa, local but fluid religions, whose elements were open to combination with those of other religions, influenced people's everyday lives, the economy and political action. We know little about the history of these religions, whose basic principles were not committed to writing. It was only the first European travellers and especially the missionaries who began to write about them. Their interpretations were motivated by the desire to organise, elevate, access and dominate a non-Christian world, as well as to bring about broad religious change in concert with a large number of likeminded people.[20] In the regions of southern Africa with a strong European presence, early missionary initiatives

---

16 Jean Brierley and Thomas Spear, 'Mutesa, the Missionaries and Christian Conversion in Buganda', *International Journal of African Historical Studies* 21, 4 (1988): 601–18; John Rowe, 'Mutesa and the Missionaries: Church and State in Pre-Colonial Buganda', in *Christian Missionaries and the State in the Third World*, ed. Holger Bernt and Michael Twaddle, 52–65. (Oxford: OUP, 2002).

17 For a brief introduction, see Jacob K. Olupona, *African Religions: A Very Short Introduction* (Oxford: OUP, 2014); for a longer one, see Adrian Hastings, *The Church in Africa, 1450–1950* (Oxford: Clarendon Press, 1995).

18 For a recent discussion of the early mission phase in Australia, see Meredith Lake, 'Salvation and Civilisation: First Missionary Encounter at Sydney Cove', in *Evangelists of Empire?*, ed. Barry et al., 87–103.

19 For a good general overview, see Max Charlesworth, Howard Morphy, Diane Bell and Kenneth Maddock (eds), *Religion in Aboriginal Australia. An Anthology*, 3rd edn (St Lucia: University of Queensland Press, 1992).

20 David Chidester, *Savage Systems: Colonialism and Comparative Religion in Southern Africa* (Charlottesville and London: University of Virginia Press, 1996).

by the Moravian Brethren coexisted with the churches of the settlers, as well as with the Islam of slaves brought from the Indian Ocean region. The Methodists began their South African work in the 1820s. Farther north, in the Transvaal, with its greater continental integration, there were no significant missionary activities before the mid-nineteenth century. We can assume, however, that migrant workers came into temporary contact with missionary enterprises on the Cape. When the first mission initiatives were launched in the Transvaal, at least some people there already had an idea of the new religion. And thus in one of our regions we may assume the existence of religious systems with a long series of historical relationships to one another, which offered a foundation for conversions in the nineteenth century, while in the other two regions the religious structures within which conversions occurred were more flexible and local, but historically less well documented, and narratives less well known. They therefore can only ever be rendered visible against the backdrop of colonisation and the Christian aspiration towards change. Using these broad scenarios of religious interaction, which we have greatly oversimplified here, we shall take a closer, actor-centred look at selected conversions in order to contextualise their inherent narratives and the phenomena of societal and religious change they helped to bring about.

Entangled Histories

The nature of these transformation processes has been widely discussed in recent historiography. Some of the most inspiring und fruitful ideas about the nature of transformation processes have been developed by scholars working in the field of critical empire studies and postcolonial studies who aim to write a more decentralised history outside the paradigms of national history.[21] Our

[21] In her *Civilising Subjects: Metropole and Colony in the English Imagination 1830–1867* (Chicago: University of Chicago Press and Cambridge: Polity Press, 2002), Catherine Hall refers directly to issues of Christianisation; as far as mission within the context of the British Empire is concerned, see Andrew Porter, *Religion Versus Empire? British Protestant Missionaries and Overseas Expansion, 1700–1914* (Manchester: Manchester University Press, 2004). Porter focuses somewhat on the colonial metropole, but is also critical of the idea of cultural hegemony. See Andrew Porter, '"Cultural Imperialism" and Protestant Missionary Enterprise, 1780–1914', *Journal of Imperial and Commonwealth History* 25, 3 (1997): 367–91. For critical histories that question the absolute power of the metropole over the colonies see, for example, Kathleen Wilson (ed.), *A New Imperial History: Culture, Identity and Modernity in Britain and the Empire 1660–1840* (Cambridge: Cambridge University Press, 2004), or Catherine Hall (ed.), *Cultures of Empire: A Reader: Colonizers in Britain and the Empire in the Nineteenth and Twentieth Centuries* (New York: Routledge, 2000). See also Norman Etherington, *Missions and Empire*; Ann Curthoys and

suggestion here is to combine the idea of the 'provincialising of Europe'[22] with the perspectives of entangled and connected histories that have evolved in the area of postcolonial studies. While more recent scholarship has been rethinking and re-exploring the relationship between such large entities as empires and nation states,[23] our aim in this book is to study individual conversions within a variety of regional contexts. Thus we wish to investigate the occurrence, contradictions and complexity of processes of transformation. We see a gap in the literature here, and believe that the theme of conversion and its narratives is particularly well suited to exploring long-term social, religious and gender transformations as they are reflected in conversion narratives.

In our study, we will focus on narratives and source material generated in the contexts of German missions[24] or missions from Germany, both at home and abroad. Debates about 'the global' have relied substantially on English-language secondary literature, or concerned themselves with the contexts of the British Empire and the so-called 'Anglo-World' (see below). We believe that we can broaden the debate by concentrating on narratives that refer to German contexts in various ways. We hope to do so not just by pondering the particular Germanness of sources and actors, but rather by reminding ourselves that non-British and non-English actors, such as Germans, constituted a major proportion of people worth reflecting upon even when we discuss the complexity of social

Marilyn Lake (eds), *Connected Worlds: History in Transnational Perspective* (Canberra: ANU E-Press, 2006); Desley Deacon, Penny Russell and Angela Woollacott, *Transnational Lives: Biographies of Global Modernity, 1700–present, Series on Transnational History*, ed. Deacon, Russell and Woollacott (Basingstoke: Palgrave Macmillan, 2010); D. Deacon, P. Russell and A. Woollacott (eds), *Transnational Ties: Australian Lives in the World* (Canberra: ANU E-Press, 2008); Angela Woollacott, *Gender and Empire* (Basingstoke: Palgrave Macmillan, 2006); Elizabeth Elbourne, 'The Bannisters and Their Colonial World: Family Networks and Colonialism in the Early Nineteenth Century', in *Within and Without the Nation: Canadian History as Transnational History*, ed. Karen Dubinsky, Adele Perry and Henry Yu (Toronto: University of Toronto Press, forthcoming); Alan Lester and David Lambert (eds), *Colonial Lives across the British Empire: Imperial Careering in the Long Nineteenth Century* (Cambridge: Cambridge University Press, 2006); Alan Lester, *Imperial Networks: Creating Identities in Nineteenth Century South Africa and Britain* (London and New York: Routledge, 2001).

22 Dipesh Chakrabarty, *Provincializing Europe: Postcolonial Thought and Historical Difference* (Princeton: Princeton University Press, 2000).

23 Jörn Leonhard and Ulrike von Hirschhausen, *Empires und Nationalstaaten im 19. Jahrhundert*, 2nd edn (Göttingen: Vandenhoeck & Ruprecht, 2011); Jane Burbank and Frederick Cooper, *Empires in World History: Power and the Politics of Difference* (Princeton: Princeton University Press, 2010).

24 The Catholic Church conceived of its re-Catholicising activities as 'mission' as well. In that sense, Volk was 'missionised' just like the many people who encountered (Protestant) mission activities in the colonies.

and religious transformation in contexts that were not particularly 'German'. Gustav Werner Volk, whom readers will get to know in Chapter 1, lived in Prussia, more specifically in Thuringia, and converted, or was missionised into Catholicism, in the Habsburg Empire; the Protestant missionaries in Chapters 2 and 3 originated in German lands and later operated in colonial territories under British or Boer rule; the African and Australian converts implicated in the conversion narratives resulting from such operations saw themselves as members of churches that came from Germany but placed themselves in colonial contexts set up by other nations, sometimes in line with 'their own' polities and at others in conflict with them. In fact, in the 1850s and 1860s, a variety of German and German-connected (mission) actors operated 'at home and abroad', and a variety of converts' stories were told, sometimes in the entangled, transnational and mutually influential way we wish to explore in German narratives.

It seems to us that the best approach to exploring the complexities of transformation is an in-depth discussion of individual cases based on limited and carefully selected source material. Reflecting upon such individual cases, the method of parallel reading offers new ways of understanding the nature of transformation. In our studies we try to analyse seemingly unconnected cases outside the framework of the national state, following some groundbreaking scholarship in the area of early modern history such Natalie Zemon Davis's work on three seventeenth-century lives,[25] or the publications of the research group 'Self-Narratives in Transcultural Perspective'[26] or by Leo Spitzer on *Lives in Between*.[27] In her account of three seventeenth-century women, one Jewish, one Catholic and one Protestant, Natalie Zemon Davis investigates the possibilities and limits of agency for educated, writing middle-class women in French and German cities. In publications on autobiographical texts in Europe, the Ottoman Empire and Japan, the research group 'Self-Narratives in Transcultural Perspective' has continued and further developed Davis's method of 'decentred comparison'.[28] *Lives in Between* focuses on three life and family histories in rather different spatial contexts and timeframes. From a historical perspective, they are connected as a variety of protagonists – a converted slave who became a prominent pastor (Sierra Leone, Nigeria), the Zweig and Brettauer families (Moravia, Vienna) and the 'mulatto' son of a tailor and a slave who became a

25 Natalie Zemon Davis, *Women on the Margins: Three Seventeenth-Century Lives* (Cambridge; Mass. and London: Harvard University Press, 1995).

26 See the website of the DFG Research Group 530 'Self-Narratives in Transcultural Perspective': http://www.geschkult.fu-berlin.de/en/e/fg530/index.html [accessed on 22 June 2013].

27 Leo Spitzer, *Lives in Between: Assimilation and Marginality in Austria, Brazil, West Africa 1780–1945* (Cambridge: Cambridge University Press, 1989).

28 Claudia Ulbrich, Hans Medick and Angelika Schaser (eds), *Selbstzeugnis und Person* (Cologne, Weimar and Vienna: Böhlau, 2012).

member of an elite Brazilian family fighting for national independence – seek to come to terms with the promises and faultlines of 'emancipation', a keyword that characterises an extended period in history.

In our many discussions we began by 'comparing' our specific case studies. We faced the challenge that our conversion accounts differed significantly and thus came to the conclusion that they stand very much on their own and demand separate treatment. The conversion portrayed in Chapter 1 comes from a study in which the convert focuses on his own developmental and educational path, locates himself within the social realm, criticises norms, values and social orders, and explains his conversion for an educated audience. Chapters 2 and 3 concern themselves with the conversion of individuals who by their very conversions became important agents for transforming whole societies, and scholars have often been keener to explore those social transformations than the individuality of any conversion. Nevertheless, common themes emerged in the course of our discussions, and we needed to classify the specific conversions we analysed within them. Thus we dedicated each of our case studies to one of these themes as its main focus. While Chapter 1 serves as exposition, Chapters 2 and 3 successively intensify the degree of reflection upon the topics and focalisations explored in the preceding chapter(s). The joint chapter offering our reflections thus serves the purpose of discussing the preceding treatments of conversion in a more structured way, integrating them and tying them together.

In our discussions we also began by examining conversions from the longer nineteenth century and comparing them. In the process, however, we found ourselves getting increasingly close chronologically, and ultimately arrived at the quite narrow time period of the 1850s and 1860s. This allowed us to undertake an examination of parallel, synchronous phenomena in the different regions we study. A parallel reading of conversion in contemporaneous but regionally diverse constellations made it possible to look anew at conversion in Germany and its discussion in a largely German-language environment in the light of the respective elaborations, which are rooted in micro-history and further developed in entangled history. For our topic we therefore favour parallel reading, among the various possible ways of looking at global, comparative and entangled history. We remain rather sceptical of the explanatory approaches emphasising master narratives and global history that have become so popular of late. To be sure, we, too, believe that conversions occurred globally and in contexts of the interconnection and intensification of mutual dependencies. We are equally convinced, however, that 'the global' does not represent a level of action and localisation. For us, empirically anchored as we are in the histories of Europe, Australia and Africa, reflecting on conversions in the sense of global transformations and reciprocal relationships means formulating a shared approach and operating on the level of reflection.

Ann Stoler and Frederick Cooper study relationships, and understand the colony and the metropole as a shared, interdependent analytical field. Their work shows that the colonising centre and the colonised periphery cannot be studied in isolation from one another.[29] A historian of Empire such as Christopher Bayly, who began by studying India, has explicitly used global history to disengage himself from the empirical and to pose new questions to historiography. Unlike Christopher Bayly, whose much-discussed thesis is that the religions actually became more structurally similar in the nineteenth century, with more uniform organising principles and forms of expression,[30] we prefer to resist such bold theses with respect to conversions. Neither did conversions themselves become more uniform, nor did they take place in increasingly uniform scenarios of religious interaction. Frequently, the opposite was the case: conversions in different parts of the world initially led to the emergence of highly diverse conversion narratives, even if their literary representations were entangled. Thus we are concerned not with uniform or standardising developments, but rather with examining a panorama of conversions, the way they were processed in language and their gender-related social transformations. We have been inspired here by the way in which Jürgen Osterhammel has sketched expansive panoramas that express the transformation of the world, while leaving the question of entanglement largely up to the reader.[31] We have been stimulated not least by his suggestion, made jointly with Niels Petersson, that we should conceive of entanglements 'from below', and in the process realise that small-scale interactions are not always consonant with an increasingly large and uniform greater whole. We are persuaded by their assertion that 'Paradoxically, it thus appears to be more promising to begin the study of worldwide integration on the level of individual action, instead of focusing on the world as a whole'.[32]

---

[29] Ann Laura Stoler and Frederick Cooper, 'Between Metropole and Colony: Rethinking a Research Agenda', in *Tensions of Empire: Colonial Cultures in a Bourgeois World*, ed. Stoler and Cooper (Berkeley: University of California Press, 1997), 1–56.

[30] On the idea of 'empires of religion', see Christopher A. Bayly, *The Birth of the Modern World, 1780–1914: Global Comparisons and Connections* (Malden, Mass.: Blackwell, *2004)*, chapter 9.

[31] Jürgen Osterhammel, *Die Verwandlung der Welt: Eine Geschichte des 19. Jahrhunderts* (Munich: Beck, 2009). This work received largely positive reviews in the German-speaking world; see, for example, the review of 13 March 2009 by Friedrich Lenger: http://hsozkult.geschichte.hu-berlin.de/rezensionen/id=12427&count=7&recno=6&type=rezbuecher&sort=datum&order=down&search=J%C3%BCrgen+Osterhammel+Verwandlung [Accessed on 7 Dec. 2012]. For an English-language introduction to his approach, see Jürgen Osterhammel and Niels P. Petersson, *Globalization. A short history* (Princeton and Oxford: Princeton University Press, 2005). Osterhammel deliberately uses open-ended terms such as 'panoramas' and 'themes' for his global history.

[32] Osterhammel and Petersson, *Globalization*, 22.

Beyond the expansive panoramas, we are thus interested in the empirically grounded. While many global histories are written by a single author, we have accepted the challenge of offering a history composed by three authors, using the level of the global for reflection and scholarly debate.[33] We are convinced that we can critically query concepts and terms from this standpoint, and thereby utilise empirical evidence and multiple perspectives to study transformation through the example of religious conversions on three continents.

The Mid-Nineteenth Century

In our parallel readings, we suggest taking a close look at a moment when the world was in motion but not yet necessarily at a crucial turning point. In the 1850s and 1860s, Europe was trying to cope with the aftermath of the Revolution of 1848/49, which touched all areas of society, including religion. Between the Revolution of 1848/49 and the founding of the German Empire in 1871, the period 'between reaction and liberalism',[34] a 'conflictual process of transformation took place, which continued for some thirty years, from 1845 until 1873'.[35]

In Australia in this period we witness the beginning of indigenous people's demands for land rights in Victoria and New South Wales against the colonial political background of strong government policies of racial segregation, which were subsequently formalised in the 1869 Aborigines Act. The establishment of government reserves for Aborigines and a stronger encouragement of missions, as well as the 1859 Coranderrk land demands, which involved Aboriginal leaders like William Barak, are examples of these tendencies.[36]

---

33 A positive example of a jointly authored history is Jochen Meissner, Ulrich Mücke and Klaus Weber, *Schwarzes Amerika: Eine Geschichte der Sklaverei* (Munich: Beck, 2008), but also, and with more immediate bearing on our source material, Mary Jo Maynes, Jennifer L. Pierce, and Barbara Laslett, *Telling Stories: The Use of Personal Narratives in the Social Sciences and History* (Ithaca and London: Cornell University Press, 2008).

34 Thomas Nipperdey, *Deutsche Geschichte 1800–1866: Bürgerwelt und starker Staat* (Munich: Beck, 1983), 674 [English: *Germany from Napoleon to Bismarck, 1800–1866*, trans. Daniel Nolan (Princeton: Princeton University Press, 1996)].

35 Hans-Ulrich Wehler, *Deutsche Gesellschaftsgeschichte*, vol. 3: *Von der 'Deutschen Doppelrevolution' bis zum Beginn des Ersten Weltkrieges 1849–1914* (Munich: Beck, 1995), 3.

36 Richard Broome, *Aboriginal Victorians: A History since 1800* (Crows Nest, NSW: Allen & Unwin, 2005); Richard Broome, *Aboriginal Australians: A History since 1788*, 4th edn, (Crows Nest, NSW: Allen & Unwin, 2010); Bain Attwood, 'Off the mission stations: Aborigines in Gippsland 1860–1890', *Aboriginal History* 10, 2 (1986): 131–150; Diane E. Barwick, *Rebellion at Coranderrk* (Canberra: Aboriginal History, 1998); Jane Lydon, 'The

Southern Africa was caught up in a set of major and ongoing changes. Since at least the late eighteenth century, polities had been emerging from protracted migrations and in a number of cases they had solidified into states. Such states arose in what is now Zimbabwe, Swaziland, Angola, Zambia, Mozambique and the northern part of South Africa. State-like formations were also emerging along the south-eastern coast on the southern African frontier, with Griqua and Oorlams consolidating into polities. Meanwhile, the region was grappling with the legacies of different varieties of slavery and serfdom, one of these concentrated in Angola and Mozambique, more particularly its coastline, and the other in the Cape Colony, which had also been a slave society from the beginning – one, however, in which, unlike Caribbean slave societies, the family members of slave owners also worked on the farms.[37]

In the great empires, religious change took on a new quality, and, last but not least, the written documentation of conversions began. Another innovative aspect of the present volume is the way we integrate the study of Europe as one region among others in a postcolonial perspective. A number of such decentralising world histories have appeared in recent years. They tend to explain the rise of Europe as a phenomenon that began only after 1800, and therefore place the long global history of earlier periods in the context of an equilibrium in which the Asian and Chinese worlds were the equals of the European world.[38] Some of these histories emphasise the before-mentioned Anglo settler world that linked the British Empire with settler colonies in North America, Australia, New Zealand and South Africa.[39] Others particularly stress the Pacific and Australian world from the time when restrictive immigration legislation became predominant as part of a process in which 'races' were redefined as either 'black' or 'white'.[40] Our study, in which converts and missionaries from German

Experimental 1860s: Charles Walter's Images of Coranderrk Aboriginal Station, Victoria', *Aboriginal History* 26 (2002): 78–130.

[37] Helmut Bley, 'Südafrikanische Welt', in *Enzyklopädie der Neuzeit*, vol. 13, ed. Friedrich Jäger (Stuttgart: Metzler, 2011), 19–27. The mineral revolution that would significantly alter the face and history of southern Africa began in 1868 (Kimberley) and, more importantly, in 1886 (Witwatersrand).

[38] Kenneth Pomeranz, *The Great Divergence: China, Europe and the Making of the Modern World Economy* (Princeton: Princeton University Press, 2000); John Darwin, *After Tamerlane: The Rise and Fall of Global Empires, 1400–2000* (London: Penguin, 2008), esp. chapters 2–5; Sanjay Subrahmanyam, *Explorations in Connected History: From the Tagus to the Ganges* (Oxford: Oxford University Press, 2005).

[39] James Belich, *Replenishing the Earth: The Settler Revolution and the Rise of the Anglo-World, 1783–1939* (Oxford: Oxford University Press, 2009); Darwin, *After Tamerlane*, esp. chapters 5–6.

[40] Marilyn Lake and Henry Reynolds, *Drawing the Global Colour Line: White Men's Countries and the Challenge of Racial Equality* (Cambridge: Cambridge University Press, 2008).

contexts, in particular, also play a role alongside converts from South Africa and Australia, thus begins before the advent of German imperialism and the phase of high imperialism more generally, and observes actors who had to find their way in a world that was already colonially (pre-)structured.

In establishing the Sacra Congregatio de Propaganda Fide commission in 1622, the Catholic Church had once targeted the mission enterprise in Europe and the New World. Catholic converts in Europe saw themselves as missionaries at home and abroad in this tradition. They frequently stated that they hoped their conversion accounts would win over their former co-religionists for the Catholic Church. Since the worldwide unity of the Christian church was their aim, they observed the Catholic mission abroad with great interest and in some cases believed that their conversion accounts could be deployed for missionary purposes. So from a Catholic viewpoint, conversion narratives offered a potential link between the old and new worlds.[41] Before the last third of the nineteenth century, the Catholic mission proceeded mainly from colonialising France. Before the founding of the German Empire, Protestant missionaries from the German territories working in Africa and Australia had to contend with the influence of the European colonial powers, notably Britain. As the example of the Moravian Brethren shows, the missions were usually quite capable of using this power productively for their own ends. In this phase of only partially formed nationalism, other Protestant groupings generally fell back on a position of not seriously intervening in the affairs of secular government, which as a rule meant supporting the status quo. Their relationship to the British authorities was frequently less conflicted than that of the non-conformist mission initiatives from Britain, which took a more critical approach to the political order.

Religious conversions to Christianity are particularly suited to such a study of transformation because they are not merely situated at the interface of religion, the nation state and colonialism, but simultaneously also bridge the subjective experiences of converts and the major social transformations of their times. In our study, we discuss religious conversions in mid-nineteenth-century Africa, Australia and Europe and demonstrate through specific regional cases how textual representations captured the religious transformation of individual people, groups and at times entire societies. Our main focus is on the emergence of new varieties of Christianity in a world characterised by mobility, transition and the start of 'something new'. In this way we focus on the mid-nineteenth century, and thereby first of all on a (for Germany) unspectacular moment in a longer period of transition. Second, and simultaneously, our studies on Australia and Africa begin at a time when increasingly densely documented texts exist as sources for these two regions. The interesting question is what conclusions these

---

41 Angelika Lozar and Angelika Schaser, 'Die Rückkehr zum "wahren Glauben". Konversionen im 17. Jahrhundert', *Frühneuzeit-Info* 13 (2002): 65–74, p. 66.

temporally parallel studies allow us to draw about this age of transformation, which was an age of more than just religious conversion.

The Structure of the Book

As we explained further above, our first objective is to acquaint the reader with conversions in three regional frameworks and to illuminate the historical context in which the selected conversions in Europe, Africa and Australia took place. Naturally, these terms for the continents and major regions can be no more than approximations that would have made little immediate sense to actors at the time, since the people who converted did not do so 'in Europe', 'in Australia' or 'in Africa', and not even 'in Germany', 'in South Africa' or 'in Victoria', but rather in very specific and far smaller societal settings, which were often characterised and organised by personal, social interactions. The book's three central chapters treat the main themes of conversion narratives, gender and 'at home and abroad' in the 1850s and 1860s. Each of the individual topics is rooted in a continent or a region: in the first chapter, the focus is on Europe, in the second, Australia and in the third, South Africa.

The first chapter explores and describes the contents and structural principles of the Christian conversion narrative developed in Europe. The geographical focus is the (at that time) Prussian city of Erfurt. In those days Erfurt was not the hub of the universe, but contemporaries considered a certain Gustav Werner Volk's conversion account to be 'one of the best works on conversion'.[42] This chapter studies the way conversion was conveyed in language in the framework of a 'family conversion' in 1855–1856 and over the long writing career of a husband and father who was perceived as the 'main convert'. This exhaustively documented conversion in Protestant-dominated Erfurt reveals the dominant patterns of the conversion narrative as it evolved in Europe from the Reformation onward. Gender relations within the family also emerge clearly. As to the social consequences, this case proves representative for the thesis that religious conversions in Europe by no means correlated with a rise in social status.

The second chapter focuses on the gendered implications of conversion. Here we explore how mission texts, in particular those concerning conversions, represent the gendered power of male and female indigenous converts. In this chapter, the geographical focus is on Victoria in Australia, where young Wotjobaluk men and women joined the Moravian Church in the 1850s and 1860s. The Moravian Brethren's mission stations of Ebenezer and Ramahyuck

---

[42] Ludwig Fränkel, 'Volk, Wilhelm'. *Allgemeine Deutsche Biographie*. vol. 40, herausgegeben von der Historischen Kommission bei der Bayerischen Akademie der Wissenschaften, 227–30. 1896. http://de.wikisource.org/wiki/ADB:Volk Wilhelm.

were in the colony of Victoria. Ebenezer was not far from Coranderrk, a state reserve for Aborigines, which under Kulin leaders such as Simon Wonga and William Barak became a political centre and starting point for important indigenous land right protest movements from the 1860s.[43]

Finally, a third chapter explores the context of interlocking transformations and transitions. Caught up as they were in times of upheaval, contemporaries often found it difficult to know for sure whether they were at the end of a phase or perhaps even facing new developments that marked the impending end of their ongoing experiences. The third chapter will treat the conversions of selected representatives of the Pedi Kingdom in South Africa from this perspective. The Lutheran Berlin Mission, which was active in the Pedi Kingdom and the adjacent Boer republic of the Transvaal, envisioned the emergence of a so-called Pedi people's church, which would be sustained, developed and shaped by men and women of varying social status. The conversions presented and focused upon in this chapter took place in the 1860s, and thus at a point when, after decades of wartime chaos, movements of population and the consolidation of larger polities, an independent, newly consolidating African kingdom like that of the Pedi had to arm itself against the settler expansion of the Boers on the one hand and a different, but also encroaching, British colonial rule on the other. In this context, the Pedi faced the loss of their land and demands for new taxes and duties as well as the forced recruitment of labourers for Boer farms and military commandos.[44] Conversions were an important means for people to reposition themselves in this drastically changing world. Ultimately they facilitated the establishment of a particular version of Christianity in this specific time and place.

A chapter offering our reflections follows the three case studies. Here, we present the findings of the parallel readings and recapitulate what we find especially useful about our approach. At the end of the chapter we ask what suggestions and inspiration we might draw from our study for possible further elaborations of our experimental approach, and thus for the further development of writing on postnational and postcolonial history.

---

[43] For an overview, see, for example, Rachel Perkins and Marcia Langton (eds), *First Australians: An Illustrated History* (Victoria: Miegunyah Press, 2008), 150ff.

[44] Peter Delius, *The Land Belongs to Us. The Pedi Polity, the Boers and the British in the Nineteenth-Century Transvaal* (London: Heinemann 1984).

Chapter 1

Conversion Narratives in a European Setting: Writing About Conversion to Catholicism in Erfurt

Introduction

There are two main sources of information on nineteenth-century religious conversions: state and church documents, and oral or written accounts by the converts themselves. This chapter will explore the possibilities and limits of these sources and elaborate on the importance of German-language conversion narratives in the context of our study. We would like to argue that models of Christian conversion narratives were developed and solidified in the core region of the Reformation that would continue to shape accounts of conversions to Christianity in Europe in the nineteenth century. Missionaries from Europe were familiar with these conversion narratives, but had to adapt and alter them in other regions of the world under the influence of local conditions and the converts who lived there. In what follows, we will introduce the regional and temporal situatedness of conversion narratives, with a focus on family conversions to Catholicism. The reason for this focus is that nineteenth-century accounts of conversion to Catholicism were generally more detailed, since they apparently required more justification than conversions to Protestantism. Accounts of conversion to Protestantism, which was far more common in the region in question in the nineteenth century,[1] since it was very much in keeping with the trends of the era, were only more voluminous if the converts had previously been Catholic priests and thus felt under great pressure to explain themselves.

Volk's conversion was selected for this chapter because he published extensive autobiographical texts both before and after his conversion, and because this conversion narrative was considered a model among Catholics, but also because his conversion was discussed publicly and additional sources have

1 Gesine Carl and Angelika Schaser, 'Konversionsberichte des 17. bis 19. Jahrhunderts als Selbstzeugnisse gelesen: Ergebnisse und Forschungsperspektiven', in *Digitale Quellenedition Konversionserzählungen*, http://www.geschkult.fu-berlin.de/e/konversionen/ergebnisse/beitraege/Konversionsberichte_als_Selbstzeugnisse_gelesen.pdf?1369918255 [2013], 38–9.

survived about him as a Prussian official. We will begin by drawing attention to the regional and temporal situatedness of nineteenth-century conversion narratives, before addressing the historical context of the conversion in a second section. The third section describes the conversion of Wilhelm Gustav Werner Volk and his family in 1855 and 1856. The fourth and final section will explore the concept of person that Volk presents in his autobiographical writings, his self-representation *before* and his writing, authentification and authorisation strategies *after* his conversion, and elaborate Volk's notions of the gender order. This section will introduce a focal theme of Chapter 3: Volk's religious conversion occurred in interaction with societal developments, and he tried in his writings and translations to help reunite Christendom in Germany and beyond and to place limits on secularisation. In closing, we will summarise this chapter's most important findings.

The Regional and Temporal Situatedness of Nineteenth-Century Conversion Narratives

Literary scholars, especially those who study autobiographies, have analysed the genre-specific patterns of conversion narratives from antiquity to the present. Conversion narratives have a long tradition stretching back to St. Augustine, and they set the standard for modern autobiography.[2] The conclusions that scholars have drawn about the genre of the conversion narrative are dominated by studies of a few key texts by writers and intellectuals, to which the literature repeatedly refers.[3] The initial concentration on the genre has meant that regional and temporal peculiarities have received little attention, since the aim of the scholarship was, after all, to elaborate the specificity of the conversion narrative. If we include a larger body of non-literary source texts, however, a far more heterogeneous picture emerges. The conversion narratives not only follow a stereotypical pattern, but also depend on the respective writing framework of the converts and are situated both regionally and within the context of their time.

---

[2] Michael Sheringham, 'Conversion and Turning Points', in *Encyclopedia of Life Writing*, vol. 1, ed. Margaretta Jolly (London: Routledge, 2001), 233–4; Angelika Schaser, '"Zurück zur heiligen Kirche' – Konversionen zum Katholizismus im säkularisierten Zeitalter', *Historische Anthropologie* 15 (2007): 1–23, and 'Schreiben um dazuzugehören. Konversionserzählungen im 19. Jahrhundert', in *Selbstzeugnis und Person: Transkulturelle Perspektiven*, ed. Claudia Ulbrich, Hans Medick, and Angelika Schaser (Cologne, Weimar, and Vienna: Böhlau, 2012), 381–98.

[3] See, for example, Frédéric Gugelot, *La conversion des intellectuels au catholicisme en France 1885–1935* (Paris: CNRS éditions, 1998), and Patrick Allitt, *Catholic Converts. British and American Intellectuals turn to Rome* (Ithaca and London: Cornell Univ. Press, 1997).

Literary scholars and sociologists have portrayed the 'turning point', which divides the convert's life into a time before and after conversion, as a key element of the conversion narrative.[4] Thus Bernd Ulmer has discovered for twentieth-century accounts of conversion that temporal structuring dominates in religious conversion narratives.[5] A chronological structure is also typical of nineteenth-century conversion accounts. If the converts themselves are writing, the period before conversion is usually presented in detail, followed by a description of the process of conversion set out as a turning point that divides the convert's biography into a before and an after. A third section depicts the time after conversion, but in the published nineteenth-century German-language conversion accounts studied here this was often very brief and impersonal or even absent altogether.

As historians we profit from the analyses of literary scholars and sociologists and inquire into the background and the historical context in which the conversion narratives arose and were read or heard and discussed. One thing that becomes evident here is that conversion narratives can be found in autobiographical and biographical accounts, and that in the records of not only oral conversion accounts, the lines between biographical and autobiographical texts disappear or are actively blurred by their authors and editors. A closer investigation, which does not focus on genre-specific traits, reveals that most conversion narratives are concerned less with a clearly defined and temporally fixed turning point in a life than in depicting conversion itself as a process whose beginning and end are not always easy to locate. The difficulty of formulating a clear system of interpretation as well as a clear attribution and delimitation in times of social change is plainly evident in these texts. The study of conversion narratives shifts the focus from the institutions of the 'major churches' to regional and local differences, the cohesion of parishes, the transformation of practices of piety and the acceptance of church norms. After all, these accounts by no means revolve solely around the religious development of the self and the discussion of theological topics. Conversion accounts frequently address themes that may have been only tangential to the personal religious development, but significant for the way of life and the social, intellectual and professional development of converts. Thus in many conversion narratives, the account of the conversion itself is integrated into broader depictions of society, the churches and the state. In this narrative, the convert appears at times as an agent, then as a disciple, critic, admonisher or outsider. We understand conversions not as ruptures and

---

4 Sheringham, 'Conversion and Turning Points', 233–234.

5 Bernd Ulmer, 'Die autobiographische Plausibilität von Konversionserzählungen', in *Wer schreibt meine Lebensgeschichte? Biographie, Autobiographie, Hagiographie und ihre Entstehungszusammenhänge*, ed. Walter Sparn (Gütersloh: Gütersloher Verlagshaus, 1990), 287–95.

turning points, but as processes of change, in which the formal act of joining a Christian church is but *one aspect*. For in this framework of the history of events, political developments, societal norms and values are discussed which render visible the gender images, the scope and limits of agency, utopias, fears and hopes. All of these aspects reveal the converts' concept of person as much as the stated motives for conversion and the description of a personal development that is not restricted to the process of religious conversion.[6] If we turn our attention from questions of genre and the search for historical facts to the narrativity of these texts, conversion accounts offer a wealth of information not just on the converts, but also on the world in motion in which they lived.

Whether the surviving conversion narratives were written when the conversion was fresh in the author's mind or decades later, on their own impetus or under pressure or coercion, whether they were altered by the censors and marked by stereotypical narrative patterns or by an impressively individual style, they always show us only what the convert chose to reveal or make public about him- or herself; they reveal their apologetic character and serve as propagandistic testimony for the new faith community.[7] Frequently, we cannot reconstruct the apparently simple matters of when, where and under what circumstances the texts were written. In most cases, the manuscripts of the published texts as well as correspondences between publishers and authors have not survived.

Many of these published accounts judge, polarise, exclude and include quite clearly. For that reason, we also repeatedly find indicators that the authors expected to cause a stir and expose themselves to slander and attacks because of their conversion. Friedrich Hurter (1787–1865), for example, a well-known former Calvinist pastor, historian and publisher from Switzerland who converted to Catholicism in 1844, notes in the preface to his three-volume autobiography: 'If those who know me not at all, or prefer to misknow me, believe that they are better informed about the inner processes of my life, I happily leave them to their belief; I assure them that I will never disturb them in this'.[8] Some

---

[6] Sociologists have increasingly emphasised that conversion is a process. See Monika Wohlrab-Sahr, Volkhard Krech, and Hubert Knoblauch, 'Religiöse Bekehrung in soziologischer Perspektive: Themen, Schwerpunkte und Fragestellungen der gegenwärtigen religionssoziologischen Konversionsforschung', in *Religiöse Konversion. Systematische und fallorientierte Studien in soziologischer Perspektive*, ed. Wohlrab-Sahr, Krech, and Knoblauch (Konstanz: UVK, 1998), 7–35.

[7] Gwendolin Herder, *Entwicklungslinien volksbildnerischer Verlagsarbeit zwischen Kölner Ereignis und Märzrevolution (1837–1848): Der christliche Buchhandel am Beispiel des Verlages Herder in Freiburg im Breisgau* (Bonn: Herder, 1989), 73 ff.; Martin Riesebrodt, *Cultus und Heilsversprechen. Eine Theorie der Religionen* (Munich: Beck, 2007), 212–19.

[8] Friedrich Hurter, 'Vorrede', in *Geburt und Wiedergeburt. Erinnerungen aus meinem Leben und Blicke auf die Kirche*, vol. 1 (Schaffhausen: Verlag der Hurter'schen Buchhandlung, 1849), iii–xv, vii.

were convinced that the people in their former faith community would never understand them. Other converts, like Volk, displayed irenicist tendencies before their conversion. In the work he published as a conversion account, however, he clearly found it indispensable to place himself firmly on the side of the 'true church' and disassociate himself from other Christian churches.

It is generally difficult to discover anything about the situations and places in which converts wrote their narratives. Many published their accounts immediately after converting, others at the end of their lives, while still others ensured that the autobiographical depictions of their conversion would only appear posthumously. Volk was not the only convert to point out in his memoirs that he had already mentioned his conversion in earlier texts. This strategy in particular clearly shows that converts embedded their conversion in the continuum of their personal biographies, thereby signalling to readers that despite this change, their lives were dominated by constancy and singleness of purpose.

Nearly all converts were accompanied in the conversion process by Catholics, and they mention in their conversion accounts encounters with Catholicism earlier in their lives, which had left an (at the time mostly unnoticed) positive impression on them. In virtually all conversion narratives these encounters are projected back into childhood and adolescence, generally combined in the narrative with the wish that they had already been Catholic back then. These stories are deployed in various ways, but they appear regularly. Portrayals of encounters with Catholicism tended to include a mention of its attraction as well as a remark that these Catholics had never proselytised the later converts, but rather had shown them tolerance as non-Catholics.

According to the conversion narratives, contact with Catholic mentors and teachers during the conversion process varied greatly. Even where they mention important relationships and role models, men describe their conversions as largely autonomous decisions. Women, in contrast, appear more frequently to have developed very close, admiring relationships with their spiritual companions. Not infrequently, however, the latter were quite reticent when it came to personal encounters.

The converts who published extensive conversion narratives were practised writers, and often already well-known authors at the time of their conversion. They integrated the conversion narratives into their body of work and authorised these texts with reference to their own competencies as well as the embedding of the autobiographical segments of their texts into the broader context of society, (church) politics and religious philosophy. Most converts point out that their accounts were intended as guides for members of their previous faith community, that is, they targeted readers of the same linguistic group. Some of the accounts, however, were translated into other languages, in order to be able to promote their own religious group abroad. Thus, for example, a striking number of conversion accounts were translated. The conversion account of Ida von Hahn-Hahn,[9] for instance, was translated from German into French in 1854 (2nd French edition 1864), after an English edition of 1851 and a Dutch one in 1852. *From Babylon to Jerusalem* was translated into Italian in 1858. The parts of the text that point beyond the autobiographical are generally far more extensive and indicate not just the propagated superiority of Catholicism, but also the desired world order and the criticised or preferred social and gender orders. They stress the superiority of the Catholic Church and Catholic countries and idealise the period before the Reformation. Positive social developments are characterised as Catholic, and negative ones as Protestant.

Although most conversion narratives begin with the protagonist's childhood, sometimes reaching far back into the history of his or her family of origin, they merely allude to the genre of autobiography. Concrete biographical information is generally replaced by an emphasis on interior spiritual and religious development. Some conversion narratives do not provide even basic biographical data. The ending of conversion narratives is often defined only indirectly, since in many, basic reflections and statements are placed at the end, and biographical conclusions are rarely drawn. Indirectly, or from additional sources, one can conclude that the conversion narrative ends shortly after the time of conversion. Since some of them were likely also written under the impression of external attacks from opponents of their conversion, these accounts often close with a defence against such portrayals.

Most conversion accounts are written in the first person, which was doubtless intended to underline the authenticity of the text. Others are written in the third person singular, for example when the accounts were published after the convert's death or recorded by third parties. These conversion accounts, too, however, usually cite the converts themselves extensively, reporting the contents of letters and other autobiographical records, in order to emphasise the authentic nature of the description. Although many conversion narratives focus on the convert's life story from childhood up to conversion, the autobiographical account is generally imbedded in the historical context of the respective country, the development of society and the churches or a general philosophico-historical treatise. In such accounts, the convert operates as a person in his or her time who shapes, experiences, criticises or propagates social and ecclesiastical conditions. Many converts composed their texts in an objective, scholarly vein, discussing various controversies and documenting their accounts with references to other publications and quotations from well-known authors. They usually touched upon the most important topics of theological controversialist literature,

[9] Ida von Hahn-Hahn, *Von Babylon nach Jerusalem* (Mainz: Kirchheim & Schott, 1851). Hahn-Hahn, a well-known and very successful German writer, justified her conversion to Catholicism (1850) in this book in the form of an historical itinerary.

mentioning the sacraments, the controversy over transubstantiation, the liturgy, the role of the pope, the veneration of saints and relics, celibacy, the belief in miracles, indulgences, interpretations of the Bible and important figures in the Reformation or Counter-Reformation. The elaboration of the varying Protestant and Catholic positions was connected not least with aspirations to participate in modern life, stressing the compatibility of Catholic standpoints with science, the modern state and patriotic or national loyalty.

Some nineteenth-century conversion narratives depict conversion as a long, often laborious and imponderable process that catapulted the protagonists into great doubts and anxieties. Others described their lives before conversion as a consistent path 'towards truth', which they pursued deliberately with divine guidance and which culminated, finally and logically, in conversion. In most cases, they emphasise not only a decisive turning point that led to the conversion, but also various relevant events, impressions and encounters with people. While regularly mentioned, the act of conversion, which represents the high- and turning point in the classic conversion narrative, is often not accorded the outstanding role within the overall text that it should theoretically have. Many converts portrayed various liminal experiences in the run-up to conversion: illness, the death of loved ones, difficulties in their professional lives and religious doubts. The search for and finding of 'true religion' could be marked by protracted detours and setbacks, and was as a rule prepared for and accompanied by intensive reading.

All converts embarked on a journey in their conversion narratives, albeit from different starting points. Some set out from a position of religious indifference, others were clerics or practising Protestants and Catholics, who portray themselves from the beginning as deeply religious persons. The paths people followed to arrive at their new faith communities differed in length, difficulty and danger. Volk repeatedly assigns travel to the Catholic South a central role in his conversion narrative. Such journeys could exist on quite different planes: reading adventures, voyages of intellectual discovery or religious evolutions that passed through various stages of doubt and reassurance. Often, however, the convert quite literally travelled from one city or landscape to another, by carriage, ship or on foot. Volk and his wife were not the only ones to undertake their conversion abroad rather than in their home country. Whatever journeys the converts recount in the run-up to conversion, what all conversion narratives share is the fact that this movement led them to the new religion. The journey constitutes an important element of all conversion narratives and for that reason one finds many travel metaphors in the conversion accounts. Converting away from home was a common phenomenon, which may have been connected in part with the anticipated difficulties of having to announce one's own conversion beforehand in a largely Protestant region. Converting in a Catholic region, in contrast, could heighten the sense of inclusion and 'coming home'.

The conversion accounts reflect the ways in which the authors grappled with the changes and demands of their time, with the rules, values, and orders that had been set in motion and in which the converts were searching for their place. The (re-)orientation towards Catholicism, which promised religion, stability, unambiguousness and clear ordering principles went hand-in-hand with the attempt to recognise these orders. While Catholic doctrine may initially have contained much that was difficult to accept, especially for non-Catholic intellectuals – for instance papal infallibility, the veneration of Mary and the saints, the doctrine of transubstantiation, celibacy or indulgences – converts eventually integrated these elements into their own worldview. In his 1961 study, Kurt Aland cites four main motivations for conversion to Catholicism in the nineteenth century, which also regularly appear in the conversion narratives: 1) The search 'for authority, safety, certainty and emotional security', 2) the search 'for religious experience' and 3) environmental influences, especially encounters with Catholics and, finally, 4) 'non-theological factors'.[10] Attraction to Catholicism generally went along with a critique of the social order. Frequently, but not always, converts sought the restoration of a previous condition of society.

Even where they largely continued to adhere to the traditional narrative, the accounts reveal not just Catholic believers but also the individual in the society of his or her time. Women and men reflected on their intellectual development, professional activities, the foundations of society and the hopes and fears that preoccupied them in connection with their conversion. Although many of the conversion narratives appear to have been written shortly after conversion, some of them hint that the conversion was not a central turning point in their own life story, and that their lives were not constructed solely around questions of faith and religious knowledge. Converts conceived of the self in relational terms: with respect to their families of origin, social status, professional and social surroundings, their role as citizens, position in the life cycle, and kin network and their old and new faith communities.

At a time when scientificity was associated with exact and unambiguous results, stressing the coherence and unambiguousness of the Roman Catholic Church and pointing to the differentiations within Protestantism declared the Catholic Church to be a bastion of truth and scientificity. Thus even unpublished conversion accounts mirror the confrontations between Catholicism and the Protestant churches in the nineteenth century, which the converts themselves, their biographers and/or mentors repeatedly inscribed into these narratives,

---

[10] Kurt Aland, *Über den Glaubenswechsel in der Geschichte des Christentums* (Berlin: Verlag Alfred Töpelmann, 1961), 119. On the limits and continuing relevance of his research approach, see Rudolf Leeb and Kurt Aland, 'Über den Glaubenswechsel in der Geschichte des Christentums', *wiener zeitschrift zur geschichte der neuzeit* 7 (2007): 123–33.

although we cannot more precisely define the importance of these conflicts and polemics in the lives of converts.

Apart from these entrenched 'historical truths' and certainties, which placed the superiority of the Catholic Church and its teachings in the foreground, while frequently appearing in these texts as excurses with little connection to the biographical development, autobiographical texts by converts often reveal ambivalences that resisted the propagandistic function of conversion narratives. The emphasis on the physical and emotional crises of the frequently long and drawn-out conversion process may well have been an obligatory element of the conversion narrative. If, however, the turning points and ruptures in a life story so obviously did not end happily with conversion to the 'true church', we may suspect why such conversion accounts remained unpublished or never received the church's seal of approval.

In their accounts, converts pointed to the same problems and weaknesses in society that were lamented by the Catholic Church. Their calls for changes to the Catholic Church, which in some cases stemmed from irenicist or ecumenical ideas, generally met with little response within the Church. The Church expected its new members to adapt, while converts quite often aspired to change the Church. The modernisation of the Church was not considered the province of converts, who personally embodied the difficulties of an incontrovertible, permanent and clear distinction between Catholicism and the Protestant churches. Bold public professions of loyalty to Catholicism did nothing to change this.

Conversions to Catholicism can only be interpreted within the broader framework of the convert's changing viewpoints on and critiques of the societies in which they lived. Many converts saw themselves as independent personalities whose development had been inspired, and also accompanied (but never dominated) by a variety of persons. In the stereotypical pattern of the conversion account, themes appear that were only tangential to religious development, but that, seen from a bird's eye view, were significant for the convert's way of life, social and intellectual development.

The Setting

It is still extremely difficult to make any empirical statements about religious conversion in nineteenth-century Germany, let alone Europe. The newest figures for the nineteenth century can be found in the atlas of religious geography compiled by Lucian Hölscher, with comparative overviews on conversions between the Christian churches from1836 to 1918.[11] For the German-speaking region in the nineteenth century, one can observe three waves in which conversion accounts by Catholic converts were published and intensively and publicly discussed. The first wave of conversions was that of Romanticism,[12] a second occurred around the time of the Revolution of 1848/49 and the third highpoint coincided with the measures undertaken by the Vatican after the First Vatican Council and the state secularisation tendencies of the final third of the nineteenth century. This trend is also evident in our collections of conversion accounts in Germany. This finding is thus based on publicly discussed but not empirical collections and studies of intra-Christian conversion during the long nineteenth century, since we only have meaningful and centrally collected data beginning in 1880,[13] but also because the nineteenth century was dominated by conversions to Protestantism.[14] The rough trends are as follows: more people at this time converted from Catholicism to Protestantism[15] (even in the southern states of the German Empire) and, in turn, the number of conversions was far higher in the East than the West. Conversions to Protestantism caused far less of a public stir, since they were in accordance with a logic of progress that was believed to include an evolution from Catholicism to Protestantism. In our view, the peaks in the less frequent conversions to Catholicism at the beginning, middle and last third of the century owed much to the fact that justifications by Catholic converts were mainly published in times of upheaval, since these changes affected not just individuals but entire societies and were directed against the trend towards secularisation and the close association between

11 Lucian Hölscher (ed.), *Datenatlas zur religiösen Geographie im protestantischen Deutschland: Von der Mitte des 19. Jahrhunderts bis zum Zweiten Weltkrieg*, 4 vols. [vol. 1: *Norden*, vol. 2: *Osten*, vol. 3: *Westen*, vol. 4: *Süden*] (Berlin and New York: de Gruyter, 2001).

12 Edith Saurer, 'Romantische KonvertitInnen. Religion und Identität in der Wiener Romantik', in *Paradoxien der Romantik. Gesellschaft, Kultur und Wissenschaft in Wien im frühen 19. Jahrhundert*, ed. Christian Aspalter et al. (Wien: Facultas, 2006) 229–55.

13 Hölscher, *Datenatlas*, vol. 1, 31.

14 Although civil registers of births, deaths and marriages had been introduced in the German *Länder* as early as 1798 or after 1815, it was not until the 'Law on the certification of civil status and marriage' of 6 February 1875 that information on religious affiliation was systematically and centrally recorded in Imperial Germany. Nevertheless, it is difficult to obtain reliable empirical figures. See Kurt Aland, *Über den Glaubenswechsel*, 123–9. Aland includes statistical information on conversions from Protestantism to Catholicism and vice-versa from 1880–1899 (p. 99) and 1880–1924 (p. 135) as well as additional statistics on people who officially joined or left the Catholic Church in Germany from 1910–1954 (pp. 136–9). See also Klaus Schatz, *Zwischen Säkularisation und Zweitem Vatikanum: Der Weg des deutschen Katholizismus im 19. und 20. Jahrhundert* (Frankfurt a. M.: Knecht, 1986).

15 The integrative terms 'Protestantism' and 'Protestants' are used here to refer to all Protestant denominations in Germany, although differences between the Lutheran, Reformed and various United churches persisted in the nineteenth century.

German nationalism and Protestantism. Converts not just in Europe were responding to social change, and the accounts they wrote of their conversions may be used to explore this development.

Several conversions to Catholicism caused a public scandal in the mid-nineteenth century. The Prussian official *Geheimer Regierungsrat* Wilhelm Gustav Werner Volk (1804–1869), who became known as a writer under his pseudonym Ludwig Clarus, was at the centre of one of these debates. This conversion lends itself particularly well to study since it is documented not only in a very detailed conversion account, but also in other source documents. A member of the provincial council in Erfurt from 1838, Volk published on various topics such as medieval Spanish literature, Hans Christian Andersen, mysticism and current political conflicts, at first anonymously and from 1846 under his pseudonym. He also translated from the Latin, Italian, English, Dutch and Danish and penned essays on state and church institutions. One of his interests was also mission work in Australia, about which he translated and wrote an introduction to an English text by the Benedictine William Bernard Ullathorne (1806–1889).[16] After converting, Volk not only published extensively on the circumstances of his conversion, but was also in close contact with David Rosenthal,[17] who began publishing the first substantial anthology of texts by nineteenth-century Catholic converts, including Wilhelm Volk, in 1865.[18] Although every conversion and every conversion account has its own particular traits, Volk's conversion narratives display both the typical mixture of autobiographical and biographical texts and a detailed 'description of the world' in which he enunciates his personal religious, philosophical and political convictions and seeks to explain them in scholarly terms. Beyond the explanation and description of the conversion, Volk's texts also underline his political notions of a German nation and a German nation-state, which display not only a growing critical distance to the Prussian government

16 [Wilhelm Gustav Volk], 'Katholische Mission in Australien', *Historisch-Politische Blätter* 4 (1839): 437–45, 454–64, 530–39.

17 The Breslau physician David August Rosenthal had converted from Judaism to Catholicism, and his anthology of Catholic converts was a continuation of the collection by the Strasbourg bishop Andreas Räß, who between 1866 and 1880 had published an anthology on early modern Catholic converts. On this, see Schaser, 'Schreiben um dazuzugehören', 392–7.

18 In the preface to the first edition Rosenthal expresses gratitude 'for the many proofs of warm and lively interest ... that I have received in great abundance' and also specifically mentions 'Geheimer Regierungsrath Volk in Erfurt'. David August Rosenthal, *Convertitenbilder aus dem neunzehnten Jahrhundert*, vol. 1: *Deutschland* (Schaffhausen: Hurter'sche Buchhandlung, 1866), xii. On the friendship between Rosenthal and Volk, see also Manfred Fleischer, *Katholische und lutherische Ireniker: Unter Berücksichtigung des 19. Jahrhunderts* (Göttingen, Frankfurt a.M., and Zurich: Musterschmidt, 1968), 112.

and Protestantism, but also accord an important place to the primacy of the Catholic Church. In the Protestant camp his conversion and publications were initially considered a 'particularly glaring' case.[19] At a distance of nearly 50 years, however, the *Allgemeine Deutsche Biographie* described his narrative as 'one ... of the best writings on conversion'.[20] Volk's conversion became part of the confessional conflicts fought out in the nineteenth-century public sphere. In reaction to Rosenthal's collection, Nippold suggested that after his conversion, Volk had shown himself to be disappointed by Catholicism: 'Those who know Volk say that his chief character trait is a pathological nervous irritability, and they explain the insane fanaticism that he displayed after his conversion with inner dissatisfaction at the contrast he experienced between his fantasy of the Catholic Church and reality'.[21] Rosenthal in turn noted in the preface to the second edition of his collection that 'shortly after the publication of his work', Nippold had been found 'to have a serious disturbance to the balance of his mind, which required admission to a mental institution'.[22]

The city of Erfurt, where Volk converted, had 33,625 inhabitants in 1855,[23] the majority of them Protestants,[24] and could look back on a turbulent past. Erfurt had been an important centre of trade in the Middle Ages, but lost its autonomy and function as a regional economic centre during the Thirty Years War. Under the rule of Electoral Mainz (from 1664), following the transfer to Prussia in 1802 and subsequent Napoleonic occupation (1807–1814) and finally after reintegration into Prussian rule following the Congress of Vienna (1815) the fronts continued to be drawn between a Protestant majority and a Catholic minority. Erfurt remained a confessionally divided city; there were Catholic and Protestant foundations, schools, orphanages, poorhouses and separate associations and clubs for Catholic and Lutheran citizens. Both the Catholic and Protestant camps came under pressure from the secularisation pushed by Prussia starting in 1802. 'The Catholic [and] Protestant school board (*Schuldeputation*) was abolished and its competences and tasks accordingly transferred to secular

---

19 Friedrich Nippold, *Welche Wege führen nach Rom? Geschichtliche Beleuchtung der römischen Illusion über die Erfolge der Propaganda* (Heidelberg: Fr. Bassermann, 1869), 285.

20 Ludwig Fränkel, 'Volk, Wilhelm Gustav Werner V.', in *Allgemeine Deutsche Biographie*, vol. 40 (1896; rept. Berlin: Duncker & Humblot, 1971), 228.

21 Nippold, *Welche Wege führen nach Rom?*, 287.

22 David August Rosenthal, *Convertitenbilder aus dem neunzehnten Jahrhundert*, vol. 1: *Deutschland*, 3rd edn (Schaffhausen: Hurter'sche Buchhandlung, 1889), xv.

23 Wilhelm Horn, *Erfurts Stadtverfassung und Stadtwirtschaft in ihrer Entwicklung bis zur Gegenwart: Ein Beispiel zur Verfassungsgeschichte und Sozialpolitik der deutschen Städte* (Jena: G. Fischer, 1904), 32.

24 There are no precise figures until 1910. At that time, more than 80 per cent of Erfurters were Protestants. See Hölscher, *Datenatlas*, vol. 2, 15.

authorities'.[25] In 1817 Prussia forced Erfurt to join the 'Old Prussian Union' (which unified Lutherans and Calvinists in a Protestant state church), and the 'Amended Municipal Ordinance' of 17 March 1831 severely limited the city's rights.[26] The population grew over the nineteenth century, interrupted by setbacks caused by the occupation and cholera outbreaks, from 17,680 (1802) to 85,191 (1900).[27] The period following the French interregnum with its high contribution payments and siege was characterised, after the founding of the German Customs Union in 1833 and the expansion of the Thuringian Railway in 1846/1847, by an economic upswing.[28]

In 1838, two years after his marriage, Volk, as councillor of Magdeburg, was transferred to the government in Erfurt. The sources tell us merely that he took his office and activities seriously and continued to publish a good deal anonymously or under a pseudonym. In this he was not exceptional, since many state officials wrote in those days. In Austria 'nearly all' writers and poets between 1780 and 1848 are said to have been civil servants.[29] For 10 years Volk was editor of the weekly *Der alte Fritz*,[30] a 'conservative paper'.[31] In response to the Revolution of 1848/49 the initiators of the weekly were anxious to offer readers political orientation at reasonable prices: 'Old Fritz only appears on Saturday, however, because then he can survey the lies of the week past and spare his readers, and also because daily newspaper reading bewilders the mind and costs much time and money'. We learn that in the year of his conversion, Volk resided at Dalbergsweg 6, on the edge of the old town. In 1866, as a widowed

25 Walter Blaha, 'Erfurt unter dem Einfluß der Französischen Bürgerlichen Revolution (1789–1814)', in *Geschichte der Stadt Erfurt*, ed. Willibald Gutsche on behalf of the Erfurt town council (Weimar: Hermann Boehlaus Nachfolger, 1986), 180–213, 190.

26 Ulrich Heß, 'Weitere Entfaltung des Kapitalismus am Vorabend der Bürgerlich-demokratischen Revolution (1815–1847)', in *Geschichte der Stadt Erfurt*, 215–242, 237.

27 Horn, *Erfurts Stadtverfassung*, 32.

28 Ibid., 13–14.

29 Waltraud Heindl, *Gehorsame Rebellen: Bürokratie und Beamte in Österreich 1780 bis 1848* (Vienna, Cologne, and Graz: Böhlau, 1991), 291.

30 Ulrich Heß, 'Bürgerlich-demokratische Revolution, Durchsetzung der kapitalistischen Gesellschaftsordnung und Gründung der Sozialdemokratischen Arbeiterpartei (1848–1870)', in *Geschichte der Stadt Erfurt*, 243–80, 265–6. By Volk's own account, he 'wrote and edited' the paper from 1853 to 1863. Joseph Kehrein, *Biographisch-literarisches Lexikon der katholischen deutschen Dichter, Volks- und Jugendschriftsteller*, vol. 2 (Zurich, Stuttgart, and Würzburg: L. Woerl, 1871), 240.

31 'Der alte Fritz, was er ist und was er will', proof sheet, Erfurt, 20 December 1851, p. 1. Volk does not appear in the paper under his name. Trippe also names Volk as the paper's editor. [Karl Friedrich Trippe], *Denkmal auf Volk's (Ludwig Clarus') Grab, gesetzt von jüngster Freundeshand, (Erlös für Volk's Stiftungen)* (Erfurt: n.p., 1869), 31.

pensioner, his address was Domgasse 2, and the address books of 1865 and 1868 have him living at Farbengasse 2.[32]

The Example of a Family Conversion: The Conversion of the Volk Family in 1855/1856

Let us begin with a brief account of how the conversion proceeded based on what we know from Volk's writings, other sources and the secondary literature. Volk had been grappling with religious questions intensely for a number of years before he and his wife Caroline (née Hausbrandt, 1810?–1858) converted. Baptised as a Protestant, he was critical of the negative attitudes towards the Catholic Church that were common in his milieu, and initially supported an irenicist position, which he expressed in his writings among other things by extensively citing statements and pronouncements by the Catholic Church or Catholic personalities before analysing these texts. This mediating position drew upon his highly critical stance towards the general development of society, especially the consequences of the French Revolution and the Revolution of 1848, as well as upon his contacts to the circle around Joseph Görres. Ever since the publication of his *Geständnisse* (Confessions, 1846) he had been publicly accused of having a 'Catholic attitude'. Volk nevertheless only converted on 22 October 1855 together with his wife in Aigen (near Salzburg, Austria), shortly after Caroline Volk contracted cholera and recognised, in the face of possible death, that she did 'not want to die a Protestant'.[33] One year after the couple's joint conversion, their only daughter, Johanna Marie Magdalena Luise (born on 1 April 1839 and known as Marie), also converted to Catholicism in the same Austrian village.

The conversion caused problems for Volk at work. According to his personnel file, the civil servant, who was well respected by his superiors, had up to then been responsible for 'the policing system and police administration in general;

[32] *Adreßbuch oder vollständiger Wohnungs-Anzeiger für die Stadt Erfurt*, ed. Trütschler von Falkenstein. Köngl. Polizei-Lieutnant (Erfurt: Druck und Verlag von Hennings und Hopf, 1855), 231; *Adreßbuch oder vollständiger Wohnungs-Anzeiger für die Stadt Erfurt*, ed. Wilh. Eduard Schubotz, Polizei-Secretair (Erfurt: printed by the editor, 1862), 135; *Adreßbuch oder vollständiger Wohnungs-Anzeiger für die Stadt Erfurt*, ed. Wilh. Eduard Schubotz, Polizei-Secretair (Erfurt: printed by the editor, 1865), 174; and *Adreßbuch oder vollständiger Wohnungs-Anzeiger für die Stadt Erfurt*, ed. Wilhelm Eduard Schubotz, Polizei-Secretair und Königlicher Polizei-Anwalt (Erfurt: printed by the editor, 1868), 183. We would like to thank Astrid Rose of the Stadtarchiv Erfurt for information and assistance in researching Volk in Erfurt.

[33] [Wilhelm Gustav Volk], *Aus dem Leben einer Convertitin. Mitgetheilt von Ludwig Clarus* [i.e., Wilhelm Gustav Volk] (Schaffhausen: Hurter'sche Buchhandlung, 1859), 111. The book's publisher was the convert Friedrich Hurter.

religious, educational and morals policy, construction policy, agricultural, forestry, hunting and rivers policy, press affairs [and] the gendarmerie'.[34] The Prussian state immediately withdrew its confidence from Volk, because, 'since his conversion to the Catholic Church full confidence cannot be placed in him for all areas covered by his department ... measures have [been taken] to no longer entrust him with such matters as touch specifically on the interests of the Catholic Church'.[35] Volk resisted attempts to pension him off, but relented when threatened with forcible transfer. He ultimately owed it to his superior that he was offered an '*honourable* resignation from the civil service' and was able to continue in his post until 1 July 1858 and retire with a full pension.[36] Compared to the converts in South Africa and Australia who will be presented in the two chapters that follow, there is little ambiguity about the impact of conversion on Volk's agency: his conversion initially imperilled and then ended his career as a jurist in the civil service.

In the years after his retirement, Volk concentrated on his writing, established charitable foundations and continued his irenicist activities. When the family returned to Aigen for a longer stay after Volk's dismissal, Caroline Volk is said to have contracted measles. While in 1855 after her conversion in Aigen she had recovered from cholera 'as by a miracle, through the divine magic of her firm, unwavering faith',[37] on her last visit there she brought home the disease that would kill her in 1858, as she allegedly already suspected before her departure. The couple's only daughter entered a Salesian convent in Mühlheim (Möhr), where she lived as a novice until 1869.[38] After the closure of the convent in Mühlheim she moved to France, to the convent in Montélimar, where she died on 11 July 1898.[39] When her father wrote his will in March 1868 it appeared

---

34 GStA PK, I. HA Rep. 77, Ministerium des Innern, Tit. 185 a, Nr. 21 Bd. 3, Acta betr. die Conduiten-Listen von den Beamten der Regierung zu Erfurt, 1848–1866, p. 101.

35 GStA PK, I. HA Rep. 77, Ministerium des Innern, Tit. 397, Nr. 4 Bd. 8 Acta betr. die Anstellung der Räthe zu Assessoren bei der Regierung zu Erfurt 1849–1862 [unpag.]: copy of a letter of 6 April 1857 from Erfurt, 'Die Arbeitskräfte bei der Abtheilung des Innern hiesiger Regierung betreffend'.

36 Ibid.: From a letter of 23 June 1857 from the *Oberpräsident* of the Saxon government to the minister of the interior [emphasis in the original].

37 Volk, *Aus dem Leben einer Convertitin*, 145.

38 Volk's will was prepared on 20 March 1869 'for Miss Marie Volk, novice of the Salesian convent at Muhlheim [i.e., Mühlheim] a. d. Möhne'. Bistumsarchiv Erfurt, Bischöfliches Generalvikariat Paderborn: Pfarrstellen u.ä., Behörden, Einrichtungen, Stiftungen etc. im Bereich des heutigen Bistums Erfurt, Acta Specialia betreffend die Mission zu Ranis. Bischöfliches General-Vicariat zu Paderborn, 1862–1930.

39 Her religious name was Peronne Marie. She probably entered the convent after the death of her mother in 1858. We would like to thank Sister M. Salesia of the Convent of the Visitation in Uedem for information on her time at the convent (communication of 21 October 2011).

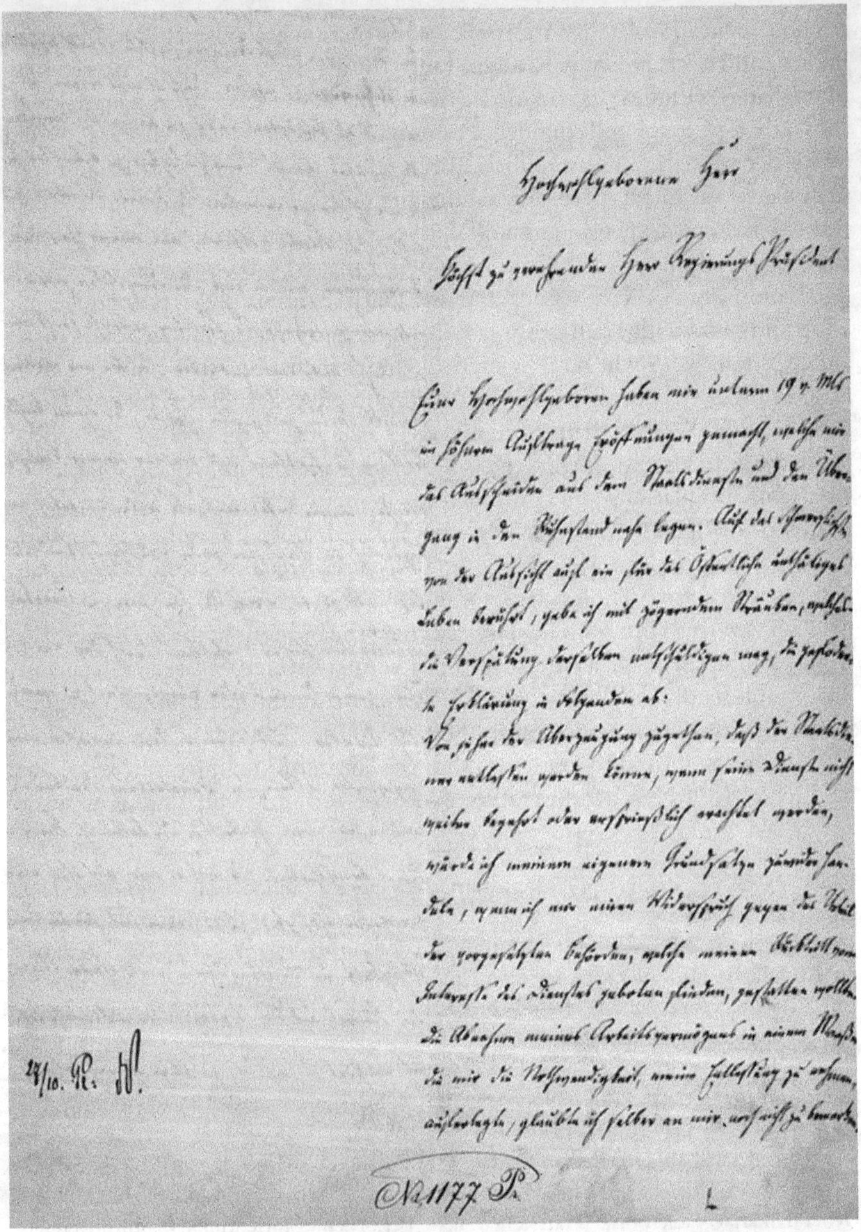

Hochwohlgeborner Herr

Höchst zu verehrender Herr Regierungs Präsident

№ 1177 P.

Figure 1.1 Letter from Volk to the president of the Saxon government, 25 October 1857 (GStA PK, I. HA Rep. 77, Ministerium des Innern, Tit. 397, Nr. 4 Bd. 8, Acta betr. die Anstellung der Räthe zu Assessoren bei der Regierung zu Erfurt 1849–1862)

unclear whether she would ultimately choose convent life, and Volk left her his entire estate. In the case that his daughter predeceased him or was prevented by religious vows from coming into her inheritance, he named the 'episcopal see of Paderborn' as his sole heir.[40]

Three topics are at the heart of Volk's last will and testament. First and foremost, he commended his soul to God and ordered 'that a requiem should be held once yearly in the cathedral here', 'whose prayers should also include my wife, who died on 16 November 1858'. Volk went on to ensure the future of the foundations he had established with his (not further specified) assets (especially the women's hospital (*Frauenpflegeanstalt*) in Erfurt and the mission in Ranis) and to guarantee an income for his daughter in case she decided not to join the convent.[41] His income included his pension, fees from his publications and an unspecified sum in donations. Thus 'Volk's Institution for Catholic Waifs' apparently regularly placed advertisements in the *Allgemeiner Anzeiger* (e.g., on Wednesday, 11 July 1860), thanking the donors ('through the donations a few months ago of handicrafts and money from our dear benefactors and benefactresses ... ') and enumerating how these donations had been spent.[42]

The attempt to reconstruct the biographical facts already shows the degree to which Volk's autobiographical account influenced what has come down to us about his conversion. Little is known about his professional and personal situation in Erfurt. His place of residence, parish and employer, like the details of his family life appear as gaps in the autobiographical and biographical depictions. The text that tells us the most about Volk's life in Erfurt is a pamphlet written about him by a 'friend' after his death.[43] The author, Karl Friedrich Trippe,[44] who had spoken at Volk's funeral, stylises him as the 'centre of Erfurt's Catholics'[45] and portrays him as a profoundly conservative man.[46] A number of motifs that recur in other publications in connection with Volk's life and conversion

---

[40] Volk composed his will on 3 March 1868 in Erfurt. An eight-page manuscript copy can be found at the Bistumsarchiv Erfurt, Bischöfliches Generalvikariat Paderborn: Pfarrstellen u.ä., Behörden, Einrichtungen, Stiftungen etc. im Bereich des heutigen Bistums Erfurt, Acta Specialia betreffend die Mission zu Ranis. Bischöfliches General-Vicariat zu Paderborn, 1862–1930.

[41] Quotations from the will in ibid.

[42] Bistumsarchiv Erfurt, Die Volk'sche Anstalt. gen. Angefangen 1856, geschlossen 1882, No 1.

[43] [Trippe], *Denkmal auf Volk's (Ludwig Clarus') Grab.*

[44] Trippe was the parish priest of St. Nicolai und Jacobi in Erfurt from 1868 to 1886. We would like to thank Michael Matscha, director of the episcopal archive (Bistumsarchiv) in Erfurt, for finding out the author of this work (communication of 21 October 2011).

[45] [Trippe], *Denkmal auf Volk's (Ludwig Clarus') Grab*, 36.

[46] He speaks of 'Volk's innate conservativism' and notes that 'he was every inch a conservative', Ibid., 8, 30.

probably appeared here first. Thus, for example, Trippe mentions that Volk was reportedly forced to retire 'against his will, and with half of his salary as a pension, after thirty-two years of exemplary, loyal and efficient execution of his official duties'.[47] Although we have evidence that this was incorrect (see above), this information was assiduously repeated.[48] This pamphlet also informs us of a large funeral and sympathetic interest in the death of Volk, his foundations and charitable activities. By this account, the boys of the Volk Foundation,[49] members of the Catholic Journeymen's Association, 'the entire Catholic clergy of Erfurt, as well as the heads and representatives of the government and municipal authorities, members of the 'Catholic Casino' (a sociable and political club) and the women's hospital attended the burial.[50] According to Trippe, Volk had also served as president of the Catholic men's association in Erfurt, and he explains the large turnout at the funeral in terms not just of Volk's foundations, but also his numerous anonymous charitable works. The words spoken at Volk's graveside also mention among the mourners members of the Catholic apprentices' association and representatives of the Catholics in and around Ranis (Thuringia),[51] where during his lifetime Volk had already had a church built and provided the salary for a missionary priest.[52] It is unclear what connection Volk had with this town.[53]

The sources on Volk's life contain no traces of the disappointment with or turning away from Catholicism that Nippold indicates. He continued his irenicist engagement after conversion. Fleischer counts him among the 'key figures of the Erfurt conference', which was intended to pave the way for a rapprochement between Protestants and Catholics. At Volk's suggestion,

47 Ibid., 20.

48 Fränkel, 'Volk, Wilhelm', in *Allgemeine Deutsche Biographie*, vol. 40 (1896), 227–230, online: http://de.wikisource.org/wiki/ADB:Volk,_Wilhelm [accessed on 14 June 2010], according to which Volk 'retired with half his salary'.

49 Bistumsarchiv Erfurt, Acta des Bischöfl. Geistlichen Gerichts zu Erfurt, betr. die von dem Herrn Geheimen Regierungsrath Volk zu Erfurt errichtete Erziehungs-Anstalt für verwahrloste katholische Kinder, 1856 [–1932].

50 [Trippe], *Denkmal auf Volk's (Ludwig Clarus') Grab*, 3–4.

51 Ibid., 40.

52 'His favourite project, however, was the founding of a mission in Ranis, for which he spent years writing, collecting, saving and sacrificing. There he built a superb little church under the protection of his patron, St William, as well as St Elizabeth. He also bought a rectory and garden there ... '. Ibid., 35.

53 The relevant documents confirm Volk's endowments for Ranis, but provide no information about his motivations. Cf. Bistumsarchiv Erfurt, Bischöfliches Generalvikariat Paderborn: Pfarrstellen u.ä., Behörden, Einrichtungen, Stiftungen etc. im Bereich des heutigen Bistums Erfurt, Acta Specialia betreffend die Mission zu Ranis. Bischöfliches General-Vicariat zu Paderborn, 1862–1930.

the meeting took place in Erfurt in 1860.[54] The Prussian government reacted harshly to this initiative and instituted criminal proceedings against Volk for 'holding an illegal assembly'. The charges were dropped and the Protestant theologian Ernst Wilhelm Hengstenberg was not the only one to mock 'the convert and foolish zealot Privy Councillor Volk'.[55] In 1867, seven years after the abortive meeting, Volk published a work under his well-known pseudonym and, unmoved by the failure of the Erfurt conference, stressed that an important step had been taken to reconcile Protestants and Catholics in Germany and that the course embarked upon must be continued. 'In the universal striving for national unity, toward whose realisation people are working so energetically, there is new inspiration to take up the idea again. ... The experiences of the summer of 1866 [the Austro-Prussian War] made it all the clearer to me how timely that push was ... '.[56] Until shortly before his death Volk published tirelessly in order, as Trippe puts it, to ensure that 'the proceeds of his continued industrious writing' would benefit his institutions.[57]

In Erfurt, where he lived for more than 30 years from 1838 until his death, he has left no public trace. Volk (like his wife years before) was buried in the Brühl cemetery in 1869. The cemetery was closed soon after his funeral.[58] There is evidence that Volk's grave was refurbished in 1901,[59] and that it could still be found there in 1914.[60] Perhaps the tombstones of the Volks were removed in 1925, when the Brühl cemetery was finally turned into a park.[61] At any

---

[54] Fleischer, *Katholische und lutherische Ireniker*, 131, 161.

[55] Both quotations are from Fleischer, *Katholische und lutherische Ireniker*, 137–8.

[56] Ludwig Clarus [i.e., Wilhelm Gustav Volk], *Die Zusammenkunft gläubiger Protestanten und Katholiken zu Erfurt im Herbste 1860 und deren Verlauf. Eine auf eigene Theilnahme und sämmtliche bekannt gewordene Quellen gegründete Darstellung und Mahnung zur Fortsetzung des Werkes* (Paderborn: Junkermann'sche Buchhandlung, 1867), 4.

[57] [Trippe], *Denkmal auf Volk's (Ludwig Clarus') Grab*, 20.

[58] Helmut Peinhardt, *Erfurt im 19. Jahrhundert. Bilderchronik: Aus Archivalien des Stadtarchivs Erfurt* [on the occasion of the city's 1250th anniversary celebrations] (Erfurt : Verl.-Haus Thüringen, 1992), 93.

[59] There is a handwritten receipt, signed on 28 June 1901 by 'Fr. Oxfort', which affirms that he had received '120 marks from Diac. Boesner for the renovation of the family grave of Geh. Regierungsrat Volk'. Bistumsarchiv Erfurt, Acta betreffend den Bau einer katholischen Kirche zu Ranis vol. II. There are also receipts concerning the care of the grave, the last of them from 1902.

[60] Wilhelm Lorenz recorded the inscriptions in 1914. See Peter-Jürgen Klippstein, 'Die Inschriften der Grabsteine auf dem Brühler Friedhof in Erfurt, aufgezeichnet von Wilhelm Lorenz', *Jahrbuch für Erfurter Geschichte* 4 (2009): 225–55.

[61] A plaque at the Brühler Straße entrance (opposite the theatre) states that the cemetery was established in the sixteenth century, but that the terrain had served as the pleasure gardens of Electoral Mainz from 1664 to 1802 before being consecrated again as a burial ground in 1820.

rate the gravestones of Caroline and Wilhelm Volk may now be found in the Episcopal Educational Centre of St Martin (the former 'Volk Foundation') at Farbengasse 2, on a wall in the interior courtyard.[62] There is no mention of the foundation Volk established in 1856 anywhere in or on the building, nor any explanation of why the two gravestones were placed there. No personal papers have yet been found for Volk,[63] who according to Trippe kept a journal and was a passionate collector.[64]

Volk's conversion not only reflects in detail the religious debates that dominated in the German-speaking region at this period: his writings address not only intra-Christian and confessional but also general societal problems and rivalries that had their origins in the various Christian confessions. Although Christian–Jewish dialogues were also being conducted, and the interest in Islam and other world religions was great in the nineteenth century, religious debates in everyday political life were influenced by these intra-Christian conflicts.

Wilhelm Gustav Werner Volk, who died at the age of 65 in 1869, 14 years after his conversion, only earned an entry in the *Allgemeine Deutsche Biographie* (ADB) in 1896. The author of the entry found it difficult to characterise his subject according to the usual professional categories: he describes Volk as a 'church and literary historian, mystic and patrologist'.[65] It is not his professional career but his path from the Lutheran to the Catholic Church that provides the basic structure for the article. Born on 25 January 1804 into a 'Lutheran, not particularly pious family in Halberstadt', during his student days in Göttingen Volk had 'still [been] without any definite faith, and never went to church'. As a jurist he had then begun with 'extensive Pietist readings' in 1829. When he arrived at the University of Berlin in 1832 for his third state examination in law, he met the Catholic convert Georg Phillips (1804–1872), who is said to have introduced him to Catholic circles in southern Germany. 'Employed from the spring of 1838 by the government in Erfurt', Volk now devoted all his creative energies 'to religious endeavours', which he had become acquainted with through Georg Phillips, Clemens Brentano and Joseph Görres. 'In this way his official career, despite his considerable gifts, never took him beyond the rank of *Regierungsrath*, as which he retired in 1858'.

---

62 The gravestone for Caroline Volk, née Hausbrandt, gives only her date of death (16 November 1858); Volk's reads: 'Wilhelm Volk, königl. Geheimer Regierungsrath, b. 25 January 1804, d. 17. March 1869'.

63 The 'Archivbestand Geistliches Gericht Erfurt, jüngerer Bestand' at the Bistumsarchiv Erfurt has not yet been made completely accessible. According to the archive's director Michael Matscha, no segments of Volk's possible collected papers have been found thus far (communication of 21 October 2011).

64 [Trippe], *Denkmal auf Volk's (Ludwig Clarus') Grab*, 30.

65 Fränkel, 'Volk, Wilhelm Gustav Werner', 227–30.

The author of the article calls Wilhelm Volk one of the 'most remarkable personalities of the movement he represented so industriously' and clearly finds it difficult to name the reasons for his conversion, although he does mention that Volk's account was considered 'one of the finest texts on conversion … '. The article thus does not, as was usual in the ADB, follow Volk's professional career, which here could have been portrayed as that of an author or a (church) historian, but rather presents a personality who preferred a life in the service of Catholicism to a prestigious professional position as a judge.

The far briefer entry in the *Deutsche Biographische Enzyklopädie* returns to the pattern of the professional career, outlining the stages in Volk's legal and administrative activities, only to mention his conversion in the final sentence, without passing any judgment. The text departs from other descriptions of Volk's profession, introducing him as a literary historian and hagiographer.[66] It merely mentions that Volk had studied law, philology and philosophy in Göttingen, and of Volk's extensive topical writings, cites only the conversion account and two texts on the veneration of saints. Although the last two citations could be considered evidence of Volk's hagiographic writings, one would be hard pressed to interpret the reference to the conversion account as proof of his activity as a literary historian. The conversion account is assigned an outstanding place within his oeuvre, while Volk's writings on literary history and religious policy are as little mentioned as his articles on current events and developments in politics and church policy. Although this article apparently assigns little significance to Volk's conversion, it accords great significance to his account of it.

Conversion is at the core of the biographical appreciation of Volk in David Rosenthal's anthology of converts. Rosenthal, whose expressed aim in his collection of German Catholic convert biographies was to create a lasting monument to them, portrays the 'Prussian *geheimer Regierungsrat* in Erfurt' as an outstanding scholar and writer, who 'possessed nearly all the languages of Europe, and provided us now with classic literary histories, now with splendid translations of the most profound foreign authors and, in a voluminous religious biography, offered a truly immeasurable wealth of magnificent material for constructing a German cultural and literary history from a Catholic viewpoint'.[67]

In summary, Volk's conversion is given great importance not just in David Rosenthal's article, but also in all the biographical entries about him. We still have no scholarly biography of Volk that does justice to his life and extensive oeuvre.[68] In the eyes of the authors who wrote about Volk, conversion was a

66 'Volk, Wilhelm Gustav', in *Deutsche biographische Enzyklopädie*, vol. 10 (Munich: deGruyter, 1999), 243–4.

67 Rosenthal, *Convertitenbilder aus dem neunzehnten Jahrhundert*, vol. 1, 853–94.

68 Albert Portmann-Tinguely, 'Volk, Wilhelm Gustav Werner', in *Biographisch-Bibliographisches Kirchenlexikon*, vol. XIX (2001), 1499–1506.

central element for understanding his personality. Clearly, converting from Protestantism to Catholicism was not regarded as a private matter of conscience in the mid-nineteenth century. The whole human being, his conduct, interests, private life, professional development, publications and political opinions were up for discussion. People who took such a step in their lives appeared to change so fundamentally that in the eyes of many, they placed themselves outside the usual biographical framework. While this path taken by converts was often described as an absolutely necessary, virtually logical evolution, contemporaries generally emphasised the rupture or transgression they saw in conversion. This applies in particular to members of the church the convert had left. Like the converts themselves, members of the faith community the convert joined, in contrast, generally interpreted this step as a logical or expected orientation towards the 'true faith'. Both sides usually perceived converts as such, and it was not uncommon for them to subject their publications, conduct and way of life to particular scrutiny and in some cases mistrust.

The Concept of Person, Family and Gender in Wilhelm Gustav Werner Volk's Self-Representation (1804–1869)

How did Volk see himself? What space did he accord to his conversion, and how did he wish others to understand it? In order to explore Volk's concept of person, we will consult not just his work *Simeon*, which is considered a conversion account, since in retrospect Volk characterised three of his biographical texts as publications on his conversion. What follows will focus not only on the three autobiographical books he mentions, but also includes a fourth work. In addition to the *Geständnisse eines im Protestantismus aufgewachsenen Christen über religiöse Erziehung und Bildung* (Confessions of a Christian Raised a Protestant on Religious Upbringing and Education) published anonymously in 1846, the *Glaubenslehrjahre eines im Protestantismus erzogenen Christen* (Religious Apprenticeship of a Christian Raised in Protestantism) published anonymously six years later and the three-volume *Simeon. Wanderungen und Heimkehr eines christlichen Forschers* (Wanderings and Homecoming of a Christian Explorer), published in 1862 and 1863 under the pseudonym Ludwig Clarus, the investigation will incorporate the conversion account by his wife, who had died in 1858, *Aus dem Leben einer Convertitin* (From the Life of a Female Convert),[69] which he brought out in 1859, also under the pseudonym

[69] [Wilhelm Gustav Volk], *Geständnisse eines im Protestantismus aufgewachsenen Christen über religiöse Erziehung und Bildung* (Mainz: Kirchheim, Schott und Thielmann, 1846); *Glaubenslehrjahre eines im Protestantismus erzogenen Christen* (Regensburg: Friedrich Regensberg, 1852); and *Aus dem Leben einer Convertitin*; Ludwig Clarus [i.e.,

Ludwig Clarus and in which he reported on his own conversion in the third person as well. He explicitly refers to this conversion narrative in *Simeon*.[70] Contemporaries already viewed these four publications as closely connected, reading them as a 'comprehensive autobiography'.[71] These texts may be read as the autobiographical testimony of a man who presents himself as a middle-class paterfamilias, thereby asserting his claim as head of household to shape and control not just his own life, but that of his family.

In 1846, nearly 10 years before their family conversion, Volk published the *Geständnisse eines im Protestantismus aufgewachsenen Christen*. In the preface he calls religion the 'mighty latent force in the Self of better humanity', and asserts that 'in every human being baptised a Christian ... there is a Simeon'.[72] The reference to the figure of the Jerusalemite Simeon, mentioned in Luke 2:25–35, who was known as a pious and god-fearing man and was said to have recognised the saviour in the child Jesus, ultimately gave the title to his conversion account of 1862/1863. The subtitle 'Wanderings and Homecoming of a Christian Explorer' emphasises the active part played by Volk, who presents himself in his conversion process as a seeker, in contrast to Simeon, whom 'the holy spirit answered' by leading him into the temple to which Jesus had been brought by his parents.

The *Geständnisse* portray the author's intellectual and religious development in childhood and youth. Biographically, the text ends with the completion of Volk's schooling. The composition of the book only partly follows the literary dramaturgy of the novel of development, however. Otherwise, it deploys a collage of Volk's various publications and closes with an appendix on 'the influence of the theatre on religious education'. Volk addresses topics in connection with stations in his biography and highlights the themes of his life, which he presents here to the public. On the one hand, he stresses the importance of classical antiquity and the church fathers, whose texts he had translated into German in order to 'suffuse myself with their spirit'.[73] On the other, Volk uses the account of his own progress to criticise political and social developments since the Enlightenment. Thus he rejects 'Wolffian philosophy, the English Deists, the Encyclopédistes and the government of Frederick the Great'.[74] For Volk, the Enlightenment represented an anti-Catholic, misguided modern age and the new Prussian rule

Wilhelm Gustav Volk], *Simeon. Wanderungen und Heimkehr eines christlichen Forschers*, 3 vols. (Schaffhausen: Hurter'sche Buchhandlung, 1862–1863).

70 'I have already acquitted myself of the duty to provide an account of the course and celebration of our conversion in advance [in *Aus dem Leben einer Convertitin*]'. Volk, *Simeon*, vol. 3, 403).

71 Friedrich Nippold, *Welche Wege führen nach Rom?*, 285–96, 286.

72 Volk, *Geständnisse*, iv, v.

73 Ibid., vii.

74 Ibid., 18.

over Erfurt, which was granted to Prussia first in 1802, and then permanently in 1815, following the French occupation (1806–1814). This forced change of allegiance was probably the occasion for Volk's anti-Prussian stance. At the time, many Germans held the enlightened Frederick II responsible for the collapse of the Holy Roman Empire of the German Nation because of his wars with Maria Theresa. Volk's rejection of these tendencies accompanied his 'penchant for the aristocracy' and 'a principle of government that emulated the kingdom of God'.[75] Volk criticises the period of the Napoleonic Wars for its 'sacralisation of nationalism' and replacement of faith with nationalism.[76] Volk, who notes his 'unbiased and impartial judgment' of political questions even as a schoolboy,[77] laments the anti-Catholicism of the commemoration of the Reformation held in Prussia in 1817 and points to the unequal treatment of Protestants and converts in the description of the state measures taken on the occasion of the pilgrimage to the Holy Robe in Trier in 1844.[78] Here he could refer back to a 38-page text published in 1845, in which he compares the Berlin Industrial Exhibition with the display of the Holy Robe in Trier, and expresses his incomprehension that 'pilgrimages by industrial and technological enthusiasts' were approved while Catholic pilgrimages were cursed as 'harbingers of the return of the Dark Ages'.[79] Volk was also of the opinion that magnetism and Mesmerism offered solutions to the alliance between natural laws and the belief in miracles, an alliance not seriously contemplated by Protestant contemporaries.[80] He was critical of the theatre and what he perceived as pleasure-loving theatrical people, believing them to be a danger to moral values, which is why he called for religious censorship of the theatre.[81]

Overall, Volk reveals himself in the various chapters of his *Geständnisse* as a knowledge-hungry boy and pupil who discovered his love of scholarship during his final years at school,[82] proved himself conservative in political matters, claimed a rational position and regarded the unity of Christendom as a worthwhile goal. Volk called his first autobiographical book *Geständnisse* (confessions, in the sense of admissions) not *Bekenntnisse* (confessions in the sense of professions) because he had written it not out of an innermost need,

---

75 Ibid., 237.

76 Ibid., 77–86.

77 Ibid., 236.

78 Ibid., 194.

79 [Wilhelm Gustav Volk], *Die Berliner Gewerbeausstellung und die Ausstellung des heiligen Rockes in Trier mit besonderer Bezugnahme auf den Rongeschen Brief. Ein Brief aus Berlin von einem Protestanten* (Münster: Friedr. Regensberg, 1845), 11–12. A second, unaltered printing appeared that same year.

80 Volk, *Geständnisse*, 258, 270–71.

81 Ibid., 322.

82 Ibid., 236.

but rather as a 'kind of self-defence against incorrect perceptions'.[83] At the end of the text Volk addresses his readers in order to inform them that he was already working on a second volume, but nevertheless aimed for his *Geständnisse*, although 'an unfinished whole', to represent 'a coherent little work'.[84]

This text already makes clear that Volk saw himself as a member of Prussia's intellectual elite, a universally learned scholar, an intelligent analyst and path-breaking political advisor. Later he would write that the *Geständnisse*, published in 1846 in Mainz anonymously, that is, without his later pseudonym, 'had unmasked the costs of the modern educational system' and had thereby awakened the 'official interest [of] ... then Prussian Education Minister Eichhorn'.[85] He also quotes extensively from a review by August Reichensperger,[86] whom he later considered a friend. Reichensperger had publicly stated that the contents of the *Geständnisse* 'were a quintessence of the moral and cultural history of Germany in the past fifty years, reflected in the life of the author',[87] and attested to his acuity of vision and love of truth.

Volk had already announced the second volume of his 'religious biography', entitled *Glaubenslehrjahre eines im Protestantismus erzogenen Christen*, for 1847.[88] Chronologically, Volk depicts his student years in Göttingen and Berlin, showing his protracted evolution from 'a dead belief in reason' to 'Christian faith', and pointing out that he underwent no Augustinian experience along the way.[89] Large segments of the volume are dedicated to addressing the reactions of Protestant critics to his *Geständnisse*. He does not deny here that his positions were in opposition to his own confession, but defends himself against accusations of having converted to Catholicism. He denies this vehemently, 'since I, on the contrary, cannot and must not but disdain it for its countless anti-biblical doctrines'.[90] In order to demonstrate this, he extensively investigates the 'business of conversion' in his *Glaubenslehrjahre*.[91]

---

83 Ibid., viii.

84 Ibid., 307.

85 Volk, *Simeon*, vol. 1, 2.

86 The reviewer August Reichensperger (1808–1895) was a lawyer, politician, art connoisseur, co-founder of the Catholic Centre Party and supporter of the Kölner Dombauverein, an association dedicated to the completion and preservation of Cologne Cathedral. In 1840 Reichensperger published an appeal for the completion of Cologne Cathedral. Georg Heinrich Kaufmann, 'Reichensperger, August', in *Allgemeine Deutsche Biographie*, vol. 53 (1907), 276–81.

87 Volk, *Simeon*, vol. 1, 2.

88 Volk, *Glaubenslehrjahre*, iii.

89 Ibid., iv.

90 Ibid., 175–6.

91 Ibid., iv.

Despite Volk's critique of this group, his passages about these converts conform to the pattern of conversion narratives. The personal history of the converts always constitutes the narrower narrative, which is inconceivable without a broader narrative, which embeds the convert's personal development in a portrayal addressing the general theological justifications for a change of confession as well as questions of canon law or church history.[92] References to the Bible, the church fathers and other ecclesiastical authorities are deployed as authentication and authorisation strategies, which also allowed the authors to demonstrate that they had seriously and carefully considered their target confession and not made the decision on a whim. The treatment of the topic follows Volk's usual working method. He begins with a general statement, then presents the first (in this case Catholic) and then the second (in this case Protestant) perspective, before weighing the arguments made by both groups in a sort of synthesis. In structuring the text, Volk emphasises his claim to objectivity, which he presents as a particular characteristic of his, both before and after conversion. He qualifies his generalising statements on converts by emphasising that they would have to be tested in a closer study of the converts' life stories.[93]

Thus Volk introduces this section with the general observation:

> Catholics could ... argue that the Protestant denominations, which in all corners of the globe have perhaps only one-quarter as many believers as the Catholic Church and boast of representing the most intelligent Christians, have seen far more conversions of illustrious individuals who have made their names in art and science to Catholicism than occurred in the other direction.[94]

Volk however also accepted the Protestant argument that most princely converts in the seventeenth and eighteenth centuries had entered the Catholic Church for secular reasons, and

> that their conversion, since most of them were impoverished younger sons, had had virtually no influence on their peoples and countries. It also could not be disputed that the assiduous efforts of the Jesuits had brought a substantial portion of these famous converts back to the old church, and that the church could by no means be proud of many of them, and that their exit from the Lutheran confession could actually be regarded as a sort of cleansing of the church.[95]

92 Volk, *Simeon*, vol. 1, 1–2.
93 Volk, *Glaubenslehrjahre*, 203.
94 Ibid., 177.
95 Ibid., 178.

In the very next sentence, however, Volk qualifies this view: 'We would be wrong, though, to give even the appearance of allowing ... this suspicion to fall on the majority or indeed on all converts'.[96] He also asks his readers to consider that Protestants frequently harbour prejudices against Catholics, and that he had only learned to overcome these prejudices 'through encounters with educated Catholics and visits to Catholic countries'.[97]

With these texts, which appeared before his conversion, Volk inserted himself into the learned world and, through his sophisticated portrayal, opened up a stringent potential interpretation of his own later conversion, despite his fundamental criticism of converts. This allowed him to expand his 'religious biography' to include these two volumes written before his conversion, thereby integrating them into his overall conversion narrative.

When composing his *Glaubenslehrjahre* Volk probably had no idea that his first extensive biographical study of a convert would be devoted to his own wife. Shortly after her death, Volk published the notes on his wife's conversion that she had prepared for him (according to him, as a birthday gift in 1858), but was never able to complete, under the title *Aus dem Leben einer Convertitin*.[98] Volk abridged and commented on this conversion narrative, quoting excerpts from his wife's diaries and letters. Passages from letters by named or anonymous correspondents were supplemented and integrated into a biographical account that lent the life of the convert (and his own) a function as examples, and Volk hoped that the book would reach not just Catholic but also Protestant readers.[99] 'After we accompanied the deceased to her resting place', Volk wrote one year after her death, ' ... we cannot help but point to several moments that allow us to accept the consoling conviction that each human life, with all of its apparent coincidences, represents a quite organic whole ordained by providence'.[100] Volk speaks little about himself in this text and when he does so, it is in the third person. The hierarchy of gender relations is already evident in the composition of his text: a highly emotional, simple account of events from his wife's pen is accompanied by extensive learned commentary, in some instances taking up more than three-quarters of the page, which illuminates the state of Catholicism in a scholarly manner and not least also describes the conversion process quite precisely, in order to counter the 'wrong notions' prevalent among Protestants.[101] In the description of his wife Caroline's life, Volk combines her autobiographical writings with his own comments in such a way as to make their marriage appear as a mirror image of the prevailing norm. He attributes deep feelings to her and

96 Ibid.

97 Ibid., 180.

98 Volk, *Aus dem Leben einer Convertitin*, 195.

99 Ibid., 125–6.

100 Ibid., 212.

101 Ibid., 125–6.

a 'very practical turn of mind'[102] and supplements her unfinished conversion narrative with historical retrospection, theological explanations and commentary. Volk justifies his additions and subtractions of text with 'consideration for living persons', the 'historical gaps' in Caroline Volk's conversion narrative and 'the wholly absent or only incompletely suggested references to the actual subject matter of faith' in her text.[103] Her husband vouched for the authenticity of the passages from Caroline Volk's autobiographical writings, which he consistently wanted to place in quotation marks, as well as 'the truthfulness' of his additions.[104] Although Wilhelm Gustav Werner Volk had dealt with Catholicism from a scholarly perspective for many years, he converted only *after* his wife, who is said to have described herself as an 'uneducated woman',[105] decided to convert in the face of grave illness, since, as stated above, she did not want to 'die a Protestant'.[106]

After her conversion Caroline Volk, having nearly died, 'recovered all of a sudden, as if by a miracle'.[107] According to her biographer, shortly before her death she had emphasised her role of selfless carer to her husband and her daughter, who had also converted in 1856. 'What would have become of the two of you had I not contracted cholera? It is the only time that I was of any use to you ....'[108] Thus Volk has his late wife wholly consumed by her role as wife and mother, recognising service to her family as the meaning of her life. He memorialises her as a woman, emphasising that she had made the right emotional, decision to convert *before* him, while his own heart had 'remained cold' up to that point, although 'his mind had been unable [for many years] to deny the infallibility of the Catholic Church'.[109] He very clearly assigns emotions to the woman and intellect to the man here, but in an inversion of the usual gender hierarchy: the husband humbly admits that Caroline Volk reached the proper decision more quickly with her heart than he had with his head.

As the convert's biographer, Volk is responsible for the book's political and scholarly commentary, dividing the German-speaking region into Protestant and Catholic worlds. While no names of towns appear in the descriptions of the couple's domiciles and moves, cities and villages in the Catholic South with their churches and monasteries are named and described. The couple's Catholic social circles (especially the Görres circle), discussions and encounters are documented and characterised in detail, accompanied by criticisms of the Protestant world. Lutheran acquaintances remain largely nameless, and the text

102 Ibid., 171.
103 Ibid., 4.
104 Ibid., 3–4.
105 Ibid., 87.
106 Ibid., 111.
107 Ibid., 145.
108 Ibid., 192.
109 Ibid., 147.

stresses their deficient understanding of Catholicism and thus of the legitimate order of the world. While the domicile and presumed place of writing Erfurt and its majority Protestant population is largely absent from the text, Catholic towns and people assume great significance for the conversion narrative. Since his conversion, Volk deems the Protestant world unworthy of description, and it appears merely as a space that evokes physical malaise and emotional pain, paving the way for conversion. Caroline Volk is not the only one to choose conversion in the face of a deadly threat. Volk, too, mentions suffering various ailments and upsets before his conversion and recovery in the Catholic South. Before converting, his illnesses often accompanied him even on his journeys south. In the summer of 1850, for example, he travelled to Bad Kreuth to start a 'cure of whey and herbs'. It was only a visit to the Passion Play in Oberammergau, however, that shook him out of his 'emotional apathy', Volk informs his readers.[110] On his last journey before his conversion, Volk's deep exhaustion persists even in the South. Only an encounter with Father Peter Singer in Salzburg puts an end to the 'enervating nervous unease that had been my companion throughout the journey'. As long as his 'soulful gaze rested upon me, all sense of sickness in me [disappeared]'.[111] This information on his own state comes not from the *Leben einer Convertitin*, but from the 'separate account' of his own conversion he promises there.[112] Wilhelm, Caroline and Marie Volk converted as a family. Since the genre of the conversion account specified that every convert must take this step on his or her own responsibility and impetus, Volk could not choose the narrative of a family conversion, instead separating his own conversion in his publications from that of his wife, who converted on the same day. He did not dedicate a text to his daughter's conversion.

Interestingly, Volk described the conversion ritual extensively in this book in order to counter Protestant misconceptions about it.[113] He pointed to the stipulation that Christian converts must 'forswear their errors before at least one priest and two witnesses and make a profession of the Catholic faith'. The priest, according to Volk, 'wearing a rochet and a violet stole, steps up to the altar or at least to a crucifix, which must be standing between two lit wax candles on a table covered with a pure linen cloth, and calls down God's grace upon the convert (who must be kneeling between the two witnesses on a stool not far from the altar)'.[114] Then the convert speaks the prescribed verses and says a prayer. An address by the priest is followed by the questions of whether the convert wishes to enter the Catholic Church, forswear 'false doctrines and heresies' and practise

110 Volk, *Simeon*, vol. 3, 201.

111 Ibid.

112 Volk, *Aus dem Leben einer Convertitin*, 125. This is a reference to his *Simeon*.

113 Ibid., 125–42.

114 Ibid., 127.

the publicly professed faith until death. Having answered all three questions in the affirmative, the convert was called upon to repeat the Catholic profession of faith 'publicly and solemnly' and to swear on the Gospel Book.[115] After additional prayers the convert was supposed to make a general confession and then participate in a mass in which he 'took the holy Eucharist'. After that the priest was to enter this in the church register and present the convert with a document to be signed by the convert, the priest and the two witnesses.[116]

In his autobiographical work *Simeon*, which, like the *Leben einer Convertitin*, he wrote after joining the Catholic Church, Volk again addresses the criticisms of his *Geständnisse* and *Glaubenslehrjahre* as well as the portrayal of his wife's conversion. The Lutheran periodical *Evangelische Kirchenzeitung* had published an anonymous review in 1859.[117] In it, the reviewer weighs the value of the conversion book:

> There is more to consider about the abovementioned work than the author's pseudonymity. There is also a masquerade about who edited the book. If it is useful to issue publications about the 'inner religious life of the convert', why not provide the whole truth? Only the full light of historical truth, which openly states the place, names and circumstances, allows the testimony and account to appear certain and tested. ... The editor laboriously (?) seeks to hide the fact that it is he, the husband himself who is writing. ... [118]

What bothered the (also anonymous) reviewer the most, however, 'is the want of sentiment, the interspersing among the recollections, in the broadest possible form, of ... tendentious sentences in favour of the dogmas of the Catholic Church and against Luther that have been rehashed, written and copied a hundred times'.[119]

The reviewer exposes central points of Volk's writing and authorisation strategies here. Volk literally incorporated the conversion of his wife (and daughter) into the two works written after his conversion by presenting the conversion as a holistic process undertaken by his nuclear family, while at the same time breaking down the shared process of family conversion into its individual components by making himself responsible for the intellectual aspects and the two women for the emotional aspects of these events.

As is already clear in the subtitle to *Simeon*, Volk was inscribing himself into the discourse of the scholarly elite; he saw himself as a 'Christian scholar' and

---

115 Ibid., 139.

116 Ibid., 142, *.

117 Volk, *Simeon*, vol. 3, 412, n. *. Volk refers here to no. 79 of the *Evangelische Kirchenzeitung*.

118 Ibid., 413, n. *.

119 Ibid., 415, n. *

measured himself against those considered experts in the fields he treated. The jurist demonstrated his universal learning by publishing in a variety of areas. He wrote as a vocation, and accorded only a secondary role to his (unwanted?) profession as a jurist in the civil service. He wrote about the 1830s:

> The two volumes of my [work on] Italian literature, consisting of nearly eleven-hundred closely-printed pages, cost me a good deal of time. On many days I spent 10–12 hours on it. In addition to my official duties, I had to truncate and restrict my hours of rest and recreation. This work was interrupted by preparing for and taking the major state examination.[120]

Volk's paid employment and legal training appear here as pursuits that took up far fewer working hours than his studies of literary history. His studies and examination were thus interruptions to his real work. Volk was aware of this discrepancy and he tried to split himself into two individuals, a civil servant and a writer.[121] Probably not least out of fear for his position, he emphasised the great distance between the two activities: 'Anonymity thus seems to me to be an essential condition of my activities as a writer. I did everything to safeguard it and therefore never negotiated with a publisher. My manuscripts were entrusted to friends elsewhere, who saw to their publication without any involvement on my part'.[122]

The Prussian authorities, however, were by no means indifferent to the confessional affiliations of their civil servants: after this declaration, an announcement appeared 'in the official section of the Preußische Staatszeitung' stating 'that the rumours concerning my conversion to the Catholic Church are baseless', which in turn moved 'well-meaning friends' to refute 'my alleged conversion in tame newspaper advertisements'.[123]

At the beginning of *Simeon*, Volk explains the origins and structure of his autobiography:

> Thus the work, undertaken out of inner necessity, spontaneously turned into a sort of religious biography. But its focus is not the insignificant life of the author, which appears only in fragments. It seeks out the universal standpoints from which one can see, and is intended to exemplify the inner life not just of the author, but also of so many of his contemporaries, who, having been led through

[120] Ibid., vol. 1, 234.

[121] Ibid., vol. 2, 23. Volk quotes here from his letter of 9 May 1844. In 1846 he then chose the pseudonym Ludwig Clarus.

[122] Ibid., 22.

[123] Ibid., 24.

similar circumstances, have managed to acquire those invisible funds upon which their hopes of the life to come depend.[124]

Thus Volk places the scientist and the scholar at the centre of his text, not his own 'insignificant life' but the 'universal standpoints', which he introduces using the example of his own thoughts and intellectual development. A continuous process of written reflection takes place in this individual's mental space, one that repeatedly takes up his own older texts as monologues and by incorporating quotations from reviews and letters enters into a public dialogue with persons named or unnamed. Volk appears to have constantly noted down and processed his thoughts, excerpts from his reading and reviews, and inserted what he had written at various points, in some cases multiple times.[125]

Around this innermost circle of reflection and exploration, which appears to constitute the internal core of his being, Volk's – vaguely sketched – family emerges. While in the *Convertitin* he allows his wife to speak in her own (quoted) words and thus to play a supporting role, his daughter remains very much a dependent child. He accords her no voice of her own and her appearance in a few passages serves mainly to demonstrate the development of her father's religious reflections. Volk had delayed his daughter's confirmation, which usually took place at the age of 14, by a year and a half. In this way he sought to keep her away from anti-Catholic instruction.[126] This episode serves as an occasion for a detailed commentary on the 'Catholicising' of the Moravians[127] and demonstration of Volk's path to Catholicism via Moravian doctrine.

Volk saw among the Moravians a number of 'quasi-Catholic attitudes on faith and life'[128] and recalled the saying, 'The road leads to Rome via Herrnhut'.[129] He mentioned the following individual points as proof of the proximity of the Moravians to Catholicism. The doctrines of Nikolaus Ludwig von Zinzendorf appeared so 'conservative' to him, so completely focused on Christ, that his religious teachings as well as his weekly fast day and the 'monastic drive' he had reportedly felt throughout his life seemed to Volk very close to Catholicism.[130] According to Volk, Zinzendorf was 'free of that Protestant spirit of privacy that treats religion as an individual matter'.[131] Moreover, Moravian communal

124 Ibid., vol. 1, 1–2.

125 Ibid., vol. 2, 293.

126 Ibid., vol. 3, 288.

127 Volk was of the opinion that in one segment of Protestantism, the 'positive, pious tendency [had never] died out'. As an example he cites Zinzendorf, whom he believed to have been on the path to Catholicism. Volk, *Simeon*, vol. 2, 358; see also p. 360.

128 Ibid., vol. 3, 289.

129 Ibid., 291.

130 Ibid.

131 Ibid.

institutions and social relations were to some extent influenced by 'quite Catholic attitudes'.[132] 'Even in Zinzendorf's day, the housing of the single brothers and sisters in their own choir houses was harshly criticised as an institution inclining towards Catholic monasticism'. [133] Among the Moravian brethren matrimony, too, was founded on 'religious ethical principles ... but not on the mere desires and inclinations of individuals'.[134] 'Caring for the poor and sick, the prayer associations which watched through the night in prayer and pious exercises',[135] were also 'quasi-Catholic'. 'Daily offices', litanies, kneeling in prayer, so-called Speakings, a kind of confession in preparation to take the Eucharist, the regular practice of foot-washing, the consecration of the dying by the laying on of hands amidst prayer and song, the synods, concern for an apostolic succession of bishops and other matters could only be understood as a repristination to Catholic forms,[136] in Volk's view.

The dry passages on his wife, whom he introduces as both an object of study and an attendant circumstance of his development, seem strangely distant. While even after 20 years of studying Catholicism Volk remained a 'stubborn aspiring convert', his wife had been so strongly moved by her will to convert and the necessity of a journey to her 'spiritual guide' in Salzburg 'that she, fearing a refusal, personally asked my superior to grant me leave, in the hope that he would give me a better reception if she intervened'.[137] Volk regarded his wife's conversion as an emotionally driven process and even he was astonished that she had arrived at her destination faster than he had after years of intensely exploring religious questions. No wonder that he identified not with her, but with male converts.[138] He describes several well-known ones, some of whom he boasted as personal acquaintances. In the portrayal of these converts some of their glory always rubs off on Volk, for instance when he points out the parallels between Hurter's conversion and his own[139] or his conversion and that of the theologian William Palmer, who became a Catholic in Rome in 1855. Palmer allegedly had only been prepared to convert after a retreat suggested to him by a cardinal in Rome. 'One of the cardinals to whom the famous Englishman was commended, and who found him to be as pigheaded as the most reverend Bishop Emmanuel found me, advised him to spend just eight days participating in the spiritual

132 Ibid., 289.

133 Ibid., 291.

134 Ibid., 292.

135 Ibid.

136 Ibid.

137 Ibid., 332.

138 One of these was Friedrich Hurter (1787–1865), who converted from Calvinism to Catholicism in 1844, and another was William Palmer (1811 –1879), whose conversion from Anglicanism to Catholicism in 1855 had caused quite a stir.

139 Volk, *Simeon*, vol. 3, 85.

exercises conducted in a certain monastery by priests of the Society of Jesus'. At this point Volk has not merely made a connection between his person and the renowned Palmer, but also placed himself in very close proximity to Wilhelm Emmanuel Freiherr von Ketteler, by mentioning the first name of the bishop who had granted him an audience shortly before his conversion.[140]

His wife and daughter formed the everyday, domestic circle that Volk at least occasionally alludes to in his conversion accounts, although he does not describe his living conditions, residence or daily life. His workplace, colleagues, superiors and professional duties are pushed to the side. The existence of his professional world and the unnamed city where Volk lived with his family are relegated to subordinate clauses.

After a description of the author's (researching and writing) 'person' and his little family, the book sketches the circle of scholars in which Volk moved or with whom he debated. These included Georg and Charlotte Phillips, a couple who played an important role in his life. While Volk's texts introduce Georg Phillips as a well-known convert and professor, she is the 'dear friend' who accompanied his literary and religious career in an intensive correspondence. Volk repeatedly mentions the Görres circle as an important source of inspiration; Wolfgang Menzel and Heinrich Thiersch, but also well-known converts such as Friedrich Hurter or William Palmer, also play a role. Protestant scholars, such as the historian Ranke, in contrast, are criticised for their works (vol. 2, chap. 8). Volk offers an equally harsh assessment of the 'pre-Catholic' writings of Ida von Hahn-Hahn, which according to him were bought in multiple copies by all the lending libraries and 'were never available on the shelves' because 'the ladies virtually gobbled them up'.[141] Finally, he introduces and treats at length the clerics who played an important role in the couple's conversion. They included in particular Franciscans from Salzburg such as Father Peter Singer and Father Rinn, Caroline Volk's 'spiritual guide'.

Volk accords a far less prominent place to political topics. He repeatedly returns to his conservatism, his admiration for the Catholic ruling dynasties and the Greater German movement to which he adhered. While Volk refers to the Frankfurt National Assembly as a farce, his sympathy was with the '13 supporters of Greater Germany, nearly all of them Catholics' with whom he sought to make contact. During the seven weeks when the parliament, 'a stillbirth', was in session, according to his own account Volk kept to his room because of an illness, so that it was only during the second half of the session that he was able to make personal contact with these men, of whom he especially

140 Ibid., 319.

141 Ibid., vol. 2, 195.

mentions the 'Reichensperger brothers, dean of the cathedral Ritter of Breslau, Privy Councillor von Linde [and] Aulic Councillor Buß'.[142]

With the emphasis on his conservative stance on political and religious matters, which Volk repeatedly stresses, he variously describes the constancy of his views, in order to make his change of religion appear not as a turning point, but as a logical culmination. This effort becomes all too plain, when, for example in the introduction to *Simeon*, he quotes from a letter to 'a female friend' that he claimed to have written in 1848. 'You will soon see the appearance of the second part [of the religious biography, the *Glaubenslehrjahre*, which would not be published until 1852]; it does not yet, however, bring the matter to its conclusion. I will only be able to write the third part when I am a Catholic'.[143] Because of his conservativism and 'instinctive admiration for all things ... traditional and tested by time', Volk notes, he was 'by nature nearly ruined for Protestantism'.[144]

In his works, Volk concentrates on the male world of learning, but also comments on gender roles. In his *Glaubenslehrjahre* he places hierarchical and courtly elements in the foreground: 'I love it when one not merely honours the ladies, but also serves them as higher beings, and seeks to compensate the weaker sex for their exclusion from civil authority by affording them such a prerogative'.[145] In 1843 he had already written anonymously of marriage, that 'no dissolution of marriage is permissible, except by death, and it is consequently impossible before the death of the other'.[146] Volk believed that the stipulations on divorce in the new Prussian Legal Code of 1794, the *Allgemeines Landrecht für die Preußischen Staaten*, enshrined 'lax and unchristian principles'.[147] Without actually referring to marriage as a sacrament, it is clear that Volk defined it as such when he placed this attitude in the mouth of the 'common man'. In particular he demanded that in cases of adultery, the guilty party must not be permitted to marry the other party involved, and he showed himself relieved 'that the common man believes it to be no marriage if it is not consecrated by a clergyman, and that no desire for civil marriage had arisen among the educated'.[148] Elsewhere, in the *Geständnisse*, he expresses his distaste for female teachers, describing his preschool years as a 'limbo in the schoolroom of Miss Hunold' and, borrowing from Horace, calls his

142 Ibid., vol. 3, 200–201.

143 Ibid., vol. 1, 4.

144 Ibid., vol. 3, 85.

145 Volk, *Geständnisse*, 173.

146 [Wilhelm Gustav Volk], 'Briefliche Mittheilungen aus Preußen über das Ehescheidungsgesetz. Von einem Protestanten', *Historisch-politische Blätter* 11 (1843): 49–56, 56.

147 Ibid., 49.

148 Ibid., 49–50.

former teacher a 'female Orbilius'.[149] For Volk, women were clearly unsuited to the teaching profession and as far as we know neither his wife nor his daughter distinguished themselves through a higher level of education. Women, we may conclude from the few sentences Volk devoted to the subject, should submit to their father or husband and were disqualified by their sex from citizenship rights and higher education. When they put pen to paper, as his wife did, they did so for practical reasons and to serve, as Volk's treatment of his wife's conversion account underlines. The splitting of the conversion process into an emotional part, which he assigns to his wife, and an intellectual one that he undertakes himself, also becomes clear. In Volk's texts, women are defined as the 'weaker sex'. While old women play a prominent and powerful role in Australia and Africa, as Chapters 2 and 3 show, Volk accords a dominant role neither to his wife nor to his contemporary and fellow convert, the successful author Ida von Hahn-Hahn. The polarisation of the sexes, to which Volk assigns unambiguous gender traits, marks Volk's autobiographical writings, as does the marginalisation of his professional and private life in Erfurt in favour of detailed descriptions of the Catholic South and Catholic acquaintances.

In summary, Volk presented his conversion narrative within the framework of an extensive autobiography, which clearly reveals the influence of Goethe's *Poetry and Truth* and is set up as a documentation of his developmental and educational path. Volk portrays himself as a scholar first and foremost, continually referring to his works and mentioning well-known intellectuals with whom he was on personal or corresponding terms, but he divulges little of the basis and quality of these contacts. While he addresses his relationships with the circle around Görres and individual Catholic personalities, he does not reveal whether, how and why he as a Protestant sought contact with these people, or whether they contacted him, and what the exchange with them meant to him. In these texts Volk also reveals himself as a conservative whose family life was a private matter not to be treated in public. These texts, but more particularly his edition of his wife's conversion account, make his views of gender roles abundantly clear.

By incorporating older writings into the conversion account, Volk appropriates the interpretation of this step and imbeds the conversion into the continuum of his life by assigning a higher value to his persistence as a scholar than to the change and conversion that Protestant contemporaries usually emphasised in his life. His conversion is embedded in the biographical narrative more or less as a logical element, and described as a deliberate, autonomous act by Volk. He may well have regarded his own life, too – like his wife's – as an 'organic

[149] Volk, *Geständnisse*, 3–5. Lucius Orbilius Pupillus (Orbilius) (113 BCE –14 BCE), Latin grammarian and educator. Because of Horace's description of his teacher, the name Orbilius is associated with strict and irascible disciplinarians.

whole ordained by providence',[150] yet it was *his* will that at first, and for many years, resisted conversion and then embraced it in 1855.[151] Volk authorises his dominant role in the conversion process through a statement that he attributes to von Ketteler:

> Through grace, faith is ingrained, through virtue it is accepted and maintained. It is sufficiently ingrained in you; it is up to you also to transform it into a virtue. ... God does not call us, however, in a manner that hinders free will. He does not coerce, but leaves human beings their free will, even after they are called.[152]

Conclusions

Volk's conversion narrative illustrates the typical nineteenth-century combination of autobiographical and biographical texts in which a person locates him- or herself within the social realm, criticises norms, values and social orders, explains the conversion and lends it an exemplary function. When the Volk family converted in the mid-nineteenth century, the German world was in the midst of a massive upheaval, in which many secularising tendencies that had not fully asserted themselves in 1789 and 1848 came into play. This wave of secularisation not only changed the relationship between the state and the churches, but also led to radical changes and innovations within the churches themselves. Thus, for example, the developments after the display of the Holy Robe in Trier in 1844 and Johannes Ronge's protest against it paved the way for the founding of the German-Catholic Church.[153]

The effects of these changes did not only radically challenge Rome's claims to primacy; they also unleashed autonomising and differentiating processes on the structural and institutional level in politics and the Christian churches. The 'erosion of organised (Christian) religion and decline in (Christian) religious practices' [154] that many authors see at work more generally on the political-cultural level in the nineteenth century, like the postulated withdrawal of religions into the private sphere, cannot be confirmed for all segments of the population, however.

[150] Volk, *Aus dem Leben einer Convertitin*, 212.

[151] Volk, *Simeon*, vol. 3, 312.

[152] Ibid., 315.

[153] One need not go as far as Charles Taylor, who asserts that religion brought forth the secular. Charles Taylor, *A Secular Age* (Cambridge: Harvard University Press, 2007).

[154] Michael Minkenberg and Ulrich Willems, 'Politik und Religion im Übergang. Tendenzen und Forschungsfragen am Beginn des 21. Jahrhunderts', in *Politik und Religion*, Politische Vierteljahresschrift, Sonderheft 33, ed. Minkenberg and Willems (Wiesbaden: Westdeutscher Verlag, 2003), 13–41, 18–19.

Converts represented these transformation processes, they posed questions to their environments, challenged their religions of origin and chafed at injustices, authorities and norms that did not appear persuasive to them (anymore). For many converts, the question of the true religion touched on areas with which they had grappled professionally or intellectually over long periods.

We can conclude from the known conversion narratives that in the 'second confessional age'[155] people consciously took up conflicts that had already been fought out in the early modern period. The arguments cited and anticipated objections were similar, as was the harsh tone that characterised the conversion accounts and the polemics published against them. In many respects, the debates traced here follow the sixteenth- and seventeenth-century literature of theological controversy. A closer analysis of the sometimes voluminous texts, however, reveals in most cases that the act of conversion was by no means addressed as the sole or exclusive turning point in the convert's life. Conversion constituted *one* important step in the development of the converts, who depict it as a confrontation with religious, social, professional and/or scholarly questions. As new arrivals, the authors wrote their way into membership in the respective faith community, thereby underlining their loyalty and sense of affiliation. In this way they enabled their mentors and church authorities to exert a control function over converts after the act of conversion, and to test whether the converts deserved the trust placed in them.

Overall, the conversion narratives show that even in the 'secularised age', a religious attitude, belief and membership in a faith community enjoyed greater importance in western European society and for individuals than modern social history has accorded them thus far. Just as Michael B. Gross has reminded us of the religious revival in Germany in the period 1848–1870 using the example of the Catholic *Volksmission* (home mission),[156] and Dagmar Günther rightly emphasises the 'influence of confession'[157] in her 2004 study of members of the educated middle class in Wilhelmine Germany, analyses of the conversion accounts also show that religious affiliation continued to play an important role, even if we can distinguish between public polarisations and the far more complex distinctions in converts' concepts of the person.

Conversion accounts like Volk's have an apologetic character and at the same time may be read as calls to convert, which generally targeted members of the confession the author had left. To what extent these missionary intentions were

---

155 Olaf Blaschke, *Konfessionen im Konflikt: Deutschland zwischen 1800 und 1970: ein zweites konfessionelles Zeitalter* (Göttingen: Vandenhoeck & Ruprecht, 2002).

156 Michael B. Gross, 'The Catholic Missionary Crusade and the Protestant Revival in Nineteenth-Century Germany', in *Protestants, Catholics and Jews in Germany*, ed. Helmut Walser Smith (Oxford: Berg, 2001), 245–65.

157 Dagmar Günther, *Das nationale Ich? Autobiographische Sinnkonstruktionen deutscher Bildungsbürger des Kaiserreichs* (Tübingen: Niemeyer, 2004), 360.

successful must remain an open question, since the authors as a rule addressed the members of the new and the abandoned faith community as well as an undefined public, the academic world or colleagues, and less commonly their families of origin or relatives. Writers, or rather people accustomed to reflecting on their actions in writing, often integrated extensive notes or reviews of their reading into their conversion accounts, drawing upon published or unpublished excerpts. The texts they treated and assessed may serve as convert reading lists. As to their own publications, some of the converts were able to draw connections between texts they had published before and after converting, and thereby to illustrate their faithfulness to values and principles at a time of religious change.

Volk's conversion narrative contains detailed theological disquisitions that go well beyond his personal conversion story and form extensive independent parts of the text. With these scholarly theological, political and historical essays Volk inscribes himself into the group that he declared to be the intellectual elite, with name-dropping a central method for underlining his membership in it. To demonstrate his own scholarly reputation, he mentions renowned universities and professors or other respected references; he also expressly outlines his own academic successes and points to previous publications. Apart from this general self-portrait as a scholar, he also engages in repeated, specific self-recommendation as a theologian: Volk demonstrates his profound specialist knowledge and describes his painstaking and untiring search for the 'true' faith, proving in this way that his decision to convert was guided by reason and clearly defensible theologically. By mentioning famous converts, he inserted himself into a corresponding line of tradition and emphasised that he was by no means ashamed of his status as a convert. On the contrary, references to well-known converts confirmed the logic and rightness of his own conversion.

By writing their accounts, converts became part of a memorial community of their confession, which regularly posed a challenge to the faith communities they had abandoned, since these models of the 'true church' were always associated with monopolistic claims. The most important result was that conversion narratives illustrated the converts' concept of the person and multiple affiliations, while the analysis of the theological and political context in which the conversion narrative proper is set broadly illuminated the social importance of confessional struggles.

The often passionate and polemical discussion of published conversion accounts suggests that religion still had great significance for nineteenth-century people. As reflected in these discussions, secularisation proves to have been a process that moved at varying speeds and through various stages during the long nineteenth century, in many cases meeting with resistance and ultimately establishing a dynamic relationship between the state and the Christian churches that diminished but did not end the churches' power.

The secularisation measures that began after 1803, which meant the loss of many centres of Catholic scholarship and education, put Catholics on the defensive. Under this pressure they sought to strengthen their position in the German cultural and educational system once again. Catholic intellectuals regarded it as their duty to demonstrate that faith could coexist with the modern age.[158] And yet political and social developments led to the growth of calls for reform within the churches as well. A religious opposition movement arose with the advent of organised religious humanism in the 1840s, which involved above all Protestants, but also Catholics (as well as a few Jews).[159] Members of this movement left the churches, established new faith communities and, in conjunction with their critique of religion, founded new democratic-utopian social models, which also included the beginnings of women's emancipation.[160] Although these dissidents remained in the minority, by formally leaving the church they ushered in a process of unchurching and dechristianisation that would in the long run offer new options for locating people in the social realm. Initially, however, especially within Catholicism, this movement led to an even stronger turn towards traditions, which the Vatican's centralisation measures and the concentration of power in Rome were now declared to be. In resistance to demands for reform, papal authority was supposed to play an increasing role as a guarantor of the 'true church'.

Volk's conversion narrative was therefore directed not merely against the Protestants, but also against the separatist movements within the Catholic Church. On the one hand he invoked the fragmentation of Protestantism as an admonitory example for Catholicism, while on the other he not only justified the authority of the pope, but also sought to reconcile Catholicism with modernity. He did not merely portray joining the Catholic Church as a rational, logical and modern decision, but also repeatedly invoked the class-transcending, democratic element in Catholicism by proposing that Catholicism also offered a faith for the uneducated, while Protestantism actually excluded the broad masses because of the intellectual challenges of independent Bible-reading. Here, he regarded the intermediary function of the Catholic priest not as paternalism, but as a prerequisite for active participation in church life, while Volk saw the uneducated Protestant faithful as excluded from the life of the congregation. Like the Protestants, among whom independent Bible-reading was presented as an essential element of personal competence and thus of the concept of the

158 Christopher Dowe, *Auch Bildungsbürger: Katholische Studierende und Akademiker im Kaiserreich* (Göttingen: Vandenhoeck & Ruprecht, 2006); Thomas Nipperdey, 'Religion und Gesellschaft: Deutschland um 1900', *Historische Zeitschrift* 246 (1988): 591–615; and *Religion im Umbruch: Deutschland 1870–1918* (Munich: Beck, 1988).

159 Sylvia Paletschek, *Frauen und Dissens: Frauen im Deutschkatholizismus und in den freien Gemeinden 1841–1852* (Göttingen: Vandenhoeck & Ruprecht, 1990), 244.

160 Ibid., 252.

person, Volk too underlined his intellectual autonomy, which in his eyes did not stand in the way of an acceptance of papal authority.

As is clearly evident from Volk's writings, Catholics characterised Prussia not as a religiously neutral, but as a Protestant state. The modernity Volk rejected offered a clearer view of the state's confessional foundations. He illustrates the discrimination against non-Protestants, and calls for the equal participation of Catholics in the life of the state and the educational sector. He presents the decision to become a Catholic as an autonomous, well-considered choice undertaken with divine guidance. There was an ambivalent, dynamic relationship between the convert's active role and divine guidance, which could be differently weighted. Volk's focus was on the reliability and infallibility of an institution solidified by tradition, which, all doubts notwithstanding, had preserved and passed on the true doctrine. References to earlier converts, salvation history and divine revelation retreat into the background and are relativised by Volk. His conversion narrative highlights the seeking after truth, individual knowledge, his active part in the search for the 'true religion', and his place in society.

Chapter 2

Gendered Conversions: Wotjobaluk Men and Women in Colonial Victoria, Australia

Introduction

Catherine Hall pointed out some years ago that 'gender hierarchy was inscribed at the heart of missionary enterprise'.[1] Gender mediated power at all levels of this enterprise: between missions in the colonies and gender discourses in the metropole, between male missionaries and their wives and between missionaries and male and female indigenous converts. Gender relations on missions were key sites of collision, compromise and collaboration, as Elizabeth Elbourne reminds us, and they were sites of colonial gendered engagements where European power hierarchies could not always be upheld.[2]

Missions, like empire itself, were highly masculine enterprises.[3] Current scholarship is reviewing the nature of this masculinisation by re-assessing gendered power relations as part of everyday mission practices. An increasing number of studies have drawn our attention to the specific gendered nature of missionary masculinity as well as its relationship to other forms of masculinity and to power.[4] What we know less about are the masculinities that indigenous

---

1 Catherine Hall, *Civilising Subjects: Metropole and Colony in the English Imagination 1830–1867* (Cambridge: Polity Press, 2002), 97.

2 Elizabeth Elbourne, 'Mother's Milk: Gender, Power and Anxiety on a South African Mission Station, 1839–1840', in *Missionaries, Indigenous Peoples and Cultural Exchange*, ed. Patricia Grimshaw and Andrew May (Brighton, Portland, Toronto: Sussex Academic Press, 2010), 10–23.

3 Philippa Levine (ed.), *Gender and Empire*, Oxford History of the British Empire Companion Series (Oxford: Oxford University Press, 2004), especially the introduction.

4 See, for example, Erik Sidenvall, *The Making of Manhood Among Swedish Missionaries in China and Mongolia, c. 1890–c. 1914* (Leiden: Brill, 2009); Yvonna Maria Werner (ed.), *Christian Masculinity: Men and Religion in Northern Europe in the 19th and 20th Centuries* (Leuven: Leuven University Press, 2011); Kristin Fjelde Tjelle, *Missionary Masculinity: the Case of Norwegian Lutheran Missions to the Zulus, 1870–1930* (Oslo: Oslo University Press, 2012); Charles Wilde, 'Acts of Faith: Muscular Christianity and Masculinity among the Gogodala of Papua New Guinea', *Oceania* 75, 1 (2004): 32–48; Jacqueline Van Gent, 'Side-wounds, Sex and Savages: Moravian Masculinities and Early Modern Protestant Missions', in

converts had to negotiate.[5] While critical historical mission studies have drawn our attention to the work of male native evangelists as a key factor in the spread of Christianity in the colonies, an explicit analysis of their gendered experiences and the construction of their masculinities is still in its infancy.[6] Male converts are rarely seen as gendered beings who acquired, maintained or lost authority by adhering to masculinity that assigned them a specific place within the mission patronage, a wider colonial society and their local indigenous communities. Mission patronage was a hierarchical and patriarchal system of gendered social power. It elevated a male European missionary into the position of governing male, assigning him the role of patriarch in the extended household of the mission. His wife and other subordinates, such as converted indigenous people, were able to occupy some position of power if they adhered to the norms. Indigenous evangelists in particular gained some degree of authority. Such mission patronage reflected colonial ideas of radicalised gender hierarchies, but of course it was also ambiguous and fragile.[7]

Earlier feminist work concentrated on the disciplinary functions of missions and highlighted the processes by which indigenous women were subjected to rigorous control of their sexuality and childrearing practices.[8] In this chapter, I will examine the gendered nature of Christian conversions for both indigenous

---

Governing Masculinities in the Early Modern Period: Regulating Selves and Others ed. Susan Broomhall and Jacqueline Van Gent (Aldershot: Ashgate, 2011), 189–208.

5 Although it does not specifically discuss Christian converts, a key study of the colonial politics of masculinity is still M. Sinha, *Colonial Masculinity: The 'Manly Englishman' and the 'Effeminate Bengali' in the Late Nineteenth Century* (Manchester: Manchester University Press, 1995).

6 Myra Rutherdale, '"It is not Soft Job to be Performed": Missionaries and Imperial Manhood in Canada, 1880–1920', in *Missionaries, Indigenous People and Cultural Change*, ed. Grimshaw and May, 52–66; Rhonda Semple, 'Missionary Manhood: Professionalism, Belief and Masculinity in the Nineteenth-Century Imperial Field', *Journal of Imperial and Commonwealth History* 36, 3 (2008): 397–415.

7 On the notion of governing masculinity and the nature of male authority and its limits, see also Susan Broomhall and Jacqueline Van Gent (eds), *Governing Masculinities in the Early Modern Period: Regulating Selves and Others* (Aldershot: Ashgate, 2011), especially the introduction.

8 Margaret Jolly and Martha Macintyre (eds), *Family and Gender in the Pacific: Domestic Contradictions and Colonial Impact* (Cambridge: Cambridge University Press, 1989); Antoinette Burton, *Burdens of History: British Feminists, Indian Women, and Imperial Culture, 1865–1915* (Chapel Hill: University of North Carolina Press, 1994); Philippa Levine, *Gender and Empire*; and Kathleen Wilson, *The Island Race: Englishness, Empire and Gender in the Eighteenth Century* (London: Routledge, 2003); Patricia Grimshaw and Andrew May (eds), *Missionaries, Indigenous Peoples and Cultural Exchange* (Brighton, Portland, and Toronto: Sussex Academic Press, 2010) 5; Elbourne, 'Mother's Milk', 10–23.

men and women at Ebenezer mission. This mission has attracted historical interest in one of the male converts, Nathanel Pepper.[9]

I would like here to place both Nathanel and other Wotjobaluk people associated with the mission into a wider gendered context that considers not just this young male convert and his male relatives and peer group, but also Wotjobaluk women and their experiences of conversion. After some brief historical background on the Moravian mission at Ebenezer and a discussion of the gendered nature of the published Ebenezer sources in German and in English Moravian mission journals, I will first explore the gendered relationships of male indigenous converts – with missionaries, other converts and non-converted indigenous men – as part of the conversion process. Male converts at Ebenezer were entitled to the gendered privilege of elevation to the position of evangelist or 'native teacher', and their actions were given greater attention in reporting (both published and unpublished) by missionaries. Indigenous converts, and potential Christian converts, were expected to adapt their gendered behaviour to conform to the Protestant ideals of manhood, which included not only baptism but also marriage. Proselytising was a privilege that only a few men were granted, but even so most young men, whether baptised or not, sought to proselytise very early on. I will then turn to a discussion of indigenous converted women, most of them associated with men of the Pepper family, in order to explore the gendered expectations, agency and limits associated with Christian conversion for them. For women, marriage and the control of their sexual behaviour was at the centre of Christian womanhood, as was their responsibility for childrearing and their domestic duties. These European middle-class expectations of marriage, motherhood, domesticity and a clear control over female sexuality were powerful tools for regulating indigenous women, but a closer reading of the mission sources, which are often silent on the experiences of indigenous women, still indicates that not all gendered power relations on the mission were so exclusively patriarchal; indeed there are suggestions that some Aboriginal women undermined this system by becoming patrons of the mission and succeeded, at least temporarily, in reversing gendered power relations.

The Setting: Wotjobaluk People and the Moravian Mission Enterprise

My case study, the first-generation conversions of Wotjobaluk people in Victoria, is drawn from Moravian missions in Victoria and Queensland, which were established in the mid-nineteenth century and run by German Moravian missionaries until the early twentieth century, when the missions formally came

[9] Most recently Robert Kenny, *The Lamb Enters the Dreaming: Nathanael Pepper and the Ruptured World* (Melbourne: Scribe, 2007).

under the umbrella of the Presbyterian Church.[10] The official mission language was English, but missionaries reported in German to the mission board in Herrnhut. In late nineteenth-century colonial Australia, formal conversions of indigenous people were linked to Christian missions of various denominations, but by and large they were Protestant.[11] German missionaries were relatively prominent; they worked in Lutheran missions in South and central Australia, in Queensland, and in Moravian missions in Victoria.

The Wotjobaluk people lived in a strongly sex-segregated society that was hierarchically based more on spiritual knowledge and age than on gender. Yet much of these indigenous egalitarian structures began to change with the arrival of European colonial society and the enforced settlement of Aboriginal people. As elsewhere in indigenous Australia, relations between husband and wife, often in polygamous relationships, were not the only gendered social links that mattered. On the contrary, it appears that a number of other kin relationships were equally (if not more) important: between siblings, between classificatory uncles and nephews, between grandparent generations and grandchildren and between ancestors and the living. Feminist anthropologists have highlighted women's social agency, including the importance of women's rituals and ceremonies, in Australian indigenous cultures.[12] Annette B. Weiner has argued

[10] For a discussion of the specific administrative character of the Moravian missions in Australia, see Felicity Jensz, 'Three Peculiarities of the Southern Australian Moravian Mission Field', *Journal of Moravian History* 7 (2009): 7–30.

[11] John Harris, *One Blood. 200 Years of Aboriginal Encounter with Christianity: A Story of Hope* (Sutherland: Albatross, 1990). On Moravians specifically, see Joseph Edmund Hutton, *A History of Moravian Missions* (London: Moravian Publication Office, 1922); B. La Trobe, *The Moravian Missions: A Glance at 164 Years of Unbroken Missionary Labours* (London: G. Norman and Sons, 1896); Bain Attwood, 'Off the Mission Stations: Aborigines in Gippsland 1860–1890', *Aboriginal History* 10, 2 (1986): 131–51; Robert B. Smyth, *The Aborigines of Victoria* (Melbourne: J. Ferres, 1876); F.A. Hagenauer, *Mission Work Among the Aborigines of Victoria* (Melbourne: Diocesan Book Society, 1880); F.A. Hagenauer, *Further Facts Relating to the Moravian Mission* (Melbourne: Fergusson and Moore, 1861–67); Susan Robertson, *The Bell Sounds Pleasantly* (Melbourne: Luther Rose Publications, 1977); Phillip Pepper with Tess De Araugo, *The Kurnai of Gippsland* (Melbourne: Hyland House, 1985); P. Pepper with T. De Araugo, *You Are What You Make Yourself to Be* (Melbourne: Hyland House, 1989).

[12] See here, for example, Diane Bell, *Daughters of the Dreaming*, 3rd edn (North Melbourne, Vic.: Spinifex Press, 2002); Françoise Dussart, *Warlpiri Women's Yawulyu Ceremonies: A Form of Socialization and Innovation* (Canberra: Australian National University, 1988), and *The Politics of Ritual in an Aboriginal Settlement: Kinship, Gender and the Currency of Knowledge* (Washington, D.C. and London: Smithsonian Institute Press, 2000); Francesca Merlan, 'Gender in Aboriginal Social Life: A Review', in *Social Anthropology and Australian Aboriginal Studies*, ed. Ronald M. Berndt and Robert Tonkinson (Canberra: Aboriginal Studies Press, 1988), 15–76.

that Aboriginal women's access to sacred objects and chants provides them with spiritual authority independent of men. In gender relations, women perhaps exercise more influence as sisters than they do as wives. A western exclusive focus on women as wives, such as we find in the missionary records, thus overlooks important gendered social relationships of power in indigenous societies.[13] Weiner suggests that we should understand sibling relationships – intimacy between sisters and brothers – as 'a major organizing principle in Aboriginal social life'.[14] And anthropologist Françoise Dussart has shown how Warlpiri women gained and transmitted ceremonial knowledge from and to other women. This social process of instructing other women also gave Warlpiri women the opportunity to acquire economic resources in the process.[15] If Aboriginal women's control of ceremonial power and transmission of knowledge that bestowed authority was enacted between women, what incentive was there for Aboriginal women to listen to the stories and songs of male Europeans who claimed new sacred power?

Missions became another colonial space with which indigenous people engaged. In indigenous eyes, missions were particular places with certain material, social and gendered regimes and hierarchies.[16] But these hierarchies were not all-encompassing, and Aboriginal people evaded mission control by moving on and off mission stations.

The conversion of Australian indigenous people was a slow and tentative process during the nineteenth century, prompting scholars in the past to assume that Australians were generally resistant to the Christian message.[17] Against the background of intensified colonial impact on indigenous communities, frontier violence and competition with settlers over resources, missions slowly became more attractive to indigenous people. While these external social conditions were important, the key factor for an increase in indigenous conversions, however, lay within indigenous communities and depended on the proselytising activities of indigenous people themselves. Indigenous responses to the missions were deeply gendered, with a mission patriarchy allowing indigenous women only a limited

---

13 See the illuminating discussion by Annette B. Weiner in *Inalienable Possessions: The Paradox of Keeping While Giving* (Berkeley: University of California Press, 1992), esp. pp. 105–13 on Pintupi and Aranda women. These fundamental gendered relationships were likely very similar for Wotjobaluk women.

14 Weiner, *Inalienable Possessions*, 110.

15 Dussart, *Warlpiri Women's Yawulyu Ceremonies.*

16. On the understanding of mission as a place of distinct ritual, see, for example, Diana Austin-Broos, '"Right way t'il I die": Christianity and Kin on Country at Hermannsburg', in *Religious Change, Conversion and Culture*, ed. L. Olsen (Sydney: Sydney Association for studies in Society and Culture, 1996), 226–53.

17 Peggy Brock, 'Introduction', to *Indigenous Peoples and Religious Change* (Leiden: Brill, 2005).

public presence. All of the known indigenous evangelists in late nineteenth- and early twentieth-century Australia, for example, were men.[18] And yet indigenous women converted to Christianity in approximately the same numbers as men.

The Moravian Church, which was approached by the Presbyterian Church and came to run missions among the Wotjobaluk people in Ebenezer, was a Protestant mission society that had started out in the eighteenth century with a radical social and gendered utopian vision: the replacement of the family with sex- and age-segregated living arrangements in so-called choirs.[19] However, by the mid-nineteenth century, much of this gendered radicalism had given way to more conservative and mainstream attitudes and arrangements in order to conform to mainstream colonial practices.[20] In contrast to eighteenth-century Moravian gender arrangements, the late nineteenth century represented a period of more pronounced stratified gender hierarchies and the relegation of women to the domestic sphere as a marker of Christian womanhood.

By the mid-nineteenth century, when Moravians established their first mission stations in Australia, they had become a patriarchal society that emphasised a husband's right to govern his household and perceived mission as an extension of the patriarchal household. While some faint memories remained of an earlier period that had afforded women more spiritual space (e.g., women as deaconesses, hymns composed by women, regular confessional meetings of women), late nineteenth-century realities privileged men over women in every Moravian mission enterprise. Men were sent into the mission field first, followed only later by women as wives, who were brought out from Germany. Such patriarchal ideas were at the heart of the mission enterprise, and male converts had to demonstrate that they had switched their loyalties from indigenous male figures of authority to missionaries.

Women had a supporting role to play, but they were increasingly excluded from the religious public realm, e.g., preaching. This basic patriarchal European axiom, which in the Australian colonial setting was expanded to include the dimension of race, made indigenous men and women subordinate to both male

---

18 Only much later, with the advent of faith missions in the early twentieth century, did Aboriginal women receive more opportunities to proselytise publicly. See Joanna Cruickshank, 'Race, Time and Modernity: Australian Faith Missions in the Early Twentieth Century' (paper presented at the Australian Historians' Association conference, Perth, July 2010).

19 See, for example, Beverly Prior Smaby, 'Female Piety Among Eighteenth-Century Moravians', *Pennsylvania History* 64 (1997): 151–67; Beverly Prior Smaby, *Transformation of Moravian Bethlehem: From Communal Mission to Family Economy* (Philadelphia: University of Pennsylvania Press, 1988).

20 Beverly Prior Smaby, 'No one should lust for power ... women least', in *Pious Pursuits: German Moravians in the Atlantic World*, ed. Michelle Gillespie and Robert Beachy (New York and Oxford: Berghahn Books, 2007), 159–73.

and female Europeans. The mission introduced a further power marker with its emphasis on conversion – here social hierarchy was further differentiated to distinguish between baptised and non-baptised indigenous people. Converted indigenous men held some power over Aboriginal women, had to be subservient to missionaries and their wives, and were in theory, but not in practice, superior to non-converted indigenous people.[21]

Mission Journals as Sources

This chapter is based on letters and reports sent by male missionaries (mainly F.W. Spieseke and F.A. Hagenauer) to their headquarters and published in the main Moravian mission journals, *Periodical Accounts*, *Nachrichten aus der Brüder Gemeine* and *Missions-Blatt* in the period of the late 1850s to the late 1870s. The *Periodical Accounts* were published in English from 1790 to reach an international audience and reflected Moravians' self-understanding as a global community. They were exclusively about Moravian mission work and intended to raise money for missions. [22] The Moravians have a long tradition of creating an audience beyond the German-speaking world by copying and sending letters and station reports. The *Gemeinnachrichten*, originally only handwritten and in German, contained memoirs, mission diaries, sermons, speeches and letters and were instrumental in shaping a common identity among the far-flung Moravian congregations. They appeared in print from 1819.[23] The *Missions-Blatt* was the journal with mission reports for German-speaking congregations. The Australian reports were published in the *Missions-Blatt* in the original German and in English translation in the *Periodical Accounts.*

Thus in contrast to the conversion texts of Wilhelm Gustav Werner Volk discussed in Chapter 1 and the *Lebensbilder* of South Africa in Chapter 3, the conversions in Ebenezer simultaneously reached a German and an international English-speaking audience. While their headquarters were in Germany, the Moravians had become a global organisation and worked in the territories of several empires at the same time. The reports addressed a very heterogeneous

21 Catherine Hall, *Civilising Subjects*, 7; Joanna Cruickshank, '"A Most Lowering Thing for a Lady": Aspiring to Respectable Whiteness on Ramahyuck Mission, 1885–1900', in *Creating White Australia*, ed. Jane Carey and Claire McLisky (Sydney: Sydney University Press, 2009), 85–102.

22 John C.S. Mason, *The Moravian Church and the Missionary Awakening in England, 1760–1800* (Woodbridge, Suffolk, UK: Royal Historical Society, and Rochester, NY: Boydell Press, 2001), 180; Gisela Mettele, *Weltbürgertum, oder Gottesreich: Die Herrnhuter Brüdergemeine als globale Gemeinschaft, 1727–1857* (Göttingen: Vandenhoeck & Ruprecht, 2009), 185–6.

23 See, for example, Mettele, *Weltbürgertum*, 147–78.

audience and wide-ranging expectations: German reports in German mission journals, but English reports in the *Periodical Accounts*, which were orientated towards fundraising and widely disseminated. Thus the English mission journal was available in print before the German mission journal, which was only distributed in printed form after 1819.

These journals contained not just mission diaries and letters by missionaries (and sometimes by converts), but also occasionally short biographies or memoirs, a literary genre for which the Moravians are well known and which had been compiled for most members since the early eighteenth century.[24] However, by the time of the establishment of Ebenezer in the 1860s, memoirs were not recorded with the same regularity for indigenous converts as they had been in the early period of Moravian mission outreach. While there are some memoirs of prominent indigenous converts from other mission fields in the nineteenth century, none seem to have been compiled for Australia. The lack of these texts could be explained by a change in mission policy, which meant that the writing of memories received less encouragement in the late nineteenth century.[25] The absence of memoirs by indigenous converts could also reflect a stronger desire on the part of missionaries to control the self-representation of Moravian missions. Nobody was admitted to baptism who could not convincingly demonstrate this experience, and the mission sources therefore pay great attention to this aspect.[26]

In addition to the decline of indigenous memoirs we seem to have fewer letters by indigenous converts compared to the 1750s. In contrast to the eighteenth century, where letters by indigenous converts were written and posted across the Atlantic relatively frequently as part of Moravian internal communication, the mission journals of the 1860s contain only a few of these letters.[27] The exception were some letters exchanged between leading indigenous converts from various Moravian mission fields (e.g., Greenland and Australia) as a way of actively forging the identity of a global community. In this case, it was the Greenlander Nathan who wrote to Ebenezer on behalf of his congregation in order to support indigenous people there (including sending money); he promptly received a reply from the convert Jackson Stewart to thank him.[28]

---

[24] Christine Lost, *Das Leben als Lehrtext: Lebensläufe aus der Herrnhuter Brüdergemeine* (= Beiheft of *Unitas Fratrum*, 14. Herrnhut: Herrnhuter Verlag, 2007).

[25] Lost, *Leben als Lehrtext.*

[26] For a similar discussion of Methodists, see Christopher White, 'A Measured Faith: Edwin Starbuck, William James, and the Scientific Reform of Religious Experience', *Harvard Theological Review* 101, 3/4 (2008): 431–50.

[27] On the letters of Moravian indigenous converts in the eighteenth century, see J. Van Gent, 'The Lives of Others: Moravian Indigenous Converts' Writings and the Politics of Colonial Autobiographies', in *Selbstzeugnis und Person, Transkulturelle Perspektiven*, ed. Ulbrich, Medick and Schaser.

[28] *Periodical Accounts*, vol. 28, 526–7.

While women at Ebenezer could also write, their letters are mentioned only once in passing in a footnote.

Letters written by women converts are a good example of the gendered nature of mission sources, for they are rarely mentioned in missionaries' reports and letters (and are not preserved in mission archives). We have one exception, in which a letter by Rebecca Pepper to another Aboriginal woman was published in the mission journals in 1869. We know that there were many more letters written by Aboriginal women, because they exist in secular colonial offices to which Aboriginal women, including some affiliated with Ebenezer mission, wrote in order to intervene in colonial structures and defend their families' interests.[29] Thus, while women's literacy was the result of their association with the mission, this skill was used to engage with a wider colonial society and, also, at times, to express criticisms of the mission. Writing outside the missionary writing machine provided the opportunity to voice critiques. Bessy Cameron's experience resulted in her total break with the mission system, for which she turned to the patronage of the colonial system by writing to the Governor: 'I can never be happy on a mission'.[30] Other women likewise complained about their treatment on the stations, for example Eda Brangy in her 15 November 1881 statement to the Royal Commission on the management of Coranderrk station. Her critique was directed at the behaviour of the manager's wife, and Eda complained that she had received no wages for doing the washing, was ordered around by the daughter of the manager, and did not receive any blankets.[31]

The conversion narratives contained in the Moravian mission journals of Ebenezer refer almost exclusively to young Wotjobaluk men, especially Nathanel Pepper. Conversion is represented as an individual (male) act of spiritual awakening and gradual integration into the Moravian community. The text is written not as a first-person narrative, but as a report by the missionary. Although the mission texts mention other peers of Pepper, they are relegated to the background when discussing spiritual development. The act of conversion is emphasised as an individual, autonomous experience, while acknowledging that mission preparation and ongoing guidance, control and correction are necessary. Although women were also baptised, their spiritual development or religious leadership are not discussed in detail.

The mission sources name a group of Wotjobaluk men and women who were related to one another. Nathanel Pepper and his brothers and half-brothers, as well as the women who were married to them, figure most prominently in the

29 Patricia Grimshaw, Elizabeth Nelson and Sandra Smith (eds), *Letters from Aboriginal Women in Victoria, 1867–1926* (Melbourne University, History Department, 2002).

30 Letters by Bessy Cameron (née Flower) to Captain Page, Secretary, BPA (Board for Protection of Aborigines, Victoria), published in Grimshaw et al. *Letters from Aboriginal Women*, 149–59, 194–201.

31 Ibid., 202–3.

sources. These included Nathanel Pepper, his brother Philip Pepper (formerly Charley), his brother Light (who did not convert) and his half-brother Lanky (who was not baptised), as well as Old Boney, his son Boney (baptised Daniel) and Tallyo (baptised Timothy).[32] The women discussed in this chapter are Rachel Pepper (first wife of Nathanel), Louise Pepper (second wife of Nathanel after Rachel's death), Rebecca Pepper (wife of Philip), Kitty (wife of Light), Susannah (wife of Timothy) and Rebecca's mother Jenny.

The complexity of gender relations in colonial contexts will become clear in the following section, which discusses male indigenous converts as gendered beings and looks at how these Aboriginal men negotiated masculinity in the mission context of Ebenezer. The social relations that indigenous converted men had to negotiate were with other indigenous men and women and with the European missionary and his wife, as well as with the wider colonial society. Missionaries demanded loyalty from the very young male converts, which brought them into competition for authority with indigenous elders.

The Making of a Male Convert – Nathanel Pepper and his Relatives

Pepper (later baptised Nathanel) and his friend Boney (later baptised Daniel) were young men when the mission sources first mention them in 1859, about one year after the German Moravian missionaries Spieseke and Hagenauer arrived in the Wimmera district in Victoria and settled in the woolshed of Adolph Ellermann's farmstead, known as Antwerp. In January 1859 they had selected a site nearby to build the Ebenezer mission. The two young men Boney and Pepper are mentioned in the mission sources as helping the missionaries in an important and exclusively male activity, which signalled their authority as heads of household who were also sedentary and superior: the building of permanent timber houses.[33] In January 1859, the mission school officially opened with three Wotjobaluk boys in attendance: Boney, aged 16, Corney aged 12, and Tallyo, aged 15. During 1859, the number of what appears to have been male pupils increased to 15. They now included two boys who would become prominent converts: Pepper and Boney and several other male youths, who all lived in Pepper's hut which he had built on the mission grounds.[34]

32 A note on the use of first names in the text: The primary sources use indigenous names (or versions of them), the English names given to indigenous people by English settlers and baptismal names. The spelling of names also varies in the primary sources. For example, Pepper was baptised Nathanel (aka Nathaniel or Nathanael), Tallyo (aka Tallio, Dallio or Tallyho) was baptised Timothy, Charley was baptised Philip and Boney (aka Young Boney) was baptised Daniel. When quoting directly, we use the spelling that appears in the sources.

33 *Periodical Accounts* 23 (1860), 217, 218, 336.

34 Ibid., 340.

Similarly, missionary masculinity entailed teaching literacy to a people with no written language and translating the catechism into the local language.[35] But there are two significant gendered aspects here: first, the sources represent all initial mission-related activities as exclusively male undertakings, in keeping with an imperial ideology of empire outreach as an expression of masculinity. Second, despite the portrayal of these young Wotjobaluk men as subordinate to missionaries, it is clear that the missionaries depended on them for the very activities that formed the basis of their claim to gendered power: building houses and being able to speak the local language in order to translate the Bible and preach in it. In fact, young men like Pepper were the main translators.

It would not be until February 1860, another full year, before Boney (later baptised Daniel) and Pepper were reported to show any interest in formal conversion to Christianity.[36] But to his surprise the missionary Spieseke found Nathanel Pepper preaching in his own language to a group of about 50 indigenous people at Ebenezer.[37] Pepper had no instruction from Spieseke to do so, and was not even baptised at that point. This was not the first time that effective indigenous proselytising took place at Ebenezer during the European missionary's absence. Several months earlier, in September 1859, a group of an estimated 75–80 Aboriginal men had arrived at the station while Spieseke was in Melbourne. Unfortunately, the German missionary refused to give rations to those who were not working, and this caused great hostility.[38] These examples show how indigenous men had their own ideas about mission patronage: they clearly seized opportunities to engage in their own independent 'spreading of the word', and those who came to listen expected hospitality to be freely given without the pressure to conform to a European work ethic in return.

Thus, on Ebenezer, religious authority was a social space that was conditionally open to young male converts, which they took up not merely by preaching to their own people independent of a missionary, but also in claiming direct access to the divine in the form of dreams. The young Aboriginal men asserted this claim to independent religious authority in ritually potent moments. For example, after the death of one of their male peers, Bulcher, in February 1860, Pepper and another young Aboriginal man, Tallyo, told the missionaries about their dreams in which heaven opened up and angels appeared.[39] Dreams as divine guidance were accepted as an expression of spiritual authority and power

[35] Rutherdale, '"It is not Soft Job to be Performed": Missionaries and Imperial Manhood', 62.

[36] *Periodical Accounts* 23 (1860), 405.

[37] Ibid., 469.

[38] Susan Robertson, *The Bell Sounds Pleasantly: Ebenezer Mission Station* (Doncaster, VIC: Luther Rose Publications, 1992), 39.

[39] *Periodical Accounts* 23 (1860), 471. For a discussion of Christian dreams at Lutheran missions in central Australia, see J. Van Gent, '*Blickwechsel*: Arrernte encounters

in Australian indigenous cultures, and European anthropologists often refer to the indigenous mythology that explains current spiritual and social laws as 'dream time'.[40] Dreams were not that unusual in the Moravian tradition either, and were accepted by the missionaries in Ebenezer. What is significant is that the men were permitted to make these claims, and that they did so not as isolated individuals but as groups of young men who already had ongoing social ties with one another.

One of the cornerstones of this male homosocial spiritual bonding between missionaries, Wotjobaluk boys and Christ was the story of Willi Wimmera, a Wotjobaluk boy who, after the death of his mother, had been taken by a Presbyterian minister first to Melbourne and later to England where he was baptised and died shortly thereafter.[41] This had happened in the 1850s, just a few years before the arrival of the Moravians. Hagenauer read the story of Willi Wimmera, which had been published, to the young Aboriginal boys who came to the mission to learn to read. The Moravian missionaries mistakenly believed these three Aboriginal boys to be the stepbrothers of Willi Wimmera,[42] and therefore thought that this encounter revealed a pre-existing godly plan, which the missionaries interpreted as a sign that the death of this Aboriginal boy (like the death of Jesus) had not been in vain.

Then events are reported in the *Periodical Accounts* in quick succession and with a dramatic edge: in 1860, the missionaries sent frequent reports about the spiritual progress of several young men, most prominently of Pepper, who 'repeatedly expressed the desire to be baptised'.[43] The mission sources emphasise that those Wotjobaluk who sought baptism, or showed any Moravian-acceptable signs of conversion, were not the elders (male or female), but male youths. The age specifics of first-generation Australian indigenous conversions in Ebenezer confirm observations that have been made in this regard for the Lutheran

---

with Lutheran missionaries in central Australia', in *Luther zwischen den Kulturen*, ed. Hans Medick and Peer Schmidt (Göttingen, Vandenhoeck & Ruprecht, 2004), 396–420.

40 The literature on the concept and anthropological use of 'dream time' is vast. For a good overview, see John Morton, 'Aboriginal religion today', in Sylvia Kleinert and Margo Neile (eds), *The Oxford Companion to Aboriginal Art and Culture* (Melbourne: Oxford University Press, 2000), 9–16. For Aboriginal women's participation in the dreaming, see Bell, *Daughters of the Dreaming*. The connections between Wotjobaluk notions of the dreaming and mission teachings are discussed in detail by Kenny, *The Lamb Enters the Dreaming*.

41 For a detailed discussion of the importance of this pre-existing link between Antwerp station and the Wotjobaluk boy, who had converted in London, see Kenny, *The Lamb Enters the Dreaming*.

42 *Periodical Accounts* 23 (1860), 168.

43 Ibid., 535.

mission in central Australia.[44] Whether the gender-specific composition of the first group of Wotjobaluk converts was a result of local decisions by Wotjobaluk elders or whether the missionaries prevented Wotjobaluk young girls from attending the school because no female Moravian Sisters were yet present, is not apparent from the sources.

As we learn later, Nathanel Pepper did not hear about Jesus Christ for the first time from the missionaries; a shepherd had conveyed this information to him long before the German Moravians arrived in the Wimmera.[45] This confirms the observation by a number of historians that missions do not necessarily represent the first points of contact with Christianity. In fact, the missionaries' arrival accorded with a pre-existing idea of an almost prophetic nature. It could be integrated into existing beliefs and assumptions and required no radical break with a traditional worldview. This myth-making was equally (or more?) important to the missionaries, who thereby affirmed the importance of their calling and their predetermination for choosing this particular mission field. This link with what had gone before also created an almost natural alliance between these men in the eyes of the missionaries. In the case of Ebenezer and Willi Wimmera, it created an all-male link between Christ, the Wotjobaluk boys and the missionaries. This link at once excluded women and laid claim to male religious leadership.

Male social bonding, as it is represented in the mission journals, was enacted daily in teaching, preaching, the translation of Bible texts and the close proximity of living spaces between Nathanel's hut and the missionaries' house. Male colonial mission networks gave Pepper some access to a wider colonial male audience, for in July 1862 Nathanel Pepper spoke at a meeting of the Moravian Missionary Association in Australia, chaired by the governor.[46] This was a gendered political realm which excluded women, both indigenous and Moravian.

But Pepper and his peers were not only interested in learning to read English from the Bible and sharing this religious literacy with white men; they actively and independently – and significantly, before their own baptism – assembled other indigenous men to speak to them about Christ. There is no mention of Pepper seeking permission from a missionary to go proselytising; instead, he again acted completely independently and with authority: 'Pepper had assembled his fellow-countrymen, and spoken to them of the love of Jesus'.[47]

Yet all this diligence and initiative on the part of Wotjobaluk youth was not sufficient for Moravian pastors to agree to baptism; they first had to demonstrate

---

44 Peggy Brock and Jacqueline Van Gent, 'Generational Religious Change Among the Arrernte at Hermannsburg, Central Australia', *Australian Historical Studies* 120 (2002): 303–18.

45 *Periodical Accounts* 23 (1860), 336, 338–339.

46 Ibid., 24 (1863), 665.

47 Ibid., 23 (1860), 532.

an emotional and spiritual awakening and inner change in the Moravian mode. This was duly observed only a few days later:

> In the evening of the 18th after the day's labour was over, I took Pepper and Boney into our hut to read the Bible. The passage was an account of our Lord's meeting with Nathaniel, with which they appeared particularly interested and on explanations being given to them, they several times exclaimed 'How sweet!' I obtained increasingly the pleasing conviction, that the Spirit of God has begun His work in the hearts of several of these deeply degraded people.[48]

Spieseke's comment on the state of indigenous men reflects the dilemma these Europeans faced in an increasingly racially stratified colonial world in which they had to take sides even though they desired indigenous conversions.

Wotjobaluk young men transmitted what they had learned to their peers, thereby translating the missionary teachings not only into their own language but no doubt also into their own religious and cultural belief system. The mission journals depict this process as a highly gendered one – only men are mentioned as transmitting the Christian message to other indigenous people:

> Towards the evening, on Sunday the 25th, I went into the camp to call the people to service, and was delighted to find Pepper sitting among his fellow-countrymen, with his New Testament and small Scripture pictures in his hand, telling them in their own tongue how Jesus had died for them, and risen again and ascended up to heaven. Charley and Dallio were especially attentive listeners, and put many questions to him respecting the salvation which is in Christ Jesus.[49]

This passage not only silences Aboriginal women, it also creates a hierarchy among young Aboriginal men by singling out Pepper and placing him in an active and superior role as teacher and portraying the others as subordinate listeners. Yet in Australian indigenous traditions, listening and asking are not expressions of subordination, but rather the common method for negotiating all matters.

The actual conversion moment is in fact very brief, but the mission sources assign it great prominence. Pepper comes to Spieseke after a nocturnal awakening experience, in which he had found himself alone and in emotional turmoil by the river, meditating on the blood of Jesus.[50] This is not a conversion story in a first-person voice, but it describes a transformation. It follows an existing Moravian pattern of conversions, in the manner of the famous Herrnhut children's revival

---

48 Ibid., 533.

49 Ibid.

50 Ibid., 406.

of 1726, where children met at night outside, crying and meditating on Christ's blood.[51] Moravian readers of Pepper's conversion would have readily recognised the description.

The conversion may have been represented as a precise emotional moment, but it was a longer lasting process. Pepper's conversion was emphasised in the mission journal as an individual act, triggered by the missionaries' reading earlier that evening, and as the independent insight of an individual. The meditation on Christ's blood and on one's own personal sins were key motifs in Moravian rituals of conversion and their narratives. While this conversion is represented as a turning point, Nathanel's previous life is not really his whole life before conversion, but only his time on the mission. It thus leaves out a significant part of his identity, that is, his pre-mission experiences. The 'after', on the other hand, is drawn out and the Moravian audience is fed regular reports about Nathanel's behaviour for the rest of his life. This is in contrast to European conversion narratives, where the person's pre-conversion life is described at great length, but the time after conversion is generally given less attention.

The conversion is the moment when Pepper is singled out and consequently assigned the status of 'first fruit' and a leading male convert with a more elevated status. As a result, the mission sources give us more information about him than they do about any other Wotjobaluk man or woman. Indeed, the *Missions-Blatt* is quite upfront about this hierarchy, and when reporting on Nathanel's brother Charley, who was a baptismal candidate, the missionary noted, 'He is very much affected, and had he been the first, as Nathanel was, we would have still more to say about him'.[52]

Nathanel Pepper remained in the public eye of the mission after his conversion, and regular reports in the mission journal monitored his subsequent behaviour, while the *Periodical Accounts*' readership waited to see whether he would be admitted to baptism:

> From our last communication, you have heard that, to our great joy, and to our shame likewise, for our want of faith, a work of grace has been begun by the Holy Spirit in the heart of the youth Pepper. Several weeks have passed away since we were privileged to observe this change. You will therefore be anxious to know what the present state of things is.[53]

---

51 Pia Schmid, 'Die Kindererweckung in Herrnhut am 17. August 1727', in *Neue Aspekte der Zinzendorfforschung*, ed. Martin Brecht und Paul Peucker (Göttingen: Vandenhoeck & Ruprecht, 2006), 114–33.

52 *Missions-Blatt* 28, 6 (1864): 123.

53 Letter from Spieseke, Ebenezer, 6 March 1860, *Periodical Accounts* 23 (1860).

This surveillance of Pepper and other potential male converts was an effective means of asserting mission power. For the next few months, things seemed to go smoothly. Every report to the mission audience confirmed Pepper's positive development, his increased verbal skills (reading aloud, singing) and his voluntary voicing of a desire for baptism:

> Early in June, it appears as if a renewed stream of blessing from the Lord had flowed into the hearts of several of the youths. Pepper was particularly lively, and repeatedly expressed the desire to be baptized. His answers in the school, his diligent reading of the Bible, his singing, and the like, are all tokens of the countenance of the gracious work of the Holy Spirit. Young Boney was sadly reduced by disease, and could no longer come to school. Few of the old people attended the meetings with any degree of regularity, but among the young men a lively interest for the good news of salvation was observable.[54]

The homosociality among missionaries, male converts and potential young male converts, which this passage emphasises, served to exclude senior Aboriginal men and their authority over young indigenous people.

A further expansion of these male social relationships was achieved with Pepper's baptism, which became a significant public event attended by many colonial dignitaries from Melbourne.[55] According to missionary Hagenauer, on Sunday, 12 August 1860, the bell rang at 11am for church service and approximately 180 people, including some 60 white visitors, were present. 'Mr Chase had made use of every opportunity to read and pray with Pepper, and the latter appeared to be wholly prepared by the Holy Spirit for admission in to the Church of Christ'.[56] Pepper was baptised by the name of Nathanel 'on his own request', which should reassure the reader that his conversion was voluntary and of his own free will.[57] The baptism of the first convert was a political event that reinforced male networks not only on the mission but also within the wider Australian colonial society in which the German missionaries sought to gain a foothold. The baptism of Nathanel Pepper was also reported in the colonial newspaper, thus making it an event of significance not only to Moravians, but also to empire outreach in Victoria.

As we have seen, the positioning of converts within a spiritual and moral hierarchy of men was an important part of the gendered experience of conversion. This position, however, was not stable or taken for granted. Even after baptism, indigenous converts were continuously monitored by the missionary, and the

54 *Periodical Accounts* 23 (1860), 535.

55 Ibid., 536.

56 Ibid.

57 Ibid.

mission public was informed of their behaviour. Pepper seems to have fulfilled at least some of the Moravian expectations. 'Nathaniel Pepper gives us satisfaction, and from time to time affords encouraging tokens of spiritual life. As yet, the influences of the gospel only extend to the younger men'.[58] The missionary's observation that only young men were responding positively to their proselytising is significant. It meant that old men and women alike were reluctant to convert, and that missionaries believed that in order to ensure the survival of the mission, they had to concentrate all their efforts on these young boys and transform them into Christian men. Spiritual progress was not a sufficient precondition for Protestant Christian masculinity; Christian marriage was also essential, and, like baptism, it had to be controlled by missionaries, not Aboriginal elders or indigenous young men themselves.

Negotiating Male Hierarchies and Status

Marriage was a key marker of a man's ability to govern a household, and by the mid-nineteenth century this patriarchal ideology was being applied to all Moravians, be they European missionaries or indigenous converts.[59] Therefore the men in power, the missionaries Spieseke and Hagenauer, needed to be married now that converts had arrived and the mission had a future.[60] Their wives naturally had to be Moravian Sisters, and they were chosen by drawing lots.[61] In May 1861 Spieseke went to Melbourne to collect Sisters Christina Fricke and Louise Knobloch, who had been sent as brides from Germany. They were married in Melbourne within a few weeks after their arrival.[62]

The marriage of their male acolytes followed a different pattern and had other obstacles to overcome in order to establish their Christian masculinity. The first man to be married was Nathanel. He had wished to marry Kitty, a local Aboriginal woman, but met with resistance from Aboriginal elders because in indigenous societies, marriages were arranged according to strict kinship rules and decided by elders. Hagenauer decided to take matters into his own hands and, drawing on his wider colonial connections, he got in touch with Anne Camfield in Western Australia, on the other side of the continent, to ask for

---

[58] Ibid., 618.

[59] See, for example, Elisabeth W. Sommer, *Serving Two Masters: Moravian Brethren in Germany and North Carolina, 1727–1801* (Lexington: University Press of Kentucky, 2000).

[60] See the letter by La Trobe, Herrnhut archive, Rubrik 15 V I a 5.

[61] For a discussion of the function of lots in the Moravian Church, see, for example, Erich Beyreuther, 'Lostheorie und Lospraxis', in *Studien zur Theologie Zinzendorfs: Gesammelte Aufsätze* (Neukirchen: Olms, 1962), 109–35.

[62] Felicity Jensz, *German Moravian Missionaries in the British Colony of Victoria, Australia, 1848–1908* (Leiden: Brill, 2011), 131–4.

a Christian (but not Moravian) Aboriginal woman to be shipped over for Nathanel. While at first glance this is not much different to his own experience, where his bride was sent to him from Germany, there are significant differences in the forms of gendered power between him and Nathanel. While Hagenauer also received a woman he barely knew who had been chosen for him, it was done not only by elders but also by the drawing of lots, which was an essential part of Moravian decision-making and applied to all significant decisions, whether marriages, travel or the acceptance of a new posting. The Moravians understood the lot to signify Christ's will. There was some leeway to refuse it. For Nathanel, on the other hand, Hagenauer assumed the function of the lot, or Christ, and he alone decided whom Nathanel would marry. It did not seem to matter that this woman was not a Moravian (in contrast to the missionary Francis, who was expelled for not marrying a Moravian woman), and Rachel, as far as we know, had no say in the matter. In May 1863 Nathanel married Rachel and they both assisted in Sunday school.[63]

To be the first to be baptised and the first to be married elevated Nathanel to a higher social position within the mission hierarchy. He was now portrayed as a definite role model for other Aboriginal men, including his brothers. Neither Boney (Daniel) nor Tallyo (Timothy) were married men at this stage, and while their proselytising efforts were noted positively, they did not occupy the same position of authority in the mission texts as, for example, their kinsman Nathanel Pepper. As one missionary writes about him in the *Periodical Accounts*, 'I wish that some of the other young men were settled in a similar manner'. Nathanel's second marriage, after Rachel's death in 1869, was also decided by the Hagenauers, as we shall see.

Not all Aboriginal men in Nathanel's peer group allowed the missionaries to arrange their marriages or were associated permanently with the mission, and not all engagements entailed conversions. On the contrary, many candidates for baptism frequently lived away from the mission, which gave them the opportunity to marry outside of the missionaries' control. For example Lanky, a half-brother of Nathanel and brother to Charley (Philip), is reported as having returned to the mission after some years of absence. Now married, but not baptised, he worked as a mission gardener and his wife served in the missionary household. Their Christian spiritual awakening was nevertheless non-existent. Lanky and his wife Sarah, although 'useful', did not seem very interested in the spiritual side of Moravian life, as Spieseke could not observe 'any token of the work of grace in their hearts'.[64] Lanky did not convert, but when he died two years later, in 1865, he asked to be buried near the church.[65]

63 Kenny, *The Lamb Enters the Dreaming.*

64 Spieseke, letter of 15 October 1863, *Periodical Accounts* 25 (1865), 126.

65 *Periodical Accounts* 25 (1865), 510.

The Aboriginal man Tallyo (Timothy) also defied the Christian marriage system by absconding from the mission. When he returned on one occasion, and was married, the missionary expressed his hope that he might be more obedient now: 'I am glad that Talliho [*sic*] has returned and is apparently well disposed. I trust that he and Susanna will be more manageable, as they are now married'.[66] The estate of marriage was a desirable one for Christian men, but they still had to submit to the moral control of the missionary. Absconding from the station was one way to avoid this, but on their return Aboriginal men were reminded of the power hierarchy: 'The day before yesterday Tallyho [*sic*] returned with his wife Susannah after an absence of some time. I hope they will both in future be more willing to take counsel and warning from us'.[67] Nathanel gave 'no cause for dissatisfaction' and his half-brother Lanky and his wife Sarah were noted for living 'in one of the huts on this station'. Nathanel and his wife were also reported as helping at Sunday school.[68]

Yet another path again was taken by Nathanel's brother Charley, who was baptised as late as May 1864 (almost four years after his brother) by the name of Philip, together with his partner Jessy (baptised Rebecca) and they were married by missionaries immediately following baptism.[69] In his negotiation of marriage, different male power patterns become visible.

The marriage of Aboriginal converts was a field for competition between missionaries and Aboriginal elders over male power. Aboriginal elders are represented as exercising excessive and thus inappropriate sexual authority over Aboriginal women. The missionary records portray Aboriginal men's intention to marry much younger women as an abuse of male power. This was the case in the above mentioned case of Charley, who wished to marry an Aboriginal woman called Jessy. The missionary reports make it clear in this instance that Aboriginal men exercised unlawful rights in 'wanting to exchange her for another woman from another tribe' 'over whom they have no rightful control whatever [*sic*], as she is an orphan'. The absence of a father is cited as her reason for coming to the missionaries to escape 'all sorts of persecution' and seeking their paternal protection. The authority of her future husband, Charley, was unimportant or ineffective. The indigenous men, the missionaries stress, had no right to exercise authority, because the protection apparently sought by the girl was 'against the cruel tyranny of King Peter, who considers himself to be the supreme head of the tribe'. The male missionaries used this conflict to assert their position within the colonial power hierarchies and to elicit the support of

66 Spieseke, letter of 15 October 1863, *Periodical Accounts* 25 (1865), 126.
67 Ibid., 186.
68 Ibid.
69 Spieseke to Reichel, 16 May 1864, Ibid., 234.

the police, who duly arrived at the mission and chased 'King Peter' away.[70] The same argument was voiced some years later, when Aboriginal men 'in the camp' were accused of unlawfully exercising paternal power. Here Aboriginal women were portrayed as choosing missionaries as their protectors and thus putting indigenous men in a subordinate position, not because they were not Christians but because of their weak masculine authority.[71] And again, missionaries drew on the colonial male network of power and employed the police to subdue indigenous men.[72] It is noticeable here that mission patronage extended beyond converts, to all indigenous people in the vicinity, just as it did for other farms where European masters held sway over them. It reflects a deep-seated colonial attitude that control over conversion implied control over other aspects of social life, such as marriage.

Their marital status afforded Philip and Rebecca the privilege of taking children into their house with the missionary's permission. This was the first step towards the so-called orphanage for Aboriginal children.[73] This form of separate housing for children was an early institution in Moravian congregations, where children were socialised in children choirs, i.e., they were housed separately from their parents. In the nineteenth century, however, this became less common. But it had strong colonial and racial connotations, in that in the Australian colonies, Aboriginal children who were deemed neglected or in some cases orphaned were brought up in institutions headed by white people from religious communities, as Rachel had been in Anne Camfield's home for children. Their parents were not always absent, as the letters of Bessy Flower to Anne Camfield show, in which she explicitly sends greetings to her mother. Only five years later, a children's home was opened at Ebenezer on 19 March 1873, with twelve girls

---

70 Letter from Spieseke to Reichel, Ebenezer, 15 December 1863, *Periodical Accounts* 25 (1865), 187–8. The relationship between the missionaries and this Aboriginal man seem to have been more ambiguous. On other occasions, Hagenauer emphasised the support that 'King Peter' gave him, and that the Aboriginal elder supposedly accepted the missionary's authority as 'teacher'. In a published excerpt from Hagenauer's private diary, he describes him as 'my friend King Peter'. *Missions-Blatt* 26, 6 (1862), 113.

71 Spieseke to Reichel, Ebenezer, 19 February 1866, *Periodical Accounts* 26 (1866), 29.

72 Ibid. 'Thus, a few days ago, an exchange of wives took place in the camp. The parties concerned, and particularly a man who occupies the lowest grade of debasement, were angry at some of our young people for telling us. Yesterday evening the above mentioned man actually beat our Elizabeth with a branch of a tree, because he thought she had said something to us on the subject. As the girl is under our protection, and came crying to complain to us, we thought it well to make an example, and therefore sent for the police, whose arrival we now look for.'

73 In 1868 the *Periodical Accounts* report that Philip and Rebecca took an Aboriginal child of mixed descent into their house. Spieseke, 2 November 1868, *Periodical Accounts* 27 (1870), 79.

and five boys under the care of Philip Pepper and his wife Rebecca. Philip and Rebecca were 'to superintend the school (independent of teaching) acting the parts of parents to the children who live in the house, more suitable persons for the post it would be impossible to select'.[74] Philip's position as convert and a married man afforded him a higher position in the mission hierarchy, which qualified him to be superintendent of the children's home.

A specific male privilege for indigenous converts was the right to evangelise, that is, to travel and preach independently to other indigenous people, to bring them to the church where the missionary would then instruct them further and administer the sacrament of baptism. Moravian missionaries across the world encouraged indigenous evangelists. But by the mid-nineteenth century women, both white and indigenous, were excluded from this privilege, which they had shared in the early decades of Moravian proselytising.

As mentioned before, Nathanel and his brother Philip and others showed considerable energy and interest in their independent proselytising of other indigenous people. In April 1864, a missionary letter noted that 'Daniel has expressed a strong desire to accompany the Brethren to Cooper's Creek' on an evangelising trip.[75] Not only was preaching and evangelising a gendered right reserved for men, in our case it was also rewarded additionally with extra payment secured from the Presbyterian Church. More baptisms followed in July 1865. The Rev Patrick Simpson of the Presbyterian Church in Horsham assisted at the christening service; he wrote to Peter La Trobe in London advising him of the grant of £30 he had obtained from the Presbyterian Church to pay Nathanel and Philip, the two head evangelists, for their services in evangelising and preaching.[76]

Mission records stress how these independent efforts to gain religious power brought young converts into conflict with their community. Sometimes they were accused of witchcraft, an accusation made in Wotjobaluk society only among males in cases of ill health. Healers wielded considerable power, and an accusation of witchcraft therefore always provoked social conflict.

> Some time ago, our good Philip took a journey westwards to preach the Gospel to the heathen dwelling there. Soon after he had left them, one of their number, named Little, became unwell, and Philip was promptly accused of having bewitched him, on this he pertinently remarked: 'I bring them best tidings; and in return they accuse me of such a thing'.

[74] Letter from Spieseke to Reichel, 5 August 1872, *Periodical Accounts* 28 (1872), 367.

[75] Spieseke to Reichel, 18 April 1864, *Periodical Accounts* 25 (1865), 233.

[76] Herrnhut Archives, Rubrik 15 V I a 5. In 1868 it was reported that Philip had returned from a journey to Lake with several young Aboriginal people and children who wished to go to school in Ebenezer. Some of them had started to build houses. Spieseke from Ebenezer, *Periodical Accounts* 27 (1870), 194.

Here the resistance to proselytising is represented as a male conflict. The authority of missionaries must have suffered significantly, when, in another case, they learned that the convert Nathanel had visited a traditional male healer regarding his own illness. Male spiritual power was reinterpreted in missionary texts as witchcraft: old men who interfered with marriages also interfered with sacred power, and were thus in direct competition with male missionaries.

Male competition over power and authority existed not only between indigenous elders and missionaries, but also among male missionaries themselves. The dependence of Moravian missionaries on young male evangelists was not merely explicitly acknowledged in reports to the mission society and the international readership; it was also a source of competition among missionaries over patronage of these young Wotjobaluk men. This competition came to a head when one of the white missionaries left Ebenezer for a new mission station in Ramahyuck in Gippsland and Nathanel followed him in 1869. The remaining missionary Spieseke contextualised the departure of the previous evangelist exclusively as a response to the death of his wife, not as continued loyalty to the missionary Hagenauer.[77] He replaced Nathanel with his brother Philip, who is henceforth mentioned in the mission sources as preaching at church and in homes[78] and holding regular prayer meetings and blessings.[79] Philip also submitted petitions to the Aboriginal Protection Board demanding more land for his people to settle on. He quickly advanced to an authority and political leader in matters beyond immediate mission concerns.[80]

---

77 *Periodical Accounts* 27 (1870), 349.

78 *Periodical Accounts* 27 (1870), 350.

79 Ibid., 514.

80 Ibid., 409. In 1870 the missionaries forwarded letters written at Ebenezer, including by Philip Pepper, to the Board for the Protection of Aborigines, requesting more land. They acknowledged the disastrous health situation of Aboriginal people and their dispossession in their request for land grants. In 1866 Aboriginal people had already asked Spieseke 'Why are we have no land at all?' *Periodical Accounts* 26 (1866), 195.

Figure 2.1 Missionary Friedrich August Hagenauer (1829–1909) in the church of Ramahyuck with an entirely indigenous audience. The Aboriginal evangelists are shown as part of the indigenous congregation, their leadership in preaching and evangelising is not depicted here. The photo was taken by Carl Walter, 7 September 1868. (Courtesy of Moravian Archives Herrnhut, FS- Australien, U1, o. Nr.)

The relative power of male converts and their position as male heads of household had to be controlled by white missionaries, who needed to assert their overall paternal authority over them. This could be done, for example, by appealing to higher (male) religious authorities such as Christ and by pointing to the 'moral floor' and thus the need for governance by missionaries. The exercise of control over male converts, especially the more prominent evangelists, also led to competition between missionaries at the station.

The conversion narratives of men involved only Christ and themselves, but their social behaviour was strongly orientated towards traditional structures, that is, towards peer groups. These young men still bowed to the authority of older Aboriginal men (for example healers), although the mission texts try to deny this. Not all of their brothers converted, and not all of their children stayed on the mission. The men were monitored as long as they associated with the mission, and their frequent lapses (such as participation in indigenous rituals and sexual relationships outside marriage) showed that they had not completely internalised the ideals of Christian masculinity. While they lived on the mission rather than in the camp, they left frequently to see relatives.

As male evangelists, both Nathanel and Philip were marked by their right to preach, even in church. Both men were part of a wider kin and peer group that was active on the mission, and went into country and brought people to the mission. Indigenous men did this to a far greater degree than any of the white missionaries. Nathanel and Philip had to mark their status as heads of (European-defined) households by building huts for themselves and their (nuclear) families on the grounds of the mission, which signalled their alliance with and submission to missionary men rather than indigenous elders in the camp. It also demonstrated a seeming acceptance of a settled lifestyle, which would force men to take up paid employment as heads of households. The men were both very young when they joined the mission, and missionaries intervened in their marriage plans and encouraged them to marry, as this was the base for governance. Mission paternalism and European men's right to rule the mission as an extension of their own households came to the fore in the explicit contrasting of paternalism and paternal rules, and in the placing of evangelists in a subordinate position to the European fathers, but in a superior and antagonistic position to their own indigenous fathers and men in authority. Male bonding and the transmission of knowledge along gender-specific lines may have made it easy for young Wotjobaluk to seek out these alien teachers, but what about the women?

Aboriginal Women, Gendered Power and Mission Control: Rachel Pepper, Louise Arbuckle and Rebecca Pepper

Like their male relatives discussed above, Aboriginal women had to negotiate the gendered hierarchies on the mission as well as in the wider colonial society and of course also within their own kin group. These three social spaces had very different gender ideologies, which were often in conflict with one another. In Australian colonial society women were subordinate to men, and racial subordination meant that both Aboriginal men and women were subordinate to white men and women. Domesticity was a normative gender ideology, but it was unattainable for both working-class and indigenous women. This failure to achieve domesticity and control over their sexuality were major criticisms levelled at Aboriginal women. The Moravians, like other missionaries, regarded Aboriginal women as morally depraved and their sexuality as dangerous and in need of strict control.[81]

---

[81] Lisa Curtis-Wendland, 'Missionary wives and the sexual narratives of German Lutheran missions to Australia', *Journal of the History of Sexuality 20, 3* (2011): 498–519; 'Corporal punishment and moral reform at Hermannsburg Mission', *History Australia* 7,

On Ebenezer and Ramahyuck missions, a global and specific Moravian gender ideology was dominant, although, as we shall see, it could not always be enforced in practice. To Moravians, women's spiritual development was important, and it was generally recorded in women's memoirs. Moravian women had some access to public space on the mission, for example as Sunday school teachers, and they carried out confessional duties with other women in confessional conversations known as Speakings.[82] At the beginning of the Moravian movement in the eighteenth century, female choirs also had special holidays and women published hymns and sermons, but by the middle of the nineteenth century much of this semi-autonomous space for women had disappeared. Moravian congregations were keen to adapt to the gender order of the colonial societies in which their missions were established.

One of the key markers of Protestant normative womanhood was marriage and the implicit control of sexuality, their own as well as their husbands'. Moravians reinforced this patriarchal ideal by allowing only married women in the mission field and by encouraging converted women to marry Christian indigenous men. While there are a few cases of converted women marrying European missionaries, they are exceptions to the rule. Moravian missionaries, and often their wives as well, controlled the marriages of converted Aboriginal women.[83]

The gendered hierarchies created as part of the conversion process for Aboriginal women certainly included not just the missionary as paterfamilias of the mission, but to a considerable extent his wife as well. At Ebenezer and Ramahyuck, Aboriginal women were supervised by missionary wives, who strongly shaped gendered practices of marriage, domesticity and spirituality. The spiritual instruction and moral reform of the female members of the household were duties that fell to the missionary's wife. On the occasion of the baptism of the first two girls at Ramahyuck station, Hagenauer reported that with the 'blessing of the influence of my good wife' one girl had 'become quite changed so that we could admit her for baptism'.[84] In Australia, Moravian missionary wives were scarcely acknowledged in their spiritual authority and influence. The existing gendered relationships imparted a Victorian notion of

1 (2010): 7.1–7.17; and *(Re)constructing Missionary Wives: Frieda Strehlow and German Lutheran Women in Central Australia, 1892–1922* (PhD diss., Monash University, 2009).

[82] These confessional conversations were meant to be conducted in a sex-segregated manner, with Moravian Sisters in charge of the 'Speakings' of younger and indigenous women. For a discussion of this practice, see Katherine Faull, '"Girls Talk" das "Sprechen" von Kindern: Herrnhutische Seelsorge an den grossen Mädchen im 18. Jahrhundert', *Unitas Fratrum* 57/58 (2006): 37–56.

[83] Felicity Jensz, 'Controlling Marriages: Friedrich Hagenauer and the Betrothal of Indigenous Western Australian Women in Colonial Victoria', *Aboriginal History* 34 (2010): 34–54.

[84] *Periodical Accounts* 27 (1870), 348–9.

femininity, which focused on domesticity and the control of female sexuality. A missionary's wife's patronage also entailed the right to discipline Aboriginal women.[85] Missionary wives were specifically responsible for the moral and spiritual conduct of converted Aboriginal women before marriage, when many of them lived as servants in the missionary household. But this gendered power of missionary wives was not unlimited, and like their husbands, these European women depended on the labour of Aboriginal people. Aboriginal women did overstep the boundaries set at the mission; they could abscond and return to their families or, thanks to literacy skills acquired at the mission, appeal to the colonial authorities for more support.

This section discusses hierarchies between women that arose as part of mission gender practices. There have been a considerable number of feminist studies on the experiences of missionary wives, but less has been done on the relationship between these women and their female charges on missions.[86] As feminist scholars have rightly pointed out, missionary women did not wield unlimited power over the indigenous girls in their charge.[87] At Ebenezer and Ramahyuck, the social space for missionary wives to work with Aboriginal

---

85 For a discussion of Aboriginal women and children as domestic servants, see Jackie Huggins, 'White Aprons, Black Hands: Aboriginal Women Domestic Servants in Queensland', *Labour History* 69 (1995): 188–95; and Shirleene Robinson, '"We don't want one that is too old": Aboriginal child domestic servants in late 19th and early 20th century Queensland', *Aboriginal History* 27 (2003): 162–82.

86 For studies of white missionary women, see Patricia Grimshaw, 'Faith, Missionary Life, and the Family', in *Gender and Empire*, Philippa Levine (ed) (Oxford: Oxford University Press, 2004), 260–80; Margaret Allen, '"That's the Modern Girl": Missionary Women and Modernity in Kolkata, c. 1907–c. 1940', *Itinerario* 34, 3 (2010): 83–96; Patricia Grimshaw, 'Reappraisals of Mission History: An Introduction', in *Missionaries, Indigenous Peoples and Cultural Exchange*, ed. Grimshaw and May, 1–9; Margaret Jolly, '"To Save the Girls for Brighter and Better Lives": Presbyterian Missions and Women in the South of Vanuatu, 1848–1870'. *The Journal of Pacific History* 26, 1 (1991): 27–48; Elbourne, 'Mother's Milk'; Rhonda Anne Semple, *Missionary Women: Gender, Professionalism and the Victorian Idea of Christian Mission* (Woodbridge, Suffolk; Rochester, NY: Boydell Press, 2003), 148–9; Elizabeth Prevost, 'Assessing Women, Gender, and Empire in Britain's Nineteenth-Century Protestant Missionary Movement', *History Compass* 7, 3 (2009): 765–99; and 'Contested Conversions: Missionary Women's Religious Encounters in Early Colonial Uganda', in *Missionaries, Indigenous Peoples and Cultural Exchange*, ed. Grimshaw and May, 37–51; Jane Haggis and Margaret Allen, 'Imperial Emotions: Affective Communities of Mission in British Protestant Women's Missionary Publications c.1880–1920', *Journal of Social History* (2008): 691–716.

87 For a recent discussion, see Margaret Allen '"A Breach of Confidence by Their Greatly Beloved Principal": A Furore at Women's Christian College, Chennai, India, 1940', in *Women's Activism: Global Perspectives from the 1890s to the Present*, ed. F. de Haan, M. Allen, K. Daskalova and J. Purvis (London: Routledge, 2013), 168–82.

women was the household and the Sunday school, where women sometimes, but not always, taught children. This gendered geography was of a domestic nature, and centred on the missionary household where Aboriginal women had to do the cooking, cleaning, washing and childminding for the missionary family and where they were taught other gender-specific skills such as sewing. Even the spiritual instruction of Aboriginal women took place in the missionary's house.[88]

This 'civilising' work of missionary wives, which focused on the domestic sphere and on Aboriginal women, is rarely mentioned as an important contribution in mission records. Missionary wives also taught Aboriginal girls reading and writing.[89] And only occasionally are Aboriginal women's educational efforts at school mentioned, as for example in 1868 when we learn that 'A very important work is carried on in the instruction and education of the children, and we have valuable assistance in this from our native female teacher, E. Flowers'.[90] And the missionary continues:

> The day-school is kept for five hours daily, and good progress is made in it. Sr. Hagenauer also has a sewing-class for the women every afternoon, which is well attended; they learn and sing psalms and hymns at their work. Another class is kept by myself for candidates of baptism and reception to full church membership.[91]

These two sentences highlight the gendered power structure: while the missionary wife informally taught Aboriginal women hymns and the catechism, often while doing domestic work such as sewing, it was a male prerogative to prepare acolytes for the sacrament of baptism and thus of 'full church membership'.

---

[88] Recent archaeological findings for Ebenezer mission confirm the centrality of the missionary household, but also suggest that Aboriginal women were able to evade the domesticity expected of them to some extent. See Jane Lydon, *Fantastic Dreaming: the Archaeology of an Aboriginal Mission* (Lanham: AltaMira Press, 2009), especially chapter 4, 'Space, power and the mission-house', 103–24, and chapter 5, 'All these little things: material culture and domesticity', 125–73.

[89] *Missions-Blatt*, 1864, No 11, 226–8. Hagenauer's wife is said to have taught eight girls, only four of whom regularly came to their lessons.

[90] *Periodical Accounts* 27 (1870), 80.

[91] Ibid., Report for Ramahyuck for 1868, p. 81

Figure 2.2 'Eight school girls from Ebenezer mission', ca 1870/75. Despite the original caption of the photo, it looks more likely that the central female figure, wearing a brooch, is an Aboriginal teacher rather than a school girl. The teaching done by Aboriginal women, such as Elizabeth (Bessy) Cameron (neé Flower) who worked at Ramahyuck mission station, was usually downplayed in mission reports. (Courtesy of Moravian Archives Herrnhut, NTP –Foto, o. Sign (49))

These gendered spaces produced not just gendered domesticity, but also the gendered power that missionary wives held over the indigenous women living in their households, although this power had its limits.[92] European women's gendered colonial power over indigenous women did, however, include the right to discipline Aboriginal girls.[93] When a young Aboriginal girl named Susannah was placed in the Spieseke household by her father, Light, she had to endure corporal punishment from Mrs Spieseke, who hit her with a rod. In describing this incident, the missionary also emphasises that Susannah absconded a short

[92] The same gendered emphasis on the domestic realm for women is apparent in an Australian newspaper article about the mission station: 'Besides this, Mrs Hagenauer teaches the girls to sew and sees to it that the young women attend to their domestic duties'. *Periodical Accounts* 27 (1870), 194, report about Ramahyuck, taken from 'an Australian newspaper', continued on p. 195.

[93] Curtis-Wendlandt, 'Corporal punishment'.

while later and refused to apologise when she returned. When she ran away again to the indigenous camp, the missionary noted that 'it is indeed no easy task to treat this girl, who is already spoilt and shameless'. Control of indigenous women's sexual behaviour was one of the main areas of the gendered power hierarchy at the mission.

As discussed above, for male converts, marriage to a Christian Aboriginal woman was a necessary step towards achieving social and religious authority on the mission. For indigenous Christian women, on the other hand, marriage only afforded them the right to their own household on the mission, but did not provide them with more religious authority in the mission context. Marriage was predominantly viewed as a means of controlling women's sexuality. The patriarchal control of Aboriginal women's sexuality is one of the recurring topics in mission records, and one of the few contexts in which indigenous women are discussed, usually in negative terms, and it applied to converted and non-converted women alike.

The example of Kitty and Nathanel is instructive. Kitty was a young local Aboriginal woman whom Nathanel Pepper desired to marry after his conversion, but the Aboriginal elders refused to give their permission.[94] The reason for this refusal was most likely that Kitty was Nathanel's future sister-in-law; shortly thereafter she married Nathanel's brother Light, who did not convert. The mission records consistently portray her in a negative light: not only did she tempt the mission's first convert and cause troubles with elders; she also reportedly stayed in a pub not far from the mission. Going to these pubs suggested not just alcohol, but also sexual liaisons with settlers.[95] In May 1862 Kitty told the inquiring missionary that 'other blacks' had forced her to go there. She subsequently returned to the mission, but did not stay for long.[96] One of Nathanel's other brothers, Charley (Philip), came to fetch Light and his wife Kitty to go to 'the lake' where Light died a short while later. When Kitty returned as a widow, her presence presented new challenges to missionary control of the sexuality of their charges. In August 1862 the missionaries made 'the sad discovery that Nathanel and Kitty had forbidden knowledge of each other'.[97] Nathanel was punished by exclusion from the Eucharist. Kitty left the mission with her mother, thereby avoiding further control by the missionaries.[98]

In this situation, it became imperative for the Moravians to arrange a Christian marriage for Nathanel, which would allow them to retain the evangelist. The solution they found was Rachel. Rachel had lived since childhood on the

---

[94] See also Kenny, *The Lamb Enters the Dreaming*261–5, 268, 271.,

[95] *Missions-Blatt*, 1864, No 11, 227. Spieseke went out to find Kitty and to return her to the mission.

[96] *Nachrichten aus der Bruedergemeine* 46, 7 (1864), 628.

[97] Ibid., 629, 631–3.

[98] Ibid., 639.

mission for Aboriginal children in Albany in Western Australia, on the other side of the continent. She was sent to Victoria as a bride for Nathanel Pepper. Her life was to be that of an evangelist's wife, adhering to Moravian expectations of womanhood. Mission representations depict wives as subordinate and in need of male control. As one missionary wrote, 'he [Nathanel] lives happily with Rachel, and is indulgent of her sometimes quite indolent nature'.[99]

The expectation of Rachel as a converted woman was not that she would assume religious leadership, but that she would lead a life of domesticity and obedience not only to her husband but also to the Moravian missionaries. To a converted Aboriginal woman at Ebenezer, marriage meant integrating into the gendered mission hierarchy as the subordinate wife of a male convert and an example of Christian womanhood. It also meant subordination as a worker in the missionary household under the supervision of the missionary's wife: 'Nathanel's wife, Rachel, is of no small use to us in our domestic work, especially at this time when my wife is not well'.[100] Thus Rachel remained linked to the Spieseke household, despite her work as a Sunday school teacher and another Aboriginal woman's assumption of her duties in the kitchen.[101]

Mrs Spieseke trained Rachel and other Aboriginal girls and women living in the missionary household in domestic duties, notably dress-making.[102] Just as house-building was a marker of Christian masculinity, dress-making was the marker of Christian womanhood. The emphasis on learning sewing skills in the missionary household was also reported some years later by Bessy Flower in her letters to Anne Camfield: 'I have begun to knit this afternoon [;] we are going to have a sewing class every afternoon'.[103]

---

99 Letter from Ebenezer dated 15 January 1863, *Missions-Blatt* 28, 6 (1864), 123.

100 Spieseke to Reichel, 16 July 1863. 'Dear Brother, Nathanael's [*sic*] wife, Rachel, is of no small use to us in our domestic work, especially at this time when my wife is not well. I wish that some of the other young men were settled in a similar manner'. *Periodical Accounts* 25 (1865), 125.

101 'His [Nathanel's] wife Rachel often comes to assist my wife'. *Periodical Accounts* 25 (1865), 186.

102 As Spieseke summed up in a report in 1863, 'Susannah is of use in our house and learns to make her own clothes. ... Other women living in the household are equally taught dress-making skills. In the morning they have lessons, in the afternoon they sew. Mary is at present engaged in making a dress for her mother'. Spieseke, 15 Oct 1863, *Periodical Accounts* 25 (1865), 186–187. For a critical discussion of clothing at missions, see Peggy Brock. 'Nakedness and Clothing in Early Encounters between Aboriginal People of Central Australia, Missionaries and Anthropologists', *Journal of Colonialism and Colonial History* 8, 1 (2007). http://musejhu.edu/journal_of_colonialism_and_colonial_history/v008/8.1brock.html.

103 Bessy Flower to Anne Camfield, August 1867, Grimshaw et al., *Letters from Aboriginal Women*, 298.

But Rachel soon transcended the domestic and took up a position of considerable responsibility as a Sunday school teacher.[104] Doubtless Rachel's pre-existing literacy, acquired under the tutelage of Mrs Camfield in Albany, accelerated her career within the mission patronage and permitted her to achieve the status of Sunday school teacher, one of the highest positions that converted women could achieve in the Moravian system in the late nineteenth century. But other considerations may have played a role as well. Perhaps Spieseke wished to reinforce the leading position of her husband Nathanel (as against his brother Philip, for instance) as evangelist by promoting his wife to Sunday school teacher.

In contrast to the detailed reports about male converts, the *Periodical Accounts* tell us nothing about Rachel's life outside the reference points of the missionary household, school or her husband. The next time we read about Rachel is in connection with her husband's serious illness in April 1864. While both Nathanel and Rachel were very ill, Nathanel's state is mentioned first and described in more detail before the discussion turns to Rachel's condition.[105] Significantly, the report then mentions grief over the death of their newborn child as the cause of their illness. But just when readers of the mission journal might be feeling great empathy for Rachel, who had lost her child, the missionary reminds them of her previous moral and spiritual weakness:

> Rachel has laid aside a good deal of the indolence of which we had to complain at first; it was quite to be expected, that, when removed from the excellent discipline, which she has been enjoying at her former home, she should at first be inclined to fall back into the faults of her race. Traces of a change of heart are now beginning to show themselves, we are thankful to say she has asked to be confirmed.[106]

It was perhaps the death of her child and her own illness that finally convinced Rachel to submit to mission discipline. And it is significantly the only time when we learn about her religious life. At a moment of loss 'she has asked to be confirmed'. The discipline that the missionary deemed necessary to control women was intended to prevent her from falling 'back into the faults of her race'. The 'excellent discipline' she had 'enjoyed at her former home' refers to the regime at Mrs Camfield's home for Aboriginal children in Albany, from where Rachel had come to Ebenezer to marry Pepper. As this example shows, the right to discipline even an already converted woman is made explicit as one of the

---

104 'Rachel now acts as teacher in our Sunday-School'. *Periodical Accounts* 25 (1865), 126, Spieseke, 15 October 1863.

105 'Nathanael's health is at present a matter of great concern to us'. *Periodical Accounts* 25 (1865), 232.

106 Ibid., 233.

main bases of missionaries' masculine power. For the remaining five years of her life we hear very little about Rachel in the published mission sources.

Her death in 1869 earned Rachel a final entry in the mission journal. Even then we only learn about the circumstances of her passing because it was deemed important to explain to the journal's readers why her husband Nathanel had switched his loyalty from Spieseke to Hagenauer and moved from Ebenezer to Ramahyuck, where the missionary Hagenauer had moved just a short while before. The report about Nathanel's move had added apologetically, 'The cause of his leaving this place is the death of his wife Rachel in Pleasant Creek Hospital.'[107] Thus even her death is mentioned only in relation to her husband, and in contrast to Nathanel, we learn nothing about Rachel's spiritual state, her thoughts or even her doubts. The different forms of gendered power for indigenous Christian women are also apparent in the examples of two other women associated with the Pepper men – Louise Arbuckle and Rebecca Pepper.

Figure 2.3 Nathanel Pepper and his second wife Louise at Ramahyuck, ca 1870/75. The couple was in charge of the mission orphanage and is here depicted with four children, of which three have been identified as children from the orphanage: Emily Milton Wood (left in the picture, born 1859), Albert and Mary Ellen Darby (1861–1879). Nathanel and Louise's own four children were Sam, Percy, Philip and Lena. (Courtesy Moravian Archives Herrnhut, FS –Australien, aus NL Kramer)

[107] *Periodical Accounts* 27 (1870), 349.

Louise Arbuckle was the Aboriginal woman whom the Hagenauers had in mind as a second wife for Nathanel Pepper. Louise Arbuckle was of Kurnai descent and worked in the Hagenauer household after they moved to Ramahyuck. Her mother had suffered from settler violence and was killed in a settler raid in which Louise, too, was wounded.[108] Louise was married on the initiative of the Hagenauers, specifically of Louise Hagenauer, to the evangelist Nathanel Pepper as his second wife after Rachel's death in 1869. This was also the pretext for bringing Nathanel from Ebenezer to Ramahyuck to work with Hagenauer. After her wedding Louise settled with her husband in their own house where she reportedly kept 'good household' and grew arrowroot for sale. Louise had four children: Sam, Lena, Percy and Philip. Unlike Bessy Flower and Rachel Pepper, Louise seems not to have become a school teacher. In official mission reports she is largely reduced to domesticity; we learn of her housekeeping skills and her successful cultivation of arrowroot, although Louise was also responsible for the children in the orphanage and managed it on her own after her husband's death in 1877.[109] The entry in the mission journal on the occasion of her husband Nathanel Pepper's death sums up the missionary's perception of normative womanhood for Aboriginal women: 'In company with his Christian wife, he kept his house and garden in good order, and lived in comparative prosperity'.[110] Louise's name is not even mentioned here.

Louise disappears from the published mission record after her husband's death, but she remarried and would bear five more children in her second marriage to John Connolly. Known as 'Grandma Connolly', she was the grandmother of Philip Pepper, author of the book *You Are What You Make Yourself To Be*.[111] This is a case where but a fragment of an Aboriginal woman's life and reality appears in the records: only her few years on the mission, and her domestic activities (in the European sense) are recorded, while her gendered identity as an indigenous woman with an extended kin group and related cultural obligations are left out. In fact, Louise had a prominent place in family memory as the one responsible for her family's Christian orientation, as alternative oral histories show.[112] In 1886, government assimilation policy forced Louise and her family to leave Ramahyuck and move to Stratford, but she continued to care for the residents at Ramahyuck. Today, a monument commemorating Louise

108 Philip Pepper, *You Are What You Make Yourself To Be*, 29.

109 'His [Nathanel's] second wife, a good Christian woman, looked well after their family of three children, and the little homestead was always neat and cleanly'. *Periodical Accounts*, vol. 30, 211.

110 Ibid., 378.

111 Philip Pepper, *You Are What You Make Yourself To Be*.

112 Ibid.

Pepper-Connolly as an Aboriginal health- and childcare worker stands in the main street of Bairnsdale in Victoria.[113]

Like Louise, Rebecca Pepper, who had married Nathanel's brother Philip and was thus Louise's sister-in-law, rarely appears in her own right in mission sources. But unlike Louise and Rachel, Rebecca had some independence in her choice of marriage partner and was able to avoid mission patronage in this regard. She also managed to use the gendered hierarchies more to her advantage, and was able to build significant patronage relations with other women, and even with the missionary.

Figure 2.4 Philip Pepper (formerly Charley) and his wife Rebecca (formerly Jessy), ca 1870. Both were baptised and married at Ebenezer mission in 1864 and took on responsibilities as managers of the newly founded orphanage in 1873. Here they are depicted with their daughter about whom we learn very little in the mission sources. (Courtesy of Moravian Archives Bethlehem, DP.Vol.1.205)

[113] David Horton (ed.), *The Encyclopaedia of Aboriginal Australia*, vol. 2 (Canberra: Aboriginal Studies Press, 1994), 857.

As a Christian convert and Philip's wife,[114] Rebecca had access to positions of authority that other indigenous women did not. Together with her husband, she took Aboriginal children into her house and later headed the orphanage in Ebenezer.[115] Rebecca and Philip had official status as 'house parents'.[116] In 1873 the new children's home opened and Rebecca and her husband are mentioned as official caretakers.[117] But shortly thereafter Rebecca fell ill and a year later the missionary reports the death of 'the matron of our school'. Rebecca's obituary sums up Moravian missionaries' main ideal of Christian womanhood for converted Aboriginal women: obedience to their husbands. Rebecca's religious agency is entirely subsumed under the authority of her husband, who is credited with her conversion to Christianity:

> I believe I mentioned in a former letter how thankful she was to her late husband Philip, our useful evangelist. She told me she did not know what would have become of her, if he had not married her – that he had been her best friend, for he had brought her to Jesus.[118]

For Moravians, a direct personal relationship with God was important for both men and women, and this is a point that the missionary mentions: 'On expressing my regret that she was so much alone, she answered: "I am not really alone, for Jesus is with me"'.[119] Her European domestic skills were at once a benchmark and a normative expectation, but they also singled her out as an 'exceptional' Aboriginal woman, thereby devaluing all others: 'The appearance of Rebecca was very superior, and her character won for her the respect of both whites and blacks. She was admirably suited for the post she held, and was, moreover, one of the few who possessed good abilities for household management.'[120]

---

114 See *Periodical Accounts* 25 (1865), 234 on the baptisms of Jessy (Rebecca), Charley (Philip) and Liberty (Matthew). Philip and Rebecca were afterwards married as Christians. See also *Periodical Accounts* 26 (1866), 420.

115 In 1868 the missionary already reported from Ebenezer, 'Philipp arrived here yesterday with an unkempt girl called Rosa. As we already have 7 girls in our house, we decided that the child should remain in Phillip and his wife Rebekka's house, to their great joy'. *Missions-Blatt* 33, 2 (1869), 54–5.

116 *Periodical Accounts* 28 (1872), 280.

117 A children's home was opened on 19 March 1873 with 12 girls and five boys under the care of Philip and Rebecca Pepper. *Periodical Accounts* 28 (1873), 525.

118 Letter from Spieseke to Reichel, 24 September 1874, on Rebecca's death, *Periodical Accounts* 29 (1874), 353.

119 Ibid.

120 Ibid.

This elevated position of Rebecca's is further reflected in the textual attention she temporarily receives in the mission journal, where she is the only Australian Aboriginal woman whose own writing is reprinted in the *Periodical Accounts* and the *Missions-Blatt*. In 1869 the journals published the following letter by Rebecca to an Aboriginal woman in the English original and also in a German translation for the *Missions-Blatt*.

> I am sorry to see you so very sick, but I hope the Lord will spare you. Trust Christ for his goodness. Pray to Him every night not only in the night but in day time whenever you can. Do not listen to the old people only love Jesus and do his will. I never forget you in my prayer. I am getting better myself. Let not your heart be troubled ye believe in God also in me Jesus saith, I am the way to the truth and the life no man cometh unto the father but by me good by my dear friend til by and by
>
> Remain your loviny [*sic*] friend Rebekah Pepper.[121]

This expression of concern for another Aboriginal woman, independent of the patriarchal structures of husband and missionary household, is rare in Ebenezer texts. But these gendered relations were of great importance to Aboriginal women. Rebecca, we are told, used some of her savings to build up her own gendered patronage, so that the Aboriginal girls in the orphanage she had headed could receive support even after her death. It is significant that the obituary mentions the 'considerable presents that she left to several of her girls' first and the church second. Rebecca was able to create a social space in which young Aboriginal girls could see an older Aboriginal woman, not a white woman, in charge of their lives. These were the ties that may have interested Rebecca the most. Within this world, Rebecca was able to publicly demonstrate her authority over missionary and husband, despite the textual representation of her as dependant in the earlier missionaries' words. It is Rebecca, and not her husband, who leaves money to the missionary: 'she made over to me four pounds fifteen shillings, as well as an ox, with which a cloth for the minister's table was to be purchased, and with the surplus a railing erected around the grave of her husband'.[122] These two material expressions of her patronage might support the authority of men – the missionary and her husband – but in the public eye of the mission community they were expressions of the status of the woman Rebecca.

Rebecca's bequest of a cloth for the minister's table in the church and for the railing around her husband's grave in the Ebenezer cemetery represents her as an influential and pious Christian woman. The mention of her will is, however,

121 *Missions-Blatt* 33, 7 (1869), 132.

122 Rebecca's death, *Periodical Accounts* 29 (1874), 353.

an exceptional moment because in most of the Ebenezer sources, Aboriginal women are not accorded any religious authority or official expressions of piety.

Silenced Religious Authority and Mission Patronage of Aboriginal Women

In contrast to mission gender ideology, Aboriginal women had a strong indigenous tradition of gendered religious authority that was transmitted between women and not dependent on men. Indigenous societies included female ritual leaders and law women to maintain gender-specific ceremonial links with country as the basis of indigenous culture and identity. Aboriginal women had their own sacred rituals, objects and links to ancestral beings. Within this sex-segregated religious culture, older women taught younger women about their ties to place and ancestors. Thus indigenous people acknowledged women's contributions and role in the maintenance of a cosmology and women's power to exclude men from certain secret sacred women's rituals. Religious knowledge was a power base for Aboriginal women.[123]

This aspect of gendered religious power in indigenous communities remained elusive to Moravian missionaries because of their deficient understanding of indigenous society as well as their own gender prejudices. Indeed, women's religious authority almost inevitably remained invisible to missionaries because in their own worldview, women did not acquire such religious authority. Missionaries, even Moravians, did not think women capable of having religious authority wholly independent of men, nor did they find it desirable. Despite the existence of semi-autonomous spaces for women in eighteenth-century Moravian communities, by the late nineteenth century men enjoyed exclusive religious authority, as expressed in their gendered privilege to preach, distribute the sacraments, lead devotional practices and prayers in the household and translate the catechism. In mid-nineteenth century Moravian communities, women no longer had any independent spiritual authority.

Not only was the role of white women diminished in late nineteenth-century Moravian societies, but Moravians also increasingly shared a widespread negative colonial view of indigenous women as devoid of any religion. In the 1860s, the Australian mission reports in the *Periodical Accounts* are on the whole dismissive of indigenous women's spirituality and their response to the Christian message. Thus for example in 1862, just three years after the establishment of the mission, the missionaries wrote to the mission board that while they were hopeful about the attendance of Aborigines at church, this optimism did not extend to women because 'the women appear to be quite unreceptive to the doctrine of

[123] See, for example, Diane Bell, *Ngarrindjeri Wuruwarrin: A World that Is, Was, and Will Be* (North Melbourne: Spinifex Press, 1998).

salvation'.[124] Similarly, upon the death of an Aboriginal woman they declared their uncertainty about her spiritual state: 'She willingly listened to the sermons of the Gospel, but was never to be moved to speak about her inner feelings'.[125]

Missionaries represented older women in particular, who wielded considerable social and spiritual power in Wotjobaluk society, as ambiguous or even reluctant in their conversions: 'The old people are quite careless about anything of spiritual importance. The women, it is true, attend the meetings daily, but there is little trace of inward impression, or movement among the dry bones'.[126] Again, two observations are important here; one is that women, like men, actually engaged at some level with the mission and its religion by attending church and daily meetings. But missionaries did not, or could not, observe the all-important individual awakening experiences among Aboriginal elders, particularly women.

Such suspicion of female spirituality is also apparent in the following example from 1870, when the missionary reported on the recent deaths of baptised Aborigines. Two men and one older woman named Linna, the mother of two prominent converts, Daniel and Philip, had passed away and the missionary reported to the mission board:

> Of the two men we have good reason to believe that they died believing in Christ as their Saviour .... As for the old woman [Linna], we cannot speak so confidently. She was baptized and expressed her hope in Jesus, who had taken away the sin of the world; but her mental powers were so far gone before her death, that we could converse but little with her.[127]

It seems, that even in death, indigenous men were more reliable than indigenous women.

The underrepresentation of female religious agency applied not just to the older women mentioned above, but also to young Aboriginal women. As we have seen, women like Jessy (Rebecca) whom I discussed above, were baptised in Ebenezer, but the mission sources remain silent on their experiences of religious awakening, which Moravians considered necessary in order to be admitted for baptism, or their spiritual development after baptism. This is in direct contrast to the detailed descriptions we encountered in the discussion of male converts like Nathanel Pepper and others, who were not only acknowledged in their religious feelings, but also granted some gendered agency in expressing this

---

124 *Nachrichten aus der Bruedergemeine* 46, 7 (1864), 637.

125 Ibid., 621. The translation is my own.

126 *Periodical Accounts* 23 (1860), 618.

127 Ibid., 27 (1870), 514.

religious authority in the form of preaching, leading devotions and prayers and translating.

In contrast to the mission sources, which give us the impression that Aboriginal women were not particularly interested in Christianity, letters by Aboriginal women outside the missionary writing machine offer us an alternative view. Although Christianity is rarely raised as an explicit topic in the letters by Aboriginal women, some interesting exceptions afford us a glimpse of women's religious agency about one generation after the founding of Ebenezer. Such exceptions include the letters by Maud Mullet, Lizzie and Mary McRae who introduced their own prayer meetings on the stations, which by that time were run by managers rather than missionaries. For their interpretation of Christianity and their attempt to proselytise, Maud was banned from visiting Coranderrk in 1916. In their letters, the women defended their right to hold religious meetings in houses on Coranderrk. They encountered more understanding from Sister Isabella Hetherington (1870–1946), an Irish female missionary who had adopted an Aboriginal child and established a small mission at Bunyip in Gippsland.[128] Hetherington was inducted into the Baptist Church, but joined the Australian United Aborigines' Mission. In 1930 she pioneered a Pentecostal Church in northern Queensland.[129] The Aboriginal women who preached at Coranderrk also advocated a religiosity that was close to many revival movements and the shaking and excitement of Pentecostalism. In 1921 Maud wrote to the Board for Aboriginal Protection that 'my husband and I can say that through Miss Hetherington we have seen and been taught more about Jesus, than ever any Manager and his wife on the aboriginal reserves in this State or any other could teach us'.[130]

Although this chapter is concerned with the spaces women could claim at the beginning of the mission period, that is, two generations earlier, these letters invite us to think about whether Aboriginal women rejected Christianity, as the missionaries claimed, or rather disliked the particularly patriarchal Moravian version of it. It seems that Aboriginal women were more likely to claim religious authority in Christianity if mission structures and control were weakened, creating a vacuum of control and male leadership because of the absence of missionaries.

While indigenous people 'on the whole' were regarded as capable of conversion, in practice the Moravian missionaries at Ebenezer did not engage very much with women in spiritual matters. They found older women in

---

[128] Grimshaw et al., *Letters from Aboriginal Women*, 229.

[129] Barry Chant, 'Hetherington, Isabella (1870–1946)', *Australian Dictionary of Biography*, National Centre of Biography, Australian National University, http://adb.anu.edu.au/biography/hetherington-isabella-12980/text23459, accessed 19 December 2011.

[130] Elizabeth and Henry McRae to Chief Commissioner of the Police, 6 September 1921. Grimshaw et al., *Letters from Aboriginal Women*, 238.

particular to be unresponsive and ambiguous in their reactions to the mission. The reports are silent on the spiritual experiences of younger women who had been baptised. Although older women attended church, the Moravians, who were looking for signs of individual awakening, could not detect any enthusiasm in them. This was very much in contrast to the spiritual responsibility and authority that indigenous women carried in their own communities.

The astonishing example of Rebecca's mission patronage in her bequest has an even deeper subtext of Aboriginal women's agency and patronage in relation to missions. Five years after Rebecca's death, the mission journal published a report that gives us a small insight into the gendered dependency of male missionaries on Aboriginal women, which is normally silenced. In 1879, missionary Hagenauer, who had set up Ebenezer with Spieseke but later moved to Ramahyuck, undertook a journey through the Wimmera district and revisited places he had first seen 21 years previously when he and Spieseke had arrived in search of a suitable place to establish a Moravian mission to the Aborigines. Hagenauer had been asked to undertake a journey to Lower Murray District with Br Kramer.

> Here we found about thirty blacks who were expecting us. Our introduction to them happened in a most interesting way. As we drew near to the camps I heard one of the well-known yelling cries indicating an event of importance, after which there was some very vigorous conversation, until an old woman stepped forward, and with a face beaming with joy saluted me with the exclamation: 'My boy come back, my boy come barly'. Our friendship with all those blacks was at once established.[131]

Twenty-one years earlier, when Hagenauer and Spieseke had been walking through the Wimmera district 'to look for blacks', they had come across an Aboriginal woman 'who was willing to carry our things and to act as a guide'.

> She was a great help to us and afterward settled at Ebenezer with her daughter Rebecca, who subsequently became well-known as a good Christian woman in the whole district. Old Jenny remained with us for some years, and then suddenly disappeared, and we could hear nothing more of her. Imagine my surprise then, when, at Swan Hill, that same old woman came forward and introduced me to the blacks as 'her boy'.[132]

---

[131] On February 21 on the way to Lake Bolga, *Periodical Accounts*, vol. 31, 184.

[132] Letter from Hagenauer, 17 March 1879, Ramahyuck, on Rebecca and old Jenny (her mother), in *Periodical Accounts*, vol. 31, 184. The 1859 report, published later in the *Periodical Accounts*, had read: 'We had read only once in the published reports before about Jenny, in 1859 shortly after the arrival of the missionaries: "In addition to the youths I have mentioned, there is a man named Joe, who appears to be impressed and who spoke on the

The gratitude that missionary Hagenauer felt towards the Aboriginal woman is repeated again in his travel report when he remarks that upon their return journey they had stopped again at Sawn Hill, and learned that a number of Aboriginal people had gone to Ebenezer, with others to follow, 'among whom is my old friend Jenny'.[133] It was highly unusual for missionaries of this era to describe an Aboriginal woman as 'my old friend', a privilege bestowed only among men, if at all. Hagenauer acknowledges his dependency in terms of fictive kinship, as 'her boy', and of emotional closeness as 'an old friend'. But if Jenny had already been 'old' 21 years previously, when in fact she had a young daughter below marriageable age, what was the missionaries' perception of 'old' Aboriginal women? Or did he make her old in order to remove any possible sexual connotations from their joint travels?

In this episode, the gendered hierarchy of mission patronage is clearly reversed and even acknowledged as such: Jenny had been instrumental in enabling these young male missionaries to set up a suitable place for the future mission of Ebenezer in 1858. The newly arrived German missionaries depended on Jenny's language skills and local knowledge. While she initially stayed at the mission, she was not baptised and eventually left. I suspect that she only appears in the mission documents 21 years later because she recognised the missionary as 'my son' and facilitated immediate positive relations with the camping group. This episode disrupts the prescribed homosocial nature of male travelling expeditions.[134]

What might this have meant for her daughter Rebecca? When Charley (Philip) is described as wanting to marry her in 1863, it was five years after her mother had guided the missionaries through the Wimmera. We might conclude that at the time her mother encountered the newly arrived missionaries, she was already a child of ten or older. Did she come along and see how the Europeans depended on her mother? The missionaries knew that Jessy (Rebecca) was Jenny's daughter; did this make a difference to the way she was treated? Did it make a difference to her independence and her agency to marry a man of her choosing? She is also not reported to have stayed in the missionaries' household before her marriage.

---

same subject to Br. Spieseke. The same is the case with the old woman, Jenny, who showed us the way, when we first came. Two of her children are also here. They told me, yesterday evening, that they do not intend to go away"'.

133 They stopped at Swan Hill again during their return journey. 'At Swan Hill we found that several had already gone to Ebenezer, and more were to follow, among whom is my old friend Jenny'. *Periodical Accounts 1878*, vol. 31, 186.

134 See, for example, Gareth Griffiths, 'Popular Imperial Adventure and the Discourse of Missionary Texts', in *Mixed Messages: Materiality, Textuality, Missions*, ed. Jamie S. Scott and Gareth Griffiths (New York, N.Y. and Houndmills: Palgrave Macmillan, 2005), 51–66.

While historical studies are increasingly recognising indigenous people's agency in their colonial engagement with Christian missions, the focus has been on men, and mostly without theorising gender. But missions were highly gendered enterprises and indigenous Australian men and women collaborated or collided with the mission process differently. This engagement left behind gendered historical sources, texts which, as other scholars have pointed out, make it difficult to find indigenous women in the archives. While Moravian mission records downplay or simply erase any religious experiences that Aboriginal women may have had, they report in great detail on the conversion process of Aboriginal men like Nathanel Pepper. However, despite the lack of details on the spiritual aspects of women's conversion, these documents do reveal aspects of women's varied agency if we read them as expressions of gendered power relationships.

Conclusions

The conversion experiences of Wotjobaluk men and women are not equally documented in the published Moravian mission journals. Their silence on women's spiritual conversion experiences and religious agency is one of the main methodological challenges for studying gender and conversion in a mission context. While the experiences of male indigenous converts are described in detail, there is little information on indigenous women, even though women were baptised and engaged with the mission in almost equal numbers as men. This marginalisation of indigenous women was the norm in colonial European recording systems, including mission primary sources, which privileged male knowledge and men's right to speak over that of women. In the missions' daily reporting on their indigenous converts, women figure far less prominently as beings with spiritual lives.

Most importantly, very little attention was paid to indigenous women's spiritual development. Although women were baptised, and thus must have convinced a missionary that they had converted, their conversion experiences are rarely noted and conveyed to an audience. They are not shown leading devotions, praying or discussing Bible texts with their peers in the way that male converts are represented. They were certainly not permitted to go out on their own to evangelise and bring other indigenous people to the mission. Spirituality, it seems, was a masculine realm. Instead, women figure prominently in mission texts as moral (especially sexual) transgressors or as victims needing missionary protection from violent older Aboriginal men. Their dependency is also shown in the emphasis on their domestic skills, either as servants living in a missionary's household (if he was married) or as wives of indigenous evangelists trying to run European-style households as expressions of their reformed femininity and gendered identity as Christian women. Skills such as sewing and gardening are frequently mentioned.

This gendered nature of mission representations, which emphasises normative behaviour, gives little direct insight into the real power that women had on and off the missions, except in cases where they violated gendered norms of behaviour. In most cases, mission texts give us only a very small and fragmented perspective on how these gendered hierarchies were conceptualised and negotiated because they assign little agency to women. Even less can be said from mission texts about the indigenous knowledge bases and religious authority of indigenous women. For example, Wotjobaluk women's traditional religious and social practices (which form the basis of their power and knowledge in indigenous communities), including links with country, authority as senior women and female traditional knowledge, are virtually absent from missionary sources. Here we learn very little specifically about women's religious knowledge and rituals because missionaries did not perceive women as holding any significant or independent gendered access to the sacred. This is the result of a Christian view in which women are barred from direct access to the sacred (except in revival movements and faith missions). Missionary wives also do not mention the traditional spiritual authority of women in more detail.

The representation of male converts was no less gendered. While male converts attracted more attention and received more space in mission reports, their gendered behaviour and spiritual authority were intertwined with and under constant scrutiny and control by male missionaries and their wives. Not only are the conversion experiences of male converts, especially the first generation of mission converts, reported publicly in detail in the mission journals, they are also followed and monitored even years after formal conversion and baptism. Indigenous converts, it seems, were never free of the danger of lapsing. Their spiritual progress, their failings, and the perceived self-evident need for male missionary guidance were written about with regularity, and were expected by the reading public. Male converts were represented as subordinate to male missionaries, but they were given space for social agency, for instance as evangelists. To the readers of the *Periodical Accounts* in the 1860s, for example, Nathanel Pepper was one of the most outstanding figures reported on with regularity.

Aboriginal women needed their literacy skills at the mission, and passed them on to Aboriginal children and other Aboriginal women. Literacy skills became instrumental in engaging with secular and mission hierarchies, as the surviving letters demonstrate. Letters by Aboriginal women were a skilled means of exercising social agency; women used them to intervene in colonial society and to defend their interests and those of their families and communities. This literacy gave Aboriginal women new tools to communicate with each other and to build and maintain gendered relationships that stood outside the colonial sphere, as Rebecca's letter to Magdalene shows.

Missions also functioned as temporary alternatives to frontier violence, as was the case for Louise Pepper, but this meant neither that missions were free of their own gendered violence nor that Aboriginal women chose to stay there for their entire lives. But as they engaged with the mission, women did so on their own account and in their own ways, which the patriarchal 'missionary writing machine' played down. Women upset gendered power relations on the mission not only by evading them, but also by establishing patronage relationships that reversed patriarchal male domination and control. Rebecca's mother Jenny was an early patron of and guide for newly arrived missionaries, who openly acknowledged their indebtedness and dependence. Yet she had no desire to stay on the mission and be part of its regime.

Chapter 3

Conversion and Religious Change in the Pedi Kingdom, South Africa: A World in Motion, at Home and Abroad

Introduction

Nineteenth-century conversions and religious change in South Africa have been extensively studied, since both had important implications for the social and political worlds that people inhabited.[1] Ever since the first Protestant mission societies arrived in the region in the late eighteenth century, the southern tip of the African continent had been a vibrant mission field.[2] By the mid-nineteenth century, some 15 mission societies, mostly from European countries such as Britain, Germany, Sweden, Norway, France and Switzerland, but also from the United States, were busy establishing themselves, culturally and religiously, in South Africa. Their activities turned the region into one of the most competitive mission fields in the world.[3] Catholic missions, however, such as might

---

[1] The majority of the studies have been conducted on mission movements that left behind archival material written in English. With regard to the Transvaal area, important exceptions are Peter Delius, *The Land Belongs to Us: The Pedi Polity, the Boers and the British in the Nineteenth-century Transvaal* (London: Heinemann, 1984); Isabel Hofmeyr's fascinating '*We Spend Our Years As A Tale That Is Told': Oral Historical Narrative in a South African Chiefdom* (London: Currey, 1994); and Lize Kriel, *The Malaboch Books: Kgaluši in the 'Civilization of the Written Word'* (Franz Steiner: Stuttgart, 2009). For a *Studienprozess* dialogue commissioned by the German Evangelical Church on its controversial history in southern Africa, see Hanns Lessing et al. (eds), *Deutsche evangelische Kirche im kolonialen südlichen Afrika: Die Rolle der Auslandsarbeit von den Anfängen bis in die 1920er Jahre [The German Protestant Church in Colonial Southern Africa: the Impact of Overseas Work from the Beginnings until the 1920s]* (Wiesbaden: Harrassowitz, 2011 [2012]). A volume on the entanglements of various missions and churches – including perspectives from the Reformed Afrikaner churches – in the twentieth century is forthcoming in 2015.

[2] Richard Elphick and Rodney Davenport (eds), *Christianity in South Africa: A Political, Social and Cultural History* (Oxford: James Currey, 1997); Henry Bredekamp and Robert Ross (eds), *Missions and Christianity in South African History* (Johannesburg: Witwatersrand Univ. Press, 1995).

[3] In the late nineteenth century, a huge number of so-called African Independent (or Initiated) Churches began to emerge in South Africa. Several hundred such churches exist in

perhaps have interested Wilhelm Gustav Werner Volk, only entered the South African mission picture in 1882 when the Trappists established themselves at Mariannhill in Natal. The Protestants kept their distance from them. There is also no evidence of converts moving between Protestant and Catholic mission establishments, although we know that they did regularly move between different sites of Protestant mission engagement.[4]

Various mission societies followed in the wake of colonial conquest. Frequently they were the vanguard of colonial expansion. In the Cape, missions soon became embroiled in conflicts with settlers who sought to distinguish themselves as human beings with political rights from so-called *schepsels* or creatures whom they deemed subhuman, and whose Christianisation they opposed. It was there in the Cape that by the mid-nineteenth century missions became most intensely embroiled in the ever more intensely unfolding tensions of slavery and abolition, advancing colonialism and land alienation. Missions moved along the Eastern Cape between 1779 and 1877, as nine frontier wars wreaked havoc on the region. A century of intermittent warfare destroyed the economic basis of the people living there on several occasions. Social ties and values were destabilised and, in turn, required redefinition. The Cape Government benefited from such dislocations, since many Africans were forced to enter their names into the colonial labour register, and as a result often had to leave their homes and families to work. Probably the most traumatic expression of the violent encounter in the region was the Xhosa cattle killing of 1857.[5] The different available religious idioms, including Christianity, merged here and provided a language in which people could express their devastating decision to kill all of their cattle in the hope that this utterly dramatic act would rid them of white domination.[6]

---

the country today, in which many different varieties of Christianity are practised.

4 Generally, not much is known about the movement of converts between mission establishments. Missionaries who wrote the archival records on which historians rely believed in the notions of congregation and community. They recorded the movement of people but not with much enthusiasm; they hinted that some converts were looking for shelter on the establishment of other mission societies. Interactions with Catholics were a virtual non-topic.

5 Jeff Peires, *The Dead Will Arise: Nongqawuse and the Great Xhosa Cattle-Killing Movement of 1856–7* (London: James Currey, 1989). For a slightly different interpretation, see Timothy J. Stapleton, 'Reluctant Slaughter: Rethinking Maqoma's Role in the Xhosa Cattle-Killing (1853–1857)', *International Journal of African Historical Studies* 26, 2 (1993): 345–69. For the history of the region, see also Clifton Crais, *White Supremacy and Black Resistance in Pre-Industrial South Africa: The Making of the Colonial Order in the Eastern Cape, 1770–1865* (Cambridge: CUP, 1992).

6 On millenarian Christianity, see Russel Viljoen, *Jan Paerl, A Khoikhoi in Cape Colonial Society 1761–1851* (Leiden: Brill, 2006).

Further to the north, in Natal, which became a British colony in 1843, missions had to struggle more tenaciously to gain converts. The communities there were still largely intact, so that mission stations primarily gathered the poor and the rejected. This tarnished their reputation among those people whom the missions had initially targeted for conversion.[7] Natal also became home to the somewhat eccentric Anglican Bishop John William Colenso, who committed himself to defending Zulu independence, or what remained of it. His passions were shared by his two daughters, Frances and particularly Harriette, who continued his activities after his death.[8] Even more dramatic encounters ensued in the Zulu Kingdom itself, which remained independent, but not untouched by encroaching colonialism, up until its military defeat in 1879. Wishing to banish unwanted political interference from his kingdom, the Zulu king had been especially suspicious of allowing missionaries among his people. After some discouraging experiences with representatives of the American Board of Missions to the Zulu and with Allen Gardiner of the Church Missionary Society in the 1830s, he permitted only two Norwegian Lutheran missionaries, Hans Paludan Schreuder and Ommund Oftebro, to live among his people in 1851. When he decided to establish relations with a handful of other missionaries in 1858, he invited Lutherans from the German Hermannsburg Mission Society into his kingdom.[9]

Kings like the Sotho paramount Moshoeshoe, by contrast, who established his mountainous kingdom in what is now Lesotho, collaborated readily with missionaries of the Paris Evangelical Mission Society.[10] He probably became a role model for many of the Sotho-Tswana leaders in the Transvaal, one of the

---

7 Norman Etherington, *Preachers, Peasants and Politics in Southeast Africa, 1835–1880: African Christian Communities in Natal, Pondoland and Zululand* (London: Royal Historical Society, 1978). In his recent book, Richard Elphick engages in a rather critical manner with Etherington's analysis and stresses that to consider the conversion of the 'flotsam and the jetsam' (Etherington) as 'inferior' represents a misconception of conversion. See Richard Elphick, *The Equality of Believers: Protestant Missionaries and the Racial Politics of South Africa* (Charlottesville: University of Virginia Press, 2012), 29–32. It does not go unnoticed, however, that among African people in the area Christianity became a resource for the poor and rejected rather than of the powerful.

8 Jeff Guy, *The Heretic: A Study of the Life of John William Colenso 1814–1883* (Johannesburg: Ravan and Pietermaritzburg: Univ. of Natal Press, 1983), and *The View across the River: Harriette Colenso and the Zulu Struggle against Imperialism* (Claremont: David Philip, 2001).

9 Jarle Simensen (ed.), *Norwegian Missions in African History*. Vol. 1, *South Africa, 1845–1906* (Oslo: Norwegian University Press, 1986).

10 For an almost novelistic account, see Tim Couzens, *Murder at Morija: Faith, Mystery, and Tragedy on an African Mission* (Charlottesville: Univ. of Virginia Press; Johannesburg: Random House, 2003) which lists the relevant literature.

two Boer Republics established in 1852. A considerable number of Sotho and Tswana communities responded positively to the adoption of Christianity.[11] They managed to use it to their own ends, while at the same time facing immense social and cultural transformations in their communities. Two of the most prominent supporters of Christianity were Secele and later his rival Khama, the leading paramount to the west of the South African Republic, in present-day Botswana.[12] Many Sotho and Tswana leaders chose Christianity and the institution of the mission station in order to bind subjects and groups from different cultural and political backgrounds to their emerging polities. In such cases, Christianity gained ground in 'outposts' of the emerging polities to which chiefs were eager to extend royal powers. Concomitantly, the religion from abroad provided a bond that helped to accommodate diversity and to provide people with a means of attachment to larger communities while retaining at least some of their language and traditions.[13]

In fact, in the views and experiences of many, colonialism was perhaps not the most disturbing dynamic in the region. In the early nineteenth century, a handful of minor clans began to transform themselves into larger polities. Fuelled by slavery and various other upheavals, a number of states started to emerge.[14] They caused smaller groups to disperse, to seek alliances, and to find their places, after migration, disruption and return, among the changed conditions of the *highveld*. The area in which the events examined in this chapter unfolded lay in the midst of such turmoil, into which settlers from the Cape had also started to penetrate around the 1840s. It is important to keep in mind that prior to the establishment of formal colonial rule, South Africa did not consist of fixed, circumscribed or ethnically defined communities. The social and political setting of regions such as the Transvaal was characterised by fluidity rather than rigid lines dividing one society from the other or separating local society from settler groups or colonialism. If people became too dissatisfied with the prevailing social and political hierarchies they withdrew to areas out of reach of those in power. In fact, Sotho and Tswana successions were marked by fragmentation, especially as rulers did not usually name which of their sons they

---

[11] Kirsten Rüther, *The Power Beyond: Mission Strategies, African Conversion, and the Development of a Christian Culture in the Transvaal* (Münster: Lit Verlag, 2001).

[12] Paul S. Landau, *The Realm of the Word: Language, Gender and Christianity in a Southern African Kingdom* (London: James Currey and Cape Town: David Philip, 1995); John and Jean Comaroff, *Of Revelation and Revolution*, Vol. I: *Christianity, Colonialism and Consciousness in South Africa*, Vol. II: *The Dialectics of Modernity on a South African Frontier* (Chicago and London: Univ. of Chicago Press, 1991, 1997).

[13] Isaac Schapera, *Tribal Innovators: Tswana Chiefs and Social Change 1795–1940* (London: Athlone, 1970).

[14] Carolyn Hamilton (ed.), *The Mfecane Aftermath: Reconstructive Debates in Southern African History* (Johannesburg: Witwatersrand Univ. Press, 1995).

wished to succeed them. As a result, sons often established their own smaller polities after a ruler's death. As was the case elsewhere, the nineteenth century brought huge changes, not just for metropolitan societies but also for people living in South Africa.

The spread of Christianity, and hence many of the conversions, was often accomplished by Africans – although missionaries reserved the privilege of baptising converts for themselves. This has been observed for the history of Christianisation in sub-Saharan Africa more generally and has been restated more recently for South Africa.[15] It applied particularly to South Africa, where knowledge of Christianity was introduced at an early stage yet missions were not very quick to follow the movement of labour migrants, itinerant preachers and other mobile individuals who spread the news that they had encountered while away from home. Long before the advent of visible and formal conversions, people responded to and sharpened their understanding of the very idea of conversion. Regardless of the fractured ways in which it was transmitted, the new religion implied new ways of being, seeing and doing things. As this chapter will suggest, however, congregations also became involved in deciding who would be admitted to the ranks of believers. Old people, in particular, who could not easily be reached by mission schooling, were baptised if the emerging congregations considered them to be worthy future members of the church.

This kind of transformation made it necessary to somehow accommodate the idea of a High God.[16] As in many African cosmologies, South Africans conceived of an otiose God in the background, who had created the world, but did not interfere immediately in people's everyday affairs, for which lesser spiritual beings were important.[17] The adoption of Christianity also entailed new conceptions of selfhood, the setup of households, and perhaps even of

---

[15] Adrian Hastings, *The Church in Africa 1450–1950* (Oxford: OUP, 1995); Elphick, *Equality of Believers*, 35. Whether 'there are few written records of the activities of African evangelists' is a matter for debate. This chapter deals with such records – albeit written *about* rather than *by* African evangelists – and the archives of various German mission societies certainly hold more material.

[16] Early mission Christianity was probably attractive for Africans more generally because it was translatable, and hence inspired them to think about conceptionalising African gods as deities with a wider scope. See Robin Horton, 'African Conversion', *Africa* 41, 2 (1971): 85–108. In their conversations, however, missionaries did not necessarily prioritise the idea of the High God to such a large degree as they insisted on the existence of sin and the need for salvation, see Elphick, *Equality of Believers*, 32–3. Missionaries also checked people's bodies and, more particularly, their outward appearance so as to judge the inner state of the converts' being. They emphasised notions of hierarchy and submission to male authority such as colonial office holders, fathers and chiefs.

[17] For more detail as well as a comprehensive overview, see Jacob K. Olupona, *African Religions: A Very Short Introduction* (Oxford: OUP, 2014), 20–37.

community. It provided the impetus for new styles of clothing, architecture, housing and furniture. It implied a new rhythm of life which was crystallised in the introduction of a seven-day week and the idea of resting on Sundays. In fact, in the Zulu Kingdom people dubbed the activity of attending church services *sonda*, or Sundaying.[18] Christianity challenged people to rethink their conceptions of health, vulnerability and death, as well as their strategies for achieving prosperity, wealth and power.[19] Missionaries invested much energy in explaining that labour and gender hierarchies had to be organised according to new rules. Hence, conversion and religious change did not occur as expressions of 'private', 'domestic' or 'personal' desires. They were part of broader changes in people's worlds. And these transformations engendered debate. The ground-breaking news was, of course, adopted unevenly. Conversion and religious change were slow, ambiguous and ambivalent processes extending over a long period of time in the course of which Christian ways of doing things became rooted in the region while some people converted and others did not. And yet a world was set in motion in more ways than one.

The number of conversions only increased towards the end of the nineteenth century when people in many parts of South Africa could no longer escape the implications of colonial conquest. Yet it remains difficult to pinpoint why exactly people began to convert at that time. Perhaps conversions owed more to the immediate experience of colonialism than to the converts' critique of their own societies. It is also likely that conversions to Christianity occurred as succeeding generations had been engaged in a long conversation about new values, changing social and political orders and the possibility of deriving, as Christians, strength and standing from this source of power.[20] For Africans, conversion represented a means of positioning themselves in their struggling, emerging or dissolving communities – in a world in motion. And because missionaries came from foreign places, the mere possibility of conversion promised to connect different parts of the world. This option frightened people, and it opened up windows of unequal interaction, although the promise was that, by converting to Christianity, people would achieve access to new sources of power and ascend the civilisational ladder.

Decisions about who converted and who did not, and about the consequences for wider kin networks, relations and the polity, had different implications. As

---

18 Jarle Simensen, 'Religious Change as Transaction: the Norwegian Mission to Zululand, South Africa 1850–1906', *Journal of Religion in Africa* 16 (1986): 82–100, esp. 87–91.

19 Although she does not refer specifically to South Africa, see Phyllis M. Martin, 'Life and Death, Power and Vulnerability: Everyday Contradictions at the Loango Mission, 1883–1904', *Journal of African Cultural Studies* 15, 1 (2002): 61–78.

20 For one of the most instructive cases, see Terence Ranger, *Are We Not Also Men? The Samkange Family & African Politics in Zimbabwe, 1920–64* (Harare: Baobab, 1995).

long as no mass conversions were taking place, the conversion of those men and women who were related to the centres of power or who were rulers themselves held particular significance. A number of rulers created the space for conversion among their people without themselves considering conversion. Others showed resistance to conversion, or became reluctant after the first conversions began to trigger political implications. Patterns of loyalty, patronage and hierarchy were frequently affected regardless of whether people converted or not. Often, what mattered more immediately was whether they stuck to their old ways or decided to 'follow the new' more generally.[21] As we will see further below, the 1860s were a period of transition when older styles and patterns of stimulating religious change dwindled and gradually – and sometimes more rapidly – new ones gained ground.

The local dynamics of conversion and religious change fed into broader contexts of historical change. This becomes evident in a published but rather underappreciated text, an account called *Lebensbilder aus Südafrika* – life portraits from South Africa – written in 1871 by the director of the Berlin Mission Society, Hermann Theodor Wangemann.[22] It cost 20 silver groschen and was thus a rather expensive product among the broad spectrum of Berlin Mission publications. Individual chapters were also available separately at a far lower cost. *Lebensbilder* recorded a selection of stories of Pedi men and women who converted in the dramatically brief time span between roughly 1860 and 1864. Even though, like many other texts, it muted the immediate voices of Africans, this extraordinary source reveals intimately embedded local religious dynamics. It also depicts them in transcontinental perspective, since the work was directed at German readers, donors and those more generally interested in foreign peoples and places. At the heart of the text were orally conceived life stories that were transposed onto 'history' in a complex process of translation and recording. Although the text portrays the conversion of prominent individuals, it reveals the dynamics of religious change and conversion as relational processes, which often involved kinship ties. Furthermore, the text was recorded while its author, the mission director, was travelling. This seems remarkable given that the mission station rather than the path between mission settlements was the actual stronghold of paternalist power. In the case of *Lebensbilder*, much recording took place outside that sphere of more immediate missionary influence.

The conversions that concern us in this chapter took place in the Pedi Kingdom, about which more will be said in the following section. Because

21 The phrase comes from Tilman Dedering, *Hate the Old and Follow the New: Khoekhoe and Missionaries in Early Nineteenth-Century Namibia* (Stuttgart: Franz Steiner, 1997).

22 Hermann Theodor Wangemann, *Lebensbilder aus Südafrika: Ein Beitrag zur Kirchen- und Culturgeschichte des neunzehnten Jahrhunderts*, 3rd edn (1st edn 1871; Berlin, 1876).

of conflicts with the king, the emerging Christian flock withdrew from his immediate reach in 1865, moving into Boer territory and the mission-owned establishment of Botšabelo, where many more conversions occurred. Both in the Pedi Kingdom and Botšabelo converts had encountered missionaries of German background since 1861. They had arrived from Germany, which was not a colonial political power, and considered themselves rather aloof from the British civilisational mission which in many ways was openly and unambiguously pursued along more commercial lines.[23] For that reason, the connections between various regional and spatial settings will have to be set out as the chapter unfolds. It will then proceed to look at the published conversion narrative, the *Lebensbilder* collection, and to provide, in a close reading, a microhistorical approach to the nature and dynamics of conversion among the Pedi people. In particular, it will explore how conversion became an affair of families and people related by kinship ties rather than an act of individual decision-making or a process of ethnicisation. Subsequently, the chapter will turn to two important themes, baptism and prayer, as they were implicated in the use and application of medicine, which link the many conversions portrayed in the *Lebensbilder* collection. Among people of less privileged status, too, both baptism and prayer figured as local political strategies and messages of power and social connection in a world of increasing colonial entanglements as well as one where space and the scope of mobility were being renegotiated for missionaries and converts of different genders. Finally, the chapter will look at how stories of African conversion affected readers back in Germany, since the idea of the religious reordering of a far-flung world contributed to the making of middle-class consciousness among religiously inclined subjects.

The Setting

The Eastern Transvaal became part of the Zuid-Afrikaanse Republiek in the late 1850s as part of efforts by Boer settlers to establish state structures while they were still expanding.[24] The Zuid-Afrikaanse Republiek was a state in which power was negotiated between groups and individuals rather than as a process driven by state institutions. Until late in the nineteenth century, the Transvaal remained a frontier society.[25] Nevertheless, these interventions disrupted and

[23] The Rhenish Mission and the Norddeutsche Mission, Bremen, were German mission societies which also adopted a rather commercial philosophy – in the German colonies, not in South Africa.

[24] On the state-building process see, for instance, the introduction in Nigel Worden, *The Making of Modern South Africa*, 2nd edn (Oxford: Blackwell, 1995).

[25] Roger Wagner, 'Zoutpansberg: The Dynamics of a Hunting Frontier, 1848–67', in *Economy and Society in Pre-industrial South Africa*, ed. Shula Marks and Anthony Atmore

inhibited the development of stable African political institutions that had been underway in the region. The settlers prospected and divided the land. Huge patches were sold to, or registered on behalf of, prospective farmers and land speculators. Even though Africans did not yet lose access to the land at this time, they would do so once the state structures of the South African Republic had been strengthened and consolidated.

The Pedi Kingdom was situated in the Zuid-Afrikaanse Republiek. In the aftermath of a prolonged period of *difaqane* wars,[26] turmoil and population movements that had lasted from around the 1820s to the 1840s, the formerly rather small lineage of the Maroteng was now becoming a hegemonic power in the area. It is possible to detect a development towards the creation of states in this process, not wholly unlike the process unfolding in Europe. Many communities dispersed, and were relocating and realigning themselves in the area at exactly the moment when the settlers moved in and, like settlers elsewhere, propounded the myth that the land they were taking had been empty.[27] The Pedi Kingdom was independent at the time under review, but commoners as well as rulers were witnessing increasing labour coercion and experiencing often violent demands for tax and tribute.

A group of Lutheran missionaries from Berlin, the capital of Prussia – but not yet of Imperial Germany – had newly arrived in the area and added yet another strand of power to the already complex setting. Unlike the position of missionaries described in the chapter on Australia, the Berlin missionaries were guests in the Pedi Kingdom. They were allotted gardens to cultivate food, and their hosts aided them in many ways to set up a material base for their existence. When compared to the parallel situation in Australia, settler society and the state were less established in the region, and missions were as yet far from providing regular school classes or living up to the ideal of the mission household. All of this was only just emerging. The missionaries were compelled, and initially willing, to respect Pedi royal authority. Their vision was to convert a whole people into a Christian nation. They did not concern themselves with how spiritual equality, once achieved through conversion, would translate into social and political equality. Rather, they believed in something akin to racial purity that kept the Pedi aloof as a *volk* or nation. This idea of aloofness was coupled with the unquestioned imperative of submission to colonial authorities. The Pedi were to be kept apart as a culture and a nation – one submissive to the powers that be.

(London: Longmans, 1980), 313–49; Stanley Trapido, 'The South African Republic: Class Formation and the State, 1850–1900', *Collected Seminar Papers on the Societies of Southern Africa in the 19th and 20th Centuries* 3 (1971/ 72): 53–65.

26 *Difaqane* is the Sotho term for the Zulu equivalent *mfecane*, meaning 'the grand dispersion'.

27 Hamilton, *The Mfecane Aftermath*.

A few years before his death the previous ruler of the Pedi, Sekwati, had enlisted the missionaries as prospective diplomats and go-betweens to keep the settlers at bay and perhaps even British colonialism, which was moving up Natal and towards the borders of the Zulu Kingdom. Pedi men and women converted against the ever more explicit will of their paramount, Sekwati, followed by Sekhukhune (r. 1861–1880, 1882–83). For Sekhukhune, the forces he faced soon became difficult to control. He noticed how conversion to Christianity facilitated the emergence of yet another force to be reckoned with. Pressed by his councillors, he asked the Christians to cultivate their new ways in their homes rather than where it was visible to others. But the face of Christianity was inevitably public. People debated and disagreed on whether the missionaries and 'the *ditaba* [news] of the white people'[28] would fortify them against affliction, harm and all kinds of mischief. Sekhukhune, eager to assert his own claim to power, reminded them that 'Myneers [the missionaries] have not come here to make rain but to teach.'[29] Too many of his subjects, however, became involved with the power of the missionaries. Sekhukhune put the believers, *madiaka*, and some of the royal wives on trial, and could only watch as an increasing number of converts and their families fled his polity. In fact, several of the royal wives became active converts and left the ambit of royal power as well – very much to the detriment of power relations between the clans they served to connect. The missionaries bought a farm they called Botšabelo, or place of refuge. This was now their own land, which they turned into a prospering Christian congregation run according to their rules. In the Pedi Kingdom, the loss of people signified an insult to royal power and authority. The price of moving there, however, was that the kingdom would be closed to the mission society until its military defeat in 1880.[30] Their vision of turning an entire people into a 'Christian nation' had thus suffered a severe backlash. For the Pedi, this implied a significant transition as far as the dynamics of religious change were concerned. New conditions that arose with the engagement of the Berlin Mission Society in their midst came to an abrupt end when the missionaries left only a few years later. Pedi who for a number of years had converted in the framework of 'their own' polity now had to move to the mission-controlled establishment of Botšabelo in order to see themselves within the new religion.

As missionaries of German origin inserted themselves into the regional setting, German historical contexts played into the situation as well. In the 1860s, Germany was not yet an imperial power in Africa (and it would never become one in the Transvaal). The German missionaries, many of whom had been on the brink of marginalisation and had entertained an uneasy relationship

[28] Wangemann, *Lebensbilder*, 72.

[29] *Berliner Missionsberichte* 1862, 254 (hereafter abbreviated as *bmb*).

[30] Delius, *The Land Belongs to Us*; Rüther, *The Power Beyond*.

with political, economic, social and religious developments back home, were themselves foreigners seeking a new home, one outside the protection of their own developing nation. Of course, while growing up, entering the world of work and discovering their own penchant for Pietist religion, they must have been exposed to at least some of the public debates in Germany surrounding desired and imagined colonial projects.[31] It is hard to know however, how far the debates dominated by liberal intellectuals or the colonial ambitions of merchants in cities like Bremen or Hamburg may have captured the imaginations of the insecure but ambitious missionaries in Berlin, most of whom came from other German states and territories and evidently aimed to improve their own lot and that of others in a colonial setting. Following the Pietist convention of proving their religious worth by personal commitment, the missionaries' memoirs and the letters of intent they sent to the Berlin Mission board before entering the institution contain little reflection of political debates.

Through their regular reports, the missionaries contributed to making the emerging German Empire an especially 'writerly one',[32] as scholars have dubbed it. Germany, which had no colonies of its own, had seen a long succession of prominent explorers venturing to Africa as part of expeditions of scientific exploration and discovery. In the first three decades of the century, missionaries of German origin, who were often also explorers, had investigated the African mission fields as members of British or other mission institutions. Once the missionaries from Berlin had established themselves in South Africa, their reports became voluminous and regular. In the mission's metropolitan centre, these reports were transformed into publications of various price categories that provided information, texts for readers' self-reflection and entertainment. The published products addressed a religiously inclined audience, but the missionaries from Berlin were also instructed to contribute to the global knowledge of foreign peoples. Headquarters proudly boasted that, more generally, 'Even for the secular-minded judge interested in science and history, it [the mission] is gradually gaining in respect and value ... Missionaries have provided us with more thorough and comprehensive knowledge of many peoples and lands'.[33]

---

31 Hans Fenske, 'Ungeduldige Zuschauer: Die Deutschen und die europäische Expansion 1815–1880', in *Imperialistische Kontinuität und nationale Ungeduld im 19. Jahrhundert*, ed. Wolfgang Reinhard (Frankfurt/ Main: Fischer, 1991), 87–123.

32 George Steinmetz, *The Devil's Handwriting: Precoloniality and the German Colonial State in Qingdao, Samoa, and Southwest Africa* (Chicago & London: University of Chicago Press, 2007).

33 *Bmb* 1834, 105. For a more general exploration of the connections between missions and knowledge recording/ production, see Patrick Harries and David Maxwell (eds), *The Spiritual in the Secular: Missionaries and Knowledge about Africa* (Grand Rapids, Michigan and Cambridge: Wm B Eerdmans, 2012).

In the various regional settings, in Berlin, Prussia and rural Pomerania, for instance, as well as in the Pedi Kingdom, the Transvaal or Botšabelo, people were not only socially mobile but willing to migrate and look towards a future in new surroundings. The prospective missionaries who ended up in South Africa did not emigrate to North America, as other disenchanted Lutherans from Prussia did.[34] Critical of the state church in Prussia, which united the Lutheran and Reformed churches in a single ecclesiastical body, they sought to strengthen 'right ways' through mission activities in South Africa. And they were often ridiculed for this in the German public, since respect for and acknowledgement of the mission enterprise would only ensue in Germany sometime around the 1880s. What mattered equally was that the German mission scene, historically connected to a transnational landscape of evangelising projects, was becoming more denominational in the mid-nineteenth century. And yet many of the missionaries' parents had been connected to the Moravian movement, which had been so important a generation or two previously for strengthening faith within existing Protestant denominations, and whose evangelising enterprise reached as far as Australia. In South Africa, the destination of the Lutheran missionaries, people and prospective converts migrated as labourers or when they attached themselves to the emerging rulers of still flexible political entities. The *Lebensbilder* collection captured these movements and permeability, and did not consider them a social feature to be commented upon negatively.[35]

---

[34] David Ellis, 'Erweckungsbewegung und Rationalismus im vormärzlichen Brandenburg und Pommern', in *Wunderwelten: Religiöse Ekstase und Magie in der Moderne*, ed. Nils Freytag and Diethard Sawicki (Munich: Wilhelm Fink, 2006), 53–82; Christopher M. Clark, 'The Politics of Revival: Pietists, Aristocrats, and the State Church in Early Nineteenth-Century Prussia', in *Between Reform, Reaction, and Resistance: Studies in the History of German Conservatism from 1789 to 1945*, ed. Larry Eugene Jones and James Retallack (Providence: Berg, 1993), 31–60; Friedrich Wilhelm Graf, 'Die Spaltung des Protestantismus: Zum Verhältnis von evangelischer Kirche, Staat und "Gesellschaft" im frühen 19. Jahrhundert', in *Religion und Gesellschaft im 19. Jahrhundert*, ed. Wolfgang Schieder (Stuttgart: Klett-Cotta, 1993), 157–90; Rudolf von Thadden, *Trieglaff: Eine pommersche Lebenswelt zwischen Kirche und Politik, 1807–1948* (Göttingen: Wallstein, 2010).

[35] This differed from the Hermannsburg Mission reporting in the same area; see Kirsten Rüther, 'Through the Eyes of Missionaries and the Archives They Created: The Interwoven Histories of Power and Authority in the Nineteenth-Century Transvaal', *Journal of Southern African Studies* 38, 2 (2012): 369–84.

The *Lebensbilder* Collection

Figure 3.1 H.T. Wangemann, mission director, and Jacob Makhoëtle, hunter and travel guide. Makhoëtle drew Wangemann's attention to a range of story tellers on their joint trip. (Illustrations from Wangemann, *D. Dr. Wangemann* (1899), front blurb; and Wangemann, *Lebensbilder* (1876), p. 189 – copyright Berliner Missionswerk, Berlin)

Lebensbilder aus Südafrika was written at a moment when the mission was still seeking public recognition and when, unlike in previous decades, a positive response to this aspiration seemed within reach.[36] The text represents an amazing narrative of African conversions. Although the text conveys views on the dynamics of religious, social and political change that the missionaries were determined to bring about (the missionaries were anything but calm observers), it allows glimpses into how religious change affected a segment of the Pedi people, not just isolated individuals. The stories were compiled either from mission reports or from interviews and late-night conversations that the mission director Theodor Wangemann[37] had conducted with various converts,

[36] Whether the *Lebensbilder* collection actually contributed to achieving this recognition is difficult to determine. Reception studies more generally are extremely difficult to conduct.

[37] Wangemann, whose parents had a Moravian background, had benefited from the opportunities for social upward mobility in the first half of the nineteenth century. Like many gifted and ambitious men of his day, he had succeeded in advancing into the respectable

especially with the help of his travel scout, Jacob Makhoëtle, while on his first grand inspection tour of South Africa in 1866 and 1867. Many of these stories may have been told in private sessions, while others perhaps originated in more public renderings of the subjects' lives. A substantial amount of editing was involved, as well as translation between Sepedi, Afrikaans and German, and between genres, languages, histories and cultures.

Wangemann and the missionaries on whose reports he drew did not write in an academic vein, although they did incorporate ethnographic sections into their narratives. They played with dialogic elements, which made their texts livelier, but which was also reminiscent of the style found in catechisms. In many respects, Wangemann and the missionaries experimented with genres and patterns of narration with which they had been socialised in their societies of origin. From time to time, however, they were also 'overpowered' by local narrative conventions, which they sometimes deployed in an ethnographic mode, but which also offered insights, at least in certain fragments, into how converts might have phrased their own understanding of conversion and religious change. As writers, the missionaries were every bit as prolific as the Catholic convert Wilhelm Gustav Werner Volk, the subject of the first case-study in this volume, but they explored more popular genres, and ones that seemed appropriate for addressing the colonial situation. Like Volk in Erfurt, the missionaries wrote themselves into being. Their Pietist inclinations, however, led them to refrain from writing and talking about themselves too directly. Instead, they used other people's conversions to suggest the respectability of their own lives and work. In their own view, it was their own initiative that had rendered those conversions possible – without any context of formal political colonisation. Quite generally, missionaries' reports emerged as textual products in close interaction with the people who informed the missionaries. The missionaries integrated their informants' styles, just as they themselves influenced local modes of presenting stories. They kept a close eye on the narrative conventions of neighbouring mission societies, which they feared as rivals on the German book market. And they often focused on topics that provoked conflict and debate among Africans and converts, and thus proved unavoidable for the missionaries.[38] This meant

middle classes through education, discipline and a certain opening of society at the time. He became a conservative Lutheran pastor and director of a teachers' seminar in Pomerania, where he was associated with Pietist aristocratic circles. But he never decided to emigrate as some of his close allies did. See Hans Wangemann, *D. Dr. Wangemann, Missionsdirektor: Ein Lebensbild* (Berlin: Wiegandt & Grieben, 1899); and von Thadden, *Trieglaff*. In 1865 he was offered the position of mission director at an institution that needed a staunch Lutheran who would, at the same time, know how to appease older Reformed tendencies in the mission body while keeping his distance from separatism.

[38] Kirsten Rüther, 'Der Streit um Englisch als Unterrichtsfach in lutherischen Missionsschulen Südafrikas, ca. 1895–1910: Impulse für eine Geschichte der Resonanzen', in

that the missionaries were not as permanently present in the texts as one might initially expect.[39]

The nineteenth-century *Lebensbilder* – literally pictures of or from life – which graphically illustrate the lives and religious commitments of individuals and are often didactic in nature, represent a popular sub-genre of modest biography, one to which the ordinary men and women involved in the mission project could also aspire.[40] *Lebensbilder aus Südafrika* was written for, and presented to, a readership in Germany. Relieving pastors of the burden of personally collecting material for the meetings of mission support groups and Sunday school classes, these texts constituted a basic ingredient in fundraising for mission work. The *Lebensbilder* also provided 'new' topics and material for a mission field in which many 'old mission tracts were already all too well known'.[41]

The narrativity and popularity of the genre harmonised almost perfectly with the originally oral renderings of lives transformed and transposed into their published version. As aptly described by Alessandro Portelli, oral history is

> a dialogic discourse, created not only by what the interviewees say, but also by what we as historians do – by the historian's presence in the field, and by the historian's presentation of the material. ... It refers to what the source and the historian do *together* at the moment of their encounter in the interview.[42]

Wangemann was such an oral historian. He was, of course, an oral historian of his time and of a religious inclination. In the *Lebensbilder*, he produced a written narrative about which it is almost impossible today to unambiguously determine who was the source and who was the historian, who created the script and who became the listener. Portelli also argues that 'oral history is more intrinsically itself when it listens to speakers who are not already recognised protagonists in the public sphere'.[43] This characteristic applies as well to the converts whom Wangemann, his colleagues or the hunter Makhoëtle, who accompanied Wangemann on his travels, brought together to be interviewed. It also applies to

Mission global: Eine Verflechtungsgeschichte seit dem 19. Jahrhundert, ed. Rebekka Habermas and Richard Hölzl (Cologne: Böhlau, 2014), 91–110; Hofmeyr, '*We Spend Our Years*'.

39 For a slightly different argument, see Gareth Griffiths, '"Trained to Tell the Truth": Missionaries, Converts, and Narration', in *Mission and Empire*, ed. Norman Etherington, Oxford History of the British Empire, Companion Series (Oxford: OUP, 2005), 153–72.

40 See also Gustav Warneck's introduction to *Johann Friedrich Riedel, ein Lebensbild aus der Minahassa auf Celebes* ed. R. Grundemann, Lebensbilder aus der Heiden-Mission Series, 2 (Gütersloh: C. Bertelsmann, 1873), 5–23.

41 Wangemann, *Lebensbilder*, 3.

42 Alessandro Portelli, 'Oral History as Genre', in *Narrative and Genre*, ed. Mary Chamberlain and Paul Thompson (London: Routledge, 1998), 23–45, quote p. 23.

43 Portelli, 'Oral History', 26.

the final product, the *Lebensbilder*, which gave shape to, and imitated the voices of, people who could easily have gone unrecorded by written history.

Through his contacts with a select number of outstanding Christians, Wangemann's narrative assigns a mediating role to both director and converts. When Christianity is conveyed as a message to ordinary Africans, the early converts preach, translate and explain. When, in the second instance, the process of religious change is conveyed to German readers, it is Wangemann who assumes the role of teaching, explaining and admonishing. It seems as if the early converts and Wangemann worked side by side. This neat cooperation is of course a textual device. In social interactions and in the course of events it was rather evident, right from the beginning, and would become even more so with time, that the missionaries wanted to teach Africans themselves, frequently sidestepping the early converts with whom they had created bonds in the first place. These early and prominent converts, in turn, themselves aspired to address Christians and leaders in the European metropole, especially in later phases of the religious and colonial encounter, when conflicts began to mount.[44]

In the South African context, Isabel Hofmeyr has argued for the necessity of understanding African people's tales as moulded by the intersection of orality and literacy. She has pointed out that it is only out of a sentimental 'wailing for purity' that we assume that the original word was less distorted.[45] Hofmeyr stresses that any oral account in nineteenth-century South Africa was touched by the written word in one way or another. One could add, as was demonstrated above, that the written accounts of missionaries and colonial administrators were naturally also touched by, and implicated in, the spoken and the performed word. It should be noted that Africans were not the only ones to achieve transcultural transformations. European actors such as missionaries strove for them as well. A mission source such as the *Lebensbilder* which has come down to us in written form and as a single-authored narrative is by no means a deliberate distortion of the narrated lives. In fact, there are many paragraphs where the text consciously tries to render and to imitate the oral – albeit often in a manner that at least resonated with the oral culture of German readers.

The *Lebensbilder* was not, however, a text like *The Pilgrim's Progress* that transformed religious reading matter into a key instrument of missionary evangelisation or, as was the case with *Pilgrim's Progress*, into some kind of missionary promotional text. *Pilgrim's Progress* later even became a basic text

44 Kirsten Rüther, '"Sekukuni, Listen!, *Banna*!, and to the Children of Frederick the Great and Our Kaiser Wilhelm": Documents in the Social and Religious History of the Transvaal, 1860–1890', *Journal of Religion in Africa* 34, 3 (2004): 207–34.

45 Isabel Hofmeyr, '"Wailing For Purity": Oral Studies in Southern African Studies', *African Studies* 54, 2 (1995): 16–31.

of the English literary canon – a fate by no means shared by the *Lebensbilder*.[46] Works such as *Pilgrim's Progress* or the *Lebensbilder* remind us that popular texts about conversion and religious achievement resonated with the particular genre of conversion accounts reviewed in the first chapter. In fact, aside from the officially defined genre of the conversion narrative, bodies such as the numerous mission societies made a much broader spectrum of narrated conversion stories available to German readers.

The *Lebensbilder* conversion narratives, the products of shared narration, listening, authorship and to a far lesser extent, presentation, remain an ambivalent source. Neither do they represent African lives and conversion experiences per se, nor do they suggest in unmediated fashion German reading tastes, German colonial fantasies or German religious consciousness. In its enmeshed perspectives, this collection of conversion narratives embodies the hopes and dilemmas of the Africans *and* missionaries who were becoming entangled in a global project of Christianisation and European colonial advance – while the results of these processes were as yet undetermined. From its inception, conversion in the African setting comprised local as well as transcontinental dynamics, ever-changing in the course of events.

The initial four chapters of the *Lebensbilder* record the lives and conversions of four prominent converts. Jan Mafadi and Jacob Mantladi, two labour migrants, had first encountered Christianity in the Cape. Martinus Sewúshan, a respected and ambitious seer and royal gunsmith, impressed the missionaries as a leader and authority on Christianity. Last but not least, Josef Kathedi, a blind man, gained the missionaries' admiration for his reflective capacities and eloquence on deeply philosophical matters. Men of family and reputation but not of office, all of them in their early thirties, they became the highly respected (male) backbone and future church elite of the Pedi Christian congregation, which, however, and as mentioned above owing to conflicts with the king, Sekhukhune, ultimately decided to leave the Pedi Kingdom. Kathedi, Mantladi, Mafadi and Sewúshan, as well as Makhoëtle, who accompanied the mission director on his travels as a scout, were men who commanded valued skills and knowledge before their conversion. This determined their power and their standing and their subsequent ability to contribute to, or manipulate, relations within their society. Conversion added another strand to this personal repertoire of power, making them individuals even better equipped to challenge the power of the king – hence the royal reluctance to accept the aggrandisement of these individuals, and the royal efforts towards halting the process of conversion among the common people more generally.

46 Isabel Hofmeyr, *The Portable Bunyan: A Transnational History of The Pilgrim's Progress* (Princeton: PUP, 2003).

The fifth and sixth chapters relate tales of cannibalism. In many ways, they represent those ordinary addressees and their 'no longer cannibalistic' offspring with whom both the missionaries and the elite converts wished to communicate. These cannibal stories have more recently been decoded as expressions of ordinary people's experiences of war, turmoil, captivity and complete disorder.[47] To contemporary readers, they probably shockingly demonstrated the abjection and degradation of humanity living 'without' religion. They forcefully point to the extraordinary trajectories covered by people in those days, and to how, in the process of regrouping, they looked for centres of power to which they could attach themselves. But cannibalism was also an emerging trope in male bourgeois discourse in Europe and in Germany.[48] Thus it is no mere coincidence that Wangemann, who had disciplined himself in order to rise into the middle classes, was so fascinated by the topic and probably himself stimulated among the Pedi a desire to relate to their foreign visitor such horrendous stories about cannibalism. The cannibal stories accord the converts a darker side, the incomprehensible background from which they themselves and their families emerged. While elite converts worked side by side with the missionaries, and the missionaries side by side with them, the common converts remained somehow associated with these scenarios. Whether these scenarios cast a shadow over African converts of loftier standing, and what status within the hierarchy of human civilisation was accorded to African converts, whose race is never mentioned, was probably left to the reader to decide for him- or herself.

Two subsequent chapters return to leaders. They focus on three royal sons, Sekhukhune, Mampuru and Dinkoanyane, and three royal wives, Tlakale, Modikisheng and Mankone, respectively. Mampuru, the original successor, was alienated from his claim to succession and sought political alliances with the royal son Dinkoanyane and the former *dingaka* Sewúshan, both of whom favoured Christianity. The royal wives' conversions, however, placed particular stress upon Sekhukhune. Within this group, 'there were considerable distinctions of rank and status ... and the importance of affinal relations in the political structure of the Pedi polity meant that conflict between the paramount and subordinate chieftaincies could have dire consequences for certain of his spouses'.[49] It appears in the narrative that the women themselves took the initiative to convert and thus, by their action, subverted the ties between the king's authority and the allied clans from which he had taken his wives. The women had been transferred from families to the royal court and, usually, gifts and favours had been

---

47 Peter Delius, 'Recapturing Captives and Conversations with "Cannibals": In Pursuit of a Neglected Stratum in South African History', *Journal of Southern African Studies* 36, 1 (2010): 7–23.

48 Eva Bischoff, *Kannibale-Werden: Eine postkoloniale Geschichte deutscher Männlichkeit um 1900* (Bielefeld: Transcript, 2011).

49 Delius, *The Land*, 113.

provided in return. This had fostered power alliances between the male heads of lineages and the king. When the women began to 'move' towards Christianity, this disturbed existing power relations. And it seems that the women did so deliberately through conversions in order to assert their own status and agency more generally. It is regrettable that we know virtually nothing about the domestic sphere of the royal Pedi household, which makes it nearly impossible to determine more fully whether what the women did – or are said to have done – was an assertion of their ancient rights, which had come under attack in the course of pressures on the king, or whether Christianity opened up a new scope of action for them. These chapters also reveal the paternalist approach of the missionaries – they introduced a cultural and religious resource to the Pedi Kingdom which, as they maintained, assisted women in defining their virtue. It was hoped that the women, in turn, would become the loyal backbone of an emerging Christian community whom the missionaries could use to exert their superior knowledge of what was good for others. Interpretations of the narrative could go in several directions, and were indeed left up to readers.

The ninth chapter is devoted to Jacob Makhoëtle, whose important function as a storyteller, hunter and go-between has already been noted. He became responsible for the military defence of the farm at Botšabelo and was reverently dubbed the leading missionary's 'prime minister'.[50] The three final chapters recount the loss of the Bopedi mission field, a traumatic experience for the Berlin Mission, narratively staged as akin to the flight from Egypt. Taken together, all of the chapters show how a new Christian Pedi community began to take shape through conversion and affiliation with the missionaries. This was a community in motion whose location and boundaries shifted as the conversions unfolded. And it was the Berlin Mission Society's favourite project of religious and national engineering.

[50] Just a note on the side: a descendant of this Jacob Makhoëtle, Botšabelo's 'prime minister', was the prime minister of the Province of Mpumalanga for some years in the early 2000s.

Conversion and Kinship in the Families and Worlds of Jan Mafadi and Ruth Mampatshe[51]

Figure 3.2 Albert Nachtigal, missionary, and Jacob Mantladi, close friend of the convert Jan Mafadi. Albert Nachtigal collected a wide variety of life stories and conversion accounts from among the Pedi. H.T. Wangemann drew extensively on his collection. Jan Mafadi, who as a migrant travelled with Jacob Mantladi, belonged to one of the early and prominent Christian converts to relate his life. Unfortunately there are no drawings of either Jan Mafadi or Ruth Mampatshe whose life stories and conversion are covered in this chapter. Illustrations from Delius, *Conversion* (1984), p.17 (reprint); Wangemann, *Lebensbilder* (1876), p. 24 – copyright Berliner Missionswerk, Berlin)

In order to back up my argument, I would like to offer a close reading of the first and penultimate stories. One is about a young man in his thirties, Jan Mafadi, and his relatives. The other deals with the life of the 85-year-old Ruth Mampatshe and her kin. These stories matter because these individual lives and religious conversions were nurtured, as well as inhibited, by the nexus of family and kinship. Even though the missionaries would have liked to manipulate Pedi

[51] A note on spelling: According to modern spelling conventions, the name would be Mampatše. The chapter will make use of the name as it is spelt in the original. This applies to other names as well where modern spelling would render the writing of names different.

ethnicity,[52] Pedi conversions were, first and foremost, a matter of kinship and family alliances. We know rather little about how the adoption of Christianity was negotiated within families or between people related by kinship – even though this constituted a vital aspect of how the new religion actually took root in the South African setting.

Jan Mafadi, an early convert portrayed in the first chapter, was responsible for bringing Christianity to Bopedi.[53] The orphaned boy was raised by his grandmother, Sewaitsheng, who later became the only family member to share his inclination towards Christianity. As a young husband, a father of a first-born son and a labour migrant, Mafadi encountered Christianity in Port Elizabeth in the Cape. It was there, beyond the immediate reach of his family, that he discovered the source that would empower him for the rest of his life. Back home he eagerly tried to persuade his family to also adopt this source of strength. This proved difficult as his wife, Mpapane, was reluctant to consent to her husband's new visions of life. Thus Mafadi associated with male companions, such as Jacob Mantladi, Josef Kathedi and Martinus Sewúshan, who assembled in prayer unions as individuals rather than family members and even managed to direct Bopedi to the Lutheran missionaries who had just arrived in the Transvaal.[54] The missionaries, they learnt, originated in Germany, not England, which, as Wangemann notes, 'represents the ends of the earth for the Bassuto'.[55] In fact, the missionaries arrived 'from Germany, far beyond even England'.[56] In a setting in which Boer settlerism and British colonialism were beginning to dominate, it was important for Wangemann, as for the other missionaries from Berlin, to locate themselves in relation to the dominant forces in the area. The phrase they used to describe their affiliation expressed geographical distance. It sought to indicate their remoteness, since for the converts the colonisers from 'England' were more familiar than the proponents of religion from yet another distant country. In addition, it linked the world from which 'English' and 'German' people came to the world of the Pedi, who were now aligned with the joint project of Christianisation. And yet, it is probably worth noting that this was

[52] Patrick Harries has described this process for the Swiss missionaries' involvement in the Tsonga-speaking people's conversion in Mozambique. See his 'Exclusion, Classification and Internal Colonialism: The Emergence of Ethnicity Among the Tsonga-Speakers of South Africa' in *The Creation of Tribalism in Southern Africa*, ed. Leroy Vail (Berkeley: Univ. of California Press; London: Currey, 1989), 82–117.

[53] Wangemann, *Lebensbilder*, 7–25.

[54] Ibid., 31–2. The missionaries also depended on permission from the Boer government to establish the mission in the Transvaal. This detail was left out of the narrative, but it is part of the broader history of the mission in the area.

[55] Wangemann, *Lebensbilder*, 7.

[56] Ibid., 7–8.

the missionaries' first contact with potential converts, not the potential converts' first contact with Christianity.

The process of conversion in Mafadi's family unfolded unevenly. He did manage to have his grandmother Sewaitsheng and his son Leboga baptised, so that for a time there was a trans-generational bond between kin who had adopted Christianity. The generation of Mafadi's parents was absent from this bond, but it did include the grandmother who had raised him in his mother's stead and who, now frail and dependent on a younger male relative for her material survival, did not have the same options of resistance as Mafadi's wife, for example. More than once, however, missionaries noted that grandmothers were especially important for the upbringing of grandsons, since they also tended to advise their widowed sons – the boys' fathers – regarding the right time for their grandsons' initiation, among other things.[57] Mafadi was then summoned to war. After her husband's death in battle in June 1862, Mafadi's wife, Mpapane, finally rejected the power that had failed to protect him. Her son's health deteriorated and the young boy, Leboga, died. The narrative insinuates that Mafadi's family was falling apart without the presence of the central figure of a living husband and father, and without Christianity. The widowed Mpapane moved in with an 'uncle' of hers who was a *dingaka* and who, as Wangemann expected from the beginning, only exacerbated Mpapane's ailments. Mpapane was indeed cast as the far from perfect wife who caused her own misery by not adhering to her prescribed role. Her independent mindset significantly contrasted with that of the ideal submissive Christian wife. Mpapane certainly did not fit in with Wangemann's vision of domesticity (and perhaps he offered information about Mpapane as a warning to his readers in Germany). In contrast to this physical deterioration and moral decay within the family, the brave but dead Mafadi still represented the Christian community's relationship to the royal Pedi. He appeared in a dream to the king, Sekhukhune, and thus made felt a presence that he did not exert over his kin.[58] In the end it was only the frail grandmother Hanna Sewaitsheng who became ever more determined to follow Jan Mafadi into the realm of eternity.[59] This probably indicates that of all the family members, she had been the most dependent on Mafadi's material support. In June 1863, a year after her grandson's death in battle, Sewaitsheng died surrounded by heathen kin determined to wrest her away from Christianity. Keeping her focus on her grandson, however, she succeeded in following him. The story conveys the message that it was highly desirable for individuals to choose Christianity against all odds. It stresses that punishment and decay lay ahead for those who

57 C. Hoffmann, *Vom Kraal zur Kanzel: Lebensgeschichte des Eingeborenenpastors Timotheus Sello* (Berlin: Ev. Missionsgesellschaft, 1914), 22–37.

58 Unfortunately, the content of his message to the king was not recorded.

59 Wangemann, *Lebensbilder*, 21.

refused to follow their wiser kin. In fact, the narrative stresses the importance of generational relations between sons, grandsons and mothers and grandmothers.

Mafadi rooted Christianity in the area. He associated with missionaries and Pedi men such as Kathedi, Mantladi and Sewúshan, who lived on and became the backbone of the emerging Christian community – or should we say family? He had spoken to the king in a dream, but died before he had the opportunity to meet Wangemann, the mission director from Berlin. All of these events created links and connections between men to whom women were attached as dependants rather than as partners. The link between the dead hero Mafadi and the director, however, was only established when Wangemann, upon leaving South Africa, took a basket woven by Mafadi, some of his books and, more importantly, his baptismal certificate, back to Berlin, where he kept examples of Mafadi's handwriting in his office:

> I have taken this testament home with me as a keepsake, and it is a valuable memento in the mission house here, along with Jan Mafadi's beloved books, with the name of this dear departed one inscribed in his own hand.[60]

This sounds almost like a kind of magical trophy that Wangemann took home with him from his adventurous expedition through Africa.[61] At the same time, the Christian hero Mafadi was associated, posthumously, with the very centre of the new religion. In this way, he left a virtual archive of his own in Berlin, 'far beyond England'. Mafadi's Bible was stored in the library and can still be seen, held in hands, or read, today, but the other objects were unfortunately not integrated into the archive, which houses only written documents.

Matters were quite different for Hanna, the grandmother. She made every effort to gain access to Christianity, but was dependent on a family that obstructed her and her grandson's decision. According to the narrative, hers was a lonely and isolated connection, which distanced and alienated her from her family and, worse still, failed to connect her with a new network of Christian relations. The narrative held that Hanna Sewaitsheng was tied to Mafadi like an appendix, which made her an honourable Christian but not able to command a position within which her faith could flourish. Yet she represented virtue. In the

---

60 Ibid., 29; the basket is mentioned on p. 83.

61 From his personal correspondence, it becomes clear that he brought several other items with him, perhaps as souvenirs. His sister was keen to receive ostrich feathers which she wished to receive directly by post, not via the mission. Archive of the Berlin Mission Society, Berlin, bmw 1/796 'Die Inspektionsreise des Herrn Direktors Wangemann in SA betreffend, 1866'. Emilie to her brother Theodor Wangemann, 12 Sept. 1866. One of his sons, about 8 years of age, was keen to receive a turtle and an *assegai* (a Zulu spear) to play with; see bmw 1/798, 'Acta die Inspectionsreise des Herrn Director Wangemann in Süd-Afrika betreffend, 1867', Dok.134, not dated.

end, however, and as we learn only much later in the narrative, this struggling woman even forgot her own name[62] – another form of languishing, withering away and disconnection.

After relating a series of life stories, the narrative comes full circle in the penultimate chapter on another 'Old grandmother and her grandchildren', which explores the life and conversion of Ruth Mampatshe.[63] The story does not merely capture a long life extending from about 1790 to 1875, and thus spanning the reign of three Pedi paramounts and a prolonged period of turbulence and violence in the region. It also portrays Mampatshe in her multiple connections to parents, cousins, daughters, sons, a husband, a king and, as the chapter title indicates, her descendants in the third generation. To that extent, her entanglement in family, kinship and political ties is recorded in much more detail than that of royal wives or other more prominent converts. The overall thrust of the story is that while Mampatshe nurtured her family through times of trouble materially, physically and emotionally, her initiation into the Christian community was possible because of a whole network of converted family and relations, especially sons and grandsons, who brought her into contact and helped her to stay in touch with the new religion. She was important for the development of a Christian community because her family needed her; although her religious knowledge may have been imperfect, she served as a genealogical, emotional and moral anchor. As Wangemann maintains, this created a perfect base for the growth of the Christian family and community. It is important to note that these connections were accorded more narrative scope than the bonds between husband and wife created through marriage.[64]

Mampatshe's family dispersed during the *difaqane* wars and famines of the period between the 1820s and 1840s. While her husband kept his food for himself, Mampatshe showed not only maternal compassion but, when caring for her mother, the obedience of a daughter.[65] Later, Mampatshe's son Nicodemus

---

62 Wangemann, *Lebensbilder*, 249.

63 Ibid., 227–51.

64 Marriage was given more relevance in the chapters on royal wives, which cannot be addressed in detail here. Royal wives were important as links between power holders of royal status and important chiefs, rather than in the context of intimate relations between husband and wife. Wangemann did, however, criticise the coercion of already-married women into sexual relations with allies of the king whom they had not chosen as 'husbands' themselves. Sometimes the missionaries even offered compensation to fathers and brothers in order to 'save' certain women from becoming entangled in these political transactions. They thus inscribed themselves into the local power matrix, although they nearly always abstained from challenging the king's right to his womenfolk. A woman whom the king wanted to keep or transfer was virtually sacrosanct to the missionary – much to his distress, at times. See Wangemann, *Lebensbilder*, 167–83.

65 Ibid., 228–9.

and her grandson Abraham, both of them labour migrants returning from the South African interior, told her about Christianity. Mampatshe remained sceptical and did not add 'her generational support' to the bond between the representatives of the family's two younger generations. Wangemann stresses the farsightedness of her reluctance. He did not approve of these ordinary young men's prayer unions, probably because in his eyes they lacked the guidance of a religiously or morally advanced person.[66] Abraham and Nicodemus also serve as counterpoints to the four noble converts whose stories are detailed in the initial chapters. Mampatshe's son and grandson were critical of existing power hierarchies, and temporarily hid from the king after being suspected of having spoken out against him. Their prayer unions were modelled on the Pietist conventicles against which the state had taken harsh police action in the mission director's Prussian homeland. No explicit link, however, is made between these meetings and the 'secretive' gatherings of African religious groupings or *dingaka*, a motif which captured the imagination of later generations of missionary writers who then tried to penetrate the 'secretive' worlds of African healers and seers. Later in life, Mampatshe had her name written into the book for baptismal classes jointly with her husband. But because he left his aging wife for a younger second one, he virtually wrote himself out of the (family) picture. The narrative makes no further reference to him. Because of pressure from King Sekhukhune on the newly Christian families, Mampatshe's family moved to Lydenburg, outside the Pedi Kingdom. The aging Mampatshe herself was unable to follow them, as the journey was physically too demanding for her.[67] The chapter describes in detail how members of the family converted and relapsed, received advice from the missionary and gradually adopted the message of Christianity. Some died as reliable Christians and 'first fruits' of the family. Thus Mampatshe's family remains in focus, but the account makes clear that they also continued to be an unreliable lot.

The important turning point came when the family decided to fetch Mampatshe from the Pedi Kingdom. Mampatshe's envisaged reunion with her Christian kin, however, also implied her separation from the authority of the king, to whom she was also related. Mampatshe was one of King Sekhukhune's 'aunts', meaning that she was one of his mother's cousins. She was considered a close relative since she sent him beer regularly, and he in turn respectfully addressed her as 'mother'.[68] At first it was opined that if Mampatshe's Christian kin fetched her from the kingdom, this would be interpreted as 'the Lydenburg Christians stealing Sekhukhune's mother'.[69] But the predicted conflict did not ensue.

66 Ibid., 230.

67 Ibid., 237–40.

68 Ibid., 242.

69 Ibid., 242.

Instead, it seems as if, by taking Mampatshe to Lydenburg, Sekhukhune was also written out of her life. This can be read as Mampatshe's major conversion: her loyalty was transferred, without provoking too much friction, from a previous alliance to the Pedi king to a new grid of converted kin. The family regrouped around Mampatshe rather than an ancestral couple or a missionary. Thus the family as a whole achieved stability. Mampatshe became their anchor, not just metaphorically, but also biographically, emotionally and morally. She was finally baptised since the entire congregation, in agreement with the missionary, decided that she deserved this initiation, despite what was perceived as her weak cognitive understanding of the divine. Wangemann relates what he had heard from his missionary in the field:

> Afterwards there was a gathering of the congregation, in which Br. Nachtigal wished to hear the opinion of the members about each of the catechumens who was supposed to take part in the next baptism. This is a widespread and laudable custom in our mission; for the blacks generally know each other better than the missionary does, and the advice of the congregation of the faithful is therefore most welcome to him. Among the baptizands was also old Mampatshe. The kindly old woman could not learn much with her weak mental powers. But she had long since understood the one necessary thing; in her heart she believed in Lord Jesus as her only Saviour and Redeemer.[70]

At first Martha,[71] Mampatshe's daughter-in-law, the wife of her son Nicodemus, put in her vote saying, 'She wants to be baptised and says, when I pray I do it with pain; but I know that the Lord will summon me soon; and I do not know where I will go then'.[72] Jonas Pudumo, the leading convert and evangelist, fell in and backed up Martha's argument. He repeated that given Mampatshe's age and the likelihood of her imminent death, it was more important to baptise her now than to demand a sophisticated knowledge of Christianity. Dorkas, the former wife of another of Mampatshe's sons, Mankoane (Noah), who had divorced her upon his conversion,[73] joined in, stressing that as a mother, Mampatshe wished to go where her children would go one day. Noah confirmed

---

[70] Ibid., 248.

[71] Martha had the option of marrying a non-Christian for bridewealth. The missionary, Nachtigal, decided to compensate her father and paid bridewealth for one of his converts, Paulus, so that she married a Christian.

[72] Wangemann, *Lebensbilder*, 248.

[73] Dorkas's former husband kept the younger Lea as his wife, but the text offers little more information about her. Dorkas remained in the congregation and was the mother of four sons and daughters who all converted and who later fetched Mampatshe into their midst. I am grateful to Carolin Knoop, who traced these family connections in a seminar assignment as part of work for her master's degree.

his mother's constant yearning for baptism. The evangelist, Jonas, then challenged the consensus. He objected that when he had seen her on a previous occasion and asked whether there was anything she needed in order to prepare for death, Mampatshe had not expressed her wish fervently enough to him. But Dorkas and Martha interjected that the evangelist's words had been too complicated for Mampatshe to understand. Finally, Andries, who seems not to have been related to Mampatshe, made the point that 'she seeks the Lord' and 'we all know that'. Thus the narrative concludes: '*Item* the decision of the congregation was: Mampatshe may receive baptism'.[74] On 21 November 1869 she wore the baptismal dress that her granddaughter Maria Ngoanankaneng[75] had worn at her baptism some three years previously on 5 August 1866, and which her son's mother-in-law, Sarah Mochole, had worn on 13 April 1868.[76] The mention of precise dates gives the appearance of the creation of a new chronology of life, or even a genealogy, through these women's successive conversions at which they all wore the same dress.[77]

Mampatshe did not figure as a powerful matron, but rather as a daughter-turned-mother-turned-grandmother (as well as an unjustly rebuked wife and later a peacefully disconnected 'aunt') whose very ways of being, seeing and doing things depended on not causing conflict and imbalance, as well as on the support she received from a grid of kin. Breaking away from the king and losing her family to the Christian setting in Lydenburg could have turned her into something like an outcast, but she regained her dignity, humanity and personhood by being an acknowledged member of the kinship group and by participating, through them, in Christian community activities. Her kin, in turn, were not whole and religiously healthy as long as their mother was absent. She behaved like many of the 'grandmothers' that the missionaries liked to set up as role models in other narratives as well – grandmothers who were respected and who made their own decisions, who served as examples of virtue and industriousness to younger women and who took care of children, mainly the sons of their sons and daughters or of the daughters of missionaries.[78]

---

74 Wangemann, *Lebensbilder*, 249.

75 Maria Ngoanankaneng bore the name of her great-grandmother Ngoanankaneng, who was Mampatshe's mother. Unfortunately I am not aware of any analysis of Pedi naming practices.

76 Wangemann, *Lebensbilder*, 251.

77 'The dress' was an important signifier of conversion. See Delius, *The Conversion*. This book is about the conversion of Rooizak, a migrant convicted of murder whom the missionary Nachtigal, with the aid of Jonas Podumo, converted in his prison cell before he was hanged.

78 Chr. Sonntag, *Anna Moschabelo* (Berlin: Buchhandlung der Berliner evangelischen Missionsgesellschaft, 1914).

It has been argued for the 'neighbouring' Hananwa and Venda that when converting, royal women were concerned about power, especially as in some societies they often participated in the exercise of power and jurisdiction. They were therefore critical of conversion and suspicious of missionaries' claims to prerogatives.[79] This accounts for Pedi royal wives as well, who could attain a certain measure of power. They tended their own gardens and moved between places, often rather independently. Through conversion, such royal women, who did not necessarily have to be 'wives', altered their range of movement and renegotiated the boundaries as they attached themselves to the mission station, often after having lost their gardens. Less is known about ordinary wives and women. Again, it has been argued for the Hananwa and Venda that when converting, ordinary women managed resources to their own advantage, particularly for keeping their families together. In this sense, Christianity was an additional resource, but not necessarily a sustainable one. As long as Christianity was not established in the region they were usually careful not to embrace that fragile structure too unambiguously.[80] Moreover, menopausal women like Mampatshe tended to be vulnerable in their own way. Mission reports sometimes mention 'abandoned' old women who tried to attach themselves to mission stations. From the logic of the narrative, Mampatshe's story describes a pattern through which conversion and religious change filtered into the very roots of a society. Christianity was not transmitted between people of different classes or ranks. It was also not a means of strengthening ethnic consciousness. Last but not least, Christianity was not passed from the missionary, who in this case remained a virtual onlooker, to the African converts. In this story, the new religion oscillated back and forth between members of a group related by kinship ties. And it was through this group as a whole that Christianity became anchored in the South African setting. In fact, the very term 'first fruit' can be read as the baptism of individuals tied to others by kinship. No individual was baptised who did not try to safeguard his position by inviting kin into the orbit of conversion. Unlike Hanna Sewaitsheng, Ruth Mampatshe did not forget her name.[81] In contrast to Hanna, who was lost and virtually 'disappeared' into pagan non-existence and non-civilisation, Mampatshe retained her name, and thus her features as an individual. She was endowed with humanity, culture and history.

Of the array of studies on mission, conversion and religious change in South Africa, only a few have touched upon the relevance of kinship. The few studies on conversion and religious change in South Africa that do treat the relevance of

---

79 Lize Kriel and Alan Kirkaldy, '"Praying is the Work of Men, Not the Work of Women": The Response of Bahananwa and Vhavhenda Women to Conversion in Late Nineteenth-Century Missionary Territories', *South African Historical Journal* 61, 2 (2009): 316–35.

80 Ibid.

81 Wangemann, *Lebensbilder*, 249.

family and kinship are based on quantitative data rather than narrative sources.[82] They focus on elite families and their emergence, over generations, as promoters of nationalist politics.[83] Probably the most interesting work on the connection between kinship and conversion is that of Elizabeth Elbourne. She argues that kinship networks are wider, more flexible and more appropriate as an analytical category than a narrow or bounded focus on ethnicity or a geographically defined region such as – in her case – the Cape Colony.[84] Elbourne traces the dynamics of conversion between people tied by blood, such as whites and former slaves (even though these ties naturally often went unrecognised). And she follows conversion trails that opened up as a result of the migrating individuals' strong links with Griqua communities on the *highveld*, and shows how people consciously subverted imposed ethnic boundaries by conversion among groups related in this way. The *Lebensbilder* are extraordinary in a different way. These texts explain conversion as a family process, one in which the social practices, resistances and interests of 'ordinary' families intersected with those who aspired to elite status. As the close reading of the two chapters shows, it also explains conversion as a family process that created chronology, genealogy and perhaps even history. In this respect, the *Lebensbilder* open up a further perspective on conversion and religious change in southern Africa, further differentiating a well-documented process in which many questions remain to be answered.

The *Lebensbilder* detail women's lives and conversions to an astonishing degree. This by no means excludes gender hierarchies, but does not particularly emphasise them either, since it was also within women's power to help create the rooted Christian congregation that was emerging in South Africa. In contrast to what we saw in Chapter 2, it is evident that a coherent narrative such as that provided in the *Lebensbilder* firmly embeds women in the stories. The narratives in Chapter 2 are marked by the fractured nature of the converts' stories, which the *Lebensbilder* merely gloss over. In that regard, the *Lebensbilder* also tell the story of how a religion was able to take root in a specific time and place despite resistance to conversion and lapses by those who did convert. Although he often focuses on individual characters, Wangemann describes family conversions that do not differ significantly from that of the Volks in Erfurt. In terms of its textual representation, the Volks' conversion was naturally rendered in a different style from accounts of the conversions of the Pedi families. An especially striking finding of the second study in this book, on the Wotjobaluk, is that elderly women who arrived at the mission were often viewed not as potential converts

[82] Mark Charles Bilbe, *Wupperthal: The Formation of a Community in South Africa 1830–1965* (Cologne: Rüdiger Köppe, 2009).

[83] Ranger, *Are We Not Also Men?*

[84] Elizabeth Elbourne, *Blood Ground: Colonialism, Missions, and the Contest for Christianity in the Cape Colony and Britain, 1799–1853* (Montreal: McGill Queens Univ. Press, 2002), 304–5.

to Christianity but rather as impediments to the missionaries' project. Perhaps the missionaries adopted a different approach to elderly women there, but it is also possible that the comportment of older women among the Pedi was more in keeping with the missionaries' notions of how grandmothers should behave. After all, both the Pedi grandmothers and the Berlin missionaries came from societies structured along hierarchical lines, which was not true of the Wotjobaluk.

Baptism, Prayer and Medicine

Across the *Lebensbilder* narratives, we find other conversion motifs that thematically link individual people's and families' affirmative responses to religious change. Through their selection of individual themes, the *Lebensbilder* rendered Pedi conversions plausible and coherent for a German audience. Baptism in particular represented a crucial ritual, and prayer a basic technique of communication, which confirmed individual people's religious experiences in the eyes of German readers, missionaries and African converts alike. The missionaries, overwhelmed by people's active search for conversion, noticed that migrants who were aware of the fact that Christianity 'is a big thing' had begun to disseminate substantial knowledge, and that, in fact, 'previous to the arrival of our missionaries, they [the migrants] had performed the most faithful and loyal services of St John [*Johannesdienste*, that is, amongst other activities, evangelising]'.[85] Prayers were accorded particular significance when assessing whether a person was 'sufficiently advanced' to receive baptism. 'Kia chu kolobetsha Ruth Mampatshe ka leina la modimo tate le la Moroa le la Moea omokchethoa (I baptise you, Ruth Mampatshe, in the name of God the Father, the Son and the Holy Spirit)'.[86] Particularly in this early phase of the religious encounter, when formal schooling and mission classes had not yet been instituted, prayer and baptism both mattered greatly. As indicators of local political strategies, they voiced messages of power and social connection in a world of colonial entanglement.

Many of the descriptions of baptism in the *Lebensbilder* collection were clad in Pietist rhetoric, which translated the experience and meaning of conversion into images familiar to the religiously inclined readers among the Berlin Mission Society's donor constituency. 'Thus she abjured the devil, his nature and his

[85] Wangemann, *Lebensbilder*, 8, 30. *Johannesdienste* in fact referred to an array of activities in addition to evangelising. The term described the calling of people to repentance and acting, as John did, more generally to prepare and pave the way for the coming of Jesus. Strikingly in the colonial context, it did not refer to Africans actually baptising other Africans even though baptisms were what John was famous for.

[86] Ibid., 250.

works',[87] or 'His soul thirsted for a sip from the water of life'[88] were phrases describing the conversion experience that were regularly attributed to Africans, but modelled on the cultural expressions of people who had undergone spiritual awakening elsewhere in the world. Such language may even have represented direct repetitions of phrases that converts had to speak at baptismal ceremonies. 'The Holy Spirit had just now ignited a fire' explained the setting of religious revival that was deemed favourable for conversions.[89] Individuals were also said to go through 'the bath of rebirth'.[90] Such phrases suggested an enthusiastic yet outside view of conversion experiences rather than the words converts themselves might have used to describe their decision. In fact, the mission director, missionaries and readers alike accorded great seriousness and authenticity to those conversions. African conversions were not to be taken lightly, and they were anything but marginal.

Another set of formulations, however, hinted at African understandings of conversion and the negotiation processes that went along with it. Upon his death, Letuchu, the father of Josef Kathedi, wished to be laid to rest with the *badimo*, the ancestors of the family. He commented upon his son's conversion as a rupture of ties: 'I no longer have a child. – You are killing me'.[91] This was a strong expression of how one man's decision and social action had not only caused harm, but actually robbed his father of his life and life force. More elaborate renderings of people's interpretations of the baptism of their loved ones came from the missionaries of the Hermannsburg Mission Society, which operated among the Tswana people in the immediate vicinity of the Pedi Kingdom. The Hermannsburg missionaries recorded, for instance, that fathers were opposed to the baptism of their daughters. They threatened to 'poison'[92] them as their daughters 'would be dead [to them] if they learnt and went for baptism'.[93] Conversion implied a severe disassociation and a loss of wealth and power to those from whom the converts distanced themselves.

Frequently, conversion and the ritual of baptism were understood as processes manipulated by powerful substances and, in turn, ones that had to be

87 Ibid., 19.

88 Ibid., 75.

89 Ibid., 71.

90 Ibid., 108.

91 Ibid., 77–8.

92 That is, to give them manipulative substances – all the translations are culturally highly charged. Medicine refers to substances which can be applied to both good and bad ends. Depending on how people interpreted them, how missionaries interpreted them, they spoke of poison. Significantly, they could be either harmful or healing, depending on who controlled them.

93 Archive of the Evangelisch-Lutherisches Missionswerk, Hermannsburg (ELM), A: S. A. 42–2 a Berseba, C.H. Backeberg, 14 January 1876.

countered, and healed, by the administration of other manipulative substances. Thus missionaries, Christians, other village residents and, if things went well, a member of the chiefly lineage, had to work out a collaborative approach to control the new ritual. As a missionary noted in 1868:

> When it became known among the people that a child was to be baptised, many came out of curiosity, who did not otherwise attend services, in order to watch the christening. For the belief has spread among the heathens that we mix the baptismal water with the brain of a dead person, and thereby work magic upon the baptizand, so that he may not return to heathenism. In order to remove this superstition from their minds, I had Makepan's wife bring me a pot of water, and before everyone's eyes I drew the baptismal water from there, whereupon all of them looked surprised, and afterwards they said publicly that what they had heard of the baptismal water before had been lies, for now they had seen with their own eyes that I used only pure water.[94]

The metaphor of the 'pure water' that this missionary used resonated peculiarly with the idealisation of baptism as 'thirsting for the water of life' mentioned by Wangemann in the *Lebensbilder*. In the South African case, however, the missionary was thought to use manipulative substances for baptism. People were also suspicious because Christianity brought with it foreign spirits, which needed to be integrated into, and harmonised with, the existing local universe of spiritual forces. Again, it is important to note that the baptism of a convert did not only establish relations between the missionary and the convert. It also created a relationship between the missionary, those who had not yet converted, the chief's family and the person newly initiated into Christianity. For conversion to become accepted in the vicinity, the ritual of baptism had to be placed in the hands, eyes and mouths of many people who together engaged in redefining notions of spiritual beings and the powers of the ancestors. It has often been argued that becoming a Christian entailed accommodating an older religious world in new guises. In this early phase, however, it seems from the responses of converts and their social networks to the possibility of conversion that conversion was clearly understood as a complete reorientation of life and social action. This rupture would only work if broader segments of the village or chiefdom participated in this event. It is unclear, however, how exactly converts broke old ties, and whether only particular social relationships were threatened.

---

[94] ELM, A: S.A. 42–26 a Cuane/ Mosetla, Backeberg, 11 July 1868. The missionary also recorded similar debates later in his evangelical career when people still believed that missionaries kept potentially harmful substances hidden in the broad sleeves of their vestments, ELM, A: S. A. 42–2 a Berseba, C.H. Backeberg 17 January 1874.

In his narrative, Wangemann describes how, prior to the arrival of the missionaries, people had assembled in a number of prayer unions or communities (*Gebetsgemeinden*).[95] Again, this is an indicator of how seriously the narrative took converts' gatherings, because likening them to these interdenominational and even transnational prayer communities was intended to resonate with readers rather than to connect African converts with the outside world. African converts were probably not even aware of this institution.

For the Pedi people, perhaps more importantly, prayers were a means to communicate directly with the divine. The divine, in turn, comprised various spiritual powers, both afflicting and appeasing. Kathedi, for instance, had talked to Mantladi about the new form of communication: 'We heard that people lose their mind when they pray and that the devil[96] will arrive among them'.[97] Again it is a pity that we do not know what exactly it was that people were thought to lose. Could it have been their sanity? Or simply their ancestral spirits, which would then have to be replaced by other spiritual forces? Conversion entailed quite a crucial reorientation as in general spirits could be at once good and evil, and it was up to the living to make them behave and interact with the living in one way or the other. Christianity was different. God was conceptualised as

---

[95] The very image of the 'Gebetsgemeinde' (prayer union) indicated how the missionaries imagined the broadening and creation of the universal community. Namely: Different Christian 'Gebetsgemeinden' were established as 'invented global circles' all over the world. Their members prayed for the unity of all Christians, be they in Japan, Brazil, on the Mauritius Islands, in Cameroon, Tunis, or China. In fact, the movement spread to Greece, Sweden, and the United States. See Manfred Fleischer, *Katholische und lutherische Ireniker* (Göttingen, Frankfurt/ Main, and Zurich, 1968), 192–198; and also M. Fleischer, 'Lutheran and Catholic Reunionists in the Age of Bismarck', *Church History* 38 (1969): 43–66.

[96] The Devil, so prominent in Christian thinking, has no immediate equivalent in African religion(s). It is probable that here, as in other societies, the word 'devil' was actually used to translate the ancestors, *badimo* and their spirits. *Badimo* could act as both evil and supportive forces. The missionaries' translation changed this concept and *badimo* became associated with major evil forces that were difficult to subdue (which living men could resist but not banish altogether). For the Ewe context in current Ghana, see Birgit Meyer, *Translating the Devil: Religion and Modernity Among the Ewe in Ghana* (Edinburgh: Edinburgh Univ. Press, 1999). Although the dynamics in South Africa were nowhere near as dramatic as among the Ewe (among whom many more Pentecostal churches flourish today, while in South Africa the African Independent Churches remain prominent). For more perspective, see Peter Delius, 'Witches and Missionaries in Nineteenth-Century Transvaal', *Journal of Southern African Studies* 27, 3 (2001): 429–43. The text explains that *badimo* represented higher spiritual beings, 'demons or spirits of the dead, who haunt the living and engage in all manner of evil' (p. 49). It also mentions 'seatane' (p. 51). We have no manuscripts that might tell us how these notions were referred to in the original.

[97] Wangemann, *Lebensbilder*, 31.

good and the devil as an evil force. Josef Kathedi, whose thoughts Wangemann narrated in some depth, was not at ease with the idea that there was said to be one *modimo*,[98] and maintained that 'there was equally a satan, and satan would be the *baas* (the more powerful of the two)'.[99] People who prayed left themselves doubly vulnerable. First, they chose not to address the *badimo* anymore, and thus risked their anger. Second, they made themselves available to a completely new evil force that the new religion brought with it, without knowing exactly, or from experience, how to control it. Mantladi had calmed Kathedi's suspicions by countering this anxiety when he explained that even though the devils, or evil forces, would come on the fifth day, it was possible to pray them away.[100] He thus advocated prayer as a technique that, while rendering people vulnerable in the first instance, would remedy the situation and – provided they were persistent – offer assistance with the new danger they faced.

Many African societies emphasised the necessity of maintaining prosperity, fertility and power – and searched for the means to cast out the evil forces that permanently threatened these achievements. In these negotiations over the meaning of prayer, the Bible itself became a medium that facilitated communication with the divine. The act of reading materialised as empowerment through the 'medicine' of the book. Mantladi, who had eased Kathedi's mind and who himself could not read well, had previously spoken to the local missionary while reading a page in a book, and noted with astonishment that 'the knowledge and wisdom of the teacher seems ever so big. He [the missionary] must have devoured a good deal of medicine, which now allowed him to know all things'. Back with his father, the sceptical Letuchu, Kathedi explained that prayer was unique because ritual intermediaries such as *dingaka*[101] (who by the way had to be paid whereas this was not the case for missionaries) were no longer needed.

> 'My father, if you wish to come to the lord, you must pray faithfully and believe the word'. 'Have you ever heard God speaking yourself, then?' 'Yes, my father. When I go to Martinus, he reads from the word of God and then God himself speaks to me'.[102]

---

98 In theological discussions between missionaries and Africans, the creator god, *modimo*, who had withdrawn after creating the world, was reactivated when missionaries constantly asked whether the Tswana people did not have a proper High God. In which ways *modimo* had been a 'High God' before that ongoing conversation is difficult to determine.

99 Wangemann, *Lebensbilder*, 71.

100 Ibid., 31.

101 *Dingaka* were ritual specialists who commanded a knowledge of health and knew how to control destructive powers. People needed their expertise to protect themselves against affliction. Christianity seemed to offer a strategy of achieving protection without these intermediaries.

102 Wangemann, *Lebensbilder*, 77.

It posed a problem for many Africans' conception of the divine that the gods did not speak in the context of Christianity, but instead seemed to manifest themselves in writing, an alien act of communication that, moreover, had occurred not recently, but a long time before. Kathedi's was a story of immediate connection to the divine, and suggested a technique for diminishing the role of religious intermediaries (though perhaps not their power). Martinus Sewúshan, the powerful seer and gunsmith, however, knew how to recast his role as a reader of the word as long as the Pedi were unable to read the book themselves but wanted to use it nonetheless.

These negotiations of conversion and religious change as manifested in conversations about baptism, prayer and medicine had implications for power and social connection. King Sekhukhune had tried to use the missionaries' power of prayer when he asked them to make rain. And indeed, at times they, who had had to struggle for acceptance from the royal power, were able to prove their powers and the power of their God by praying for rain.[103] But according to the will of Sekhukhune, the missionaries were essentially there to teach rather than to make rain. In their quest for acceptance by the royal authority, the missionaries remained focused on the king and reluctant to empower rival rulers.

The administration of medicines empowered others, such as the king or ritual specialists. In contrast to these men or the culturally comparatively open missionaries, the new, emerging elite radically disassociated themselves from the administration of medicine and manipulative substances. After converting they refused even to participate in important rituals in which fortifying medicines were administered to protect the polity. When the old king, Sekwati, had died in 1861, Kathedi had already refused to join the mourning ceremony, believing it to be incompatible with Christian ways.[104] The people around him understood this attitude as indicative of Christians more generally who, they believed, now kept a range of powerful substances to themselves, and refused to share their knowledge and power with them any more. Kathedi and other Christians also declined to participate in ceremonies in which weapons were fortified. Thus they violated not only the authority of a royal command, but also an age-old strategy for gathering strength against the military foe.[105] A considerable degree of tension built up. People felt endangered, and the converts tried to tackle the problem by bringing the king over to their side. At the same time, they remained obstinate, and advocated an alternative (source of) power rather than enlarging its scope. Dinkoanyane, the youngest of the royal sons, for whom conversion was far easier and more promising than it was for those who stood to succeed to the throne, strictly held that 'The power of the believers is not based on sorcery

[103] Ibid., 140, 135.

[104] Ibid., 75.

[105] Ibid., 154.

and medicine. When we fight we ask God to send us power'.[106] He obviously had to argue hard for this conceptual distinction. Dinkoanyane had already assigned himself to protect Sewúshan even before the option of conversion to Christianity existed. Their alliance continued into the new era, when both of them decided to become Christians. With Dinkoanyane and Sewúshan, two men who had once been *dingaka* withheld their power from further protecting the Pedi polity.[107] They now advocated a new and independent source of power and authority. The king had tried to discipline the two men. The story went that he had sent an execution commando to kill them. When the commando arrived, however, the two men had started to read aloud from the Book. Apparently, this threatened the men in the commando to such a degree that they instantly fled the scene.[108] Whatever the factual value of this story, it reinforced the idea that Sewúshan and Dinkoanyane held the power to frighten away others. Later, on Botšabelo, Dinkoanyane became a crucial leader who commanded his own followers.[109]

Mampuru, the brother whose claims to political authority Sekhukhune had managed to push aside, had many reasons to bolster his power against his rival. Christianity promised to assist him in controlling the powers at work in the Pedi Kingdom, and thus in adding to his authority. He himself was, of course, unable to convert, as this would have disrupted the alliances he had cultivated, and would have to cultivate in future, with other leaders via matrimonial bonds. Mampuru tried hard, but ultimately to no avail, to enlist the missionaries' support for his claim to power. Like his brother Dinkoanyane, Mampuru had once been fortified and protected by Sewúshan's powers. But the former seer-gunsmith turned Christian and refused to provide medicines to him or to any other non-Christian Pedi. Here conversion, as manifested in baptisms and prayer,

---

106 Ibid., 155.

107 Ibid., 56. This attitude remained essentially unchanged. Even in the 1880s and 1890s, the local missionary was aghast at how obstinately the new elite refused to allow old practices for dealing with affliction, while the missionary himself tried to incorporate 'African' features into the expression of Christianity!

108 Ibid., 146. For similar scenarios in Zulu conversions, see Kirsten Rüther, 'Imminent Colonialism: Violence on Lutheran Mission Stations and the Ending of the Pre-Colonial Zulu State', in *Development, Modernism and Modernity in Africa*, ed. Augustine Agwuele (London: Routledge, 2012), 278–93.

109 Over the years a rivalry developed between him and the missionaries, who also aspired to chiefly power. In 1871, when the *Lebensbilder* were published, Dinkoanyane and some three hundred of his followers broke away from Botšabelo to establish their own settlement (which was located in a mountainous retreat where also the Boer regime would be unable to exact taxes). They lived as a Christian community even though no missionary was prepared to serve them. In 1876 the community was defeated militarily and crushed by the Boers.

clearly assumed a political significance. Authorities with claims to local power used these techniques and rituals as political strategies. In order to maintain a position at the top of the political hierarchy, Sekhukhune needed to control not just his councillors and *dingaka*, but the missionaries as well. His subjects and some of his royal brothers, however, withdrew. They made it clear that they were forming their own centres of power, connecting to the divine and its protective substances, and gathering their own followers. In the early 1860s, this strategy, which was a well known one in Sotho, Tswana and Pedi politics, unsettled the already fragile power balance in the Pedi Kingdom. By allowing Christianity into their polities, rulers could manoeuvre themselves into a position to bolster and reinforce their authority – as long as they commanded the new power and the community of those who held it. More generally, however, the meaning of the teachings and trappings of Christianity was changing at this time. What had once been regarded as 'relatively benign curiosities that might be employed in some way for the benefit of their communities' came to be 'appropriate[d] ... as a supplemental source of politico-religious authority'.[110]

Mampuru's authority also suffered a severe blow when he lost Tlakale, a woman who had been given in marriage to his father, Sekwati, and whom his father had handed on during his lifetime to his favourite son, Mampuru.[111] When Sekhukhune managed to sideline Mampuru's claim he ordered Tlakale to return to his own royal household. After all, she was a symbol and a token of the alliances between men and families in power. Sekhukhune promised to pay significant bridewealth, which had not yet been transferred from Sekwati to Tlakale's family, and raised her status considerably over that of many of the other royal wives. Tlakale's daughter was assigned to the care of Tlakale's mother. Her father was himself interested in the power of Christianity, but wished at the same time to maintain the bonds of loyalty to the Pedi ruler. After initially toying with Christianity, he stepped back from his experiment so as not to endanger his ties with Sekhukhune. His daughter, however, was less subservient to both her father and her husband, and was considering how to raise her own status (or perhaps the status of her family?). As it is portrayed in the narrative, her continued interest in Christianity angered Sekhukhune and he sent her back to her family, retreating from his earlier promise concerning the bridewealth. Tlakale's father was eager to reconcile with Sekhukhune, and wanted him to reintegrate Tlakale into the royal household. Back at the royal court she cultivated an alliance with Dinkoanyane's wife Maria, and Mankubo,

---

110 Stephen Volz, 'Them Who Kill the Body: Christian Ideals and Political Realities in the Interior of Southern Africa during the 1850s', *Journal of Southern African Studies* 36, 1 (2010): 41–56, quote p. 41.

111 Wangemann, *Lebensbilder*, 133.

the wife of Mampatshe's son Nicodemus.[112] When Sekhukhune began to enforce his instructions more strictly, it was another woman, Machlobo, mother of Jacob Makhoëtle, the hunter who accompanied Wangemann on his travels, who provided Tlakale with food.[113] In the end she converted against the king's will and was renamed Maria Magdalena. On her return she informed him: 'My king, I have been with the Word of God!'[114] She later left for Botšabelo. In 1866, she married another man of high rank, Sewúshan, the respectable preacher and former seer and gunsmith, who must have increased his power and prestige still further by means of this marriage.

The themes of baptism, prayer and medicine suggest that conversion meant renegotiating power in the political sense as well. While the conversion of families with 'ordinary' grandmothers became a conduit for Christianity to 'trickle down' into society, kinship alliances between those in power had to be resettled as well. The reshaping of power connections set the framework within which family conversions could take place or be inhibited.

Gaining Respectability in the Metropole by Supporting African Conversion

These were the conversion narratives that engendered a sense of respectability among readers back home in Germany. Wangemann's intention was to use emerging African Christianity to strengthen the 'church at home', since it was there that he perceived an urgent need to recast religious faith. In his biography, his biographer states Wangemann's words, 'That which was created in distant lands shall also be a blessing to and revitalise the church at home'.[115] It has been argued that the making of a bourgeois world would have been unthinkable without empire. This particularly applies to the middle classes that were evolving in the context of colonially committed (nation) states. Missionaries were recruited from among these groups, which had ascended from their lowly status in the early nineteenth century into an emerging middle-class world that they were eager to shape. Their rise depended upon achieving conversions outside Europe, upon enlarging the world of Christianity and, through it, of civilisation. They were caught in the ambivalence or 'tensions of empire' as others have termed it, since their opportunities for social mobility were far more limited at home.

---

[112] Ibid., 165–8. Maria was the former Molate, wife of Dinkoanyane, baptised on 25 June 1865, p. 148.

[113] Ibid., 176.

[114] Ibid., 175.

[115] Hermann Petrich, *Hermann Theodor Wangemann: Sein Leben und Wirken für Gottes Reich und für das Missionswerk insonderheit* (Berlin: Buchhandlung der Berliner evangelischen Missionsgesellschaft, 1895), 33.

The involvement of middle-class circles in the German colonial venture is thought to have been largely an affair of the 1870s and later. But there was an important prelude. Perhaps not the majority, but a sufficient number of bourgeois and entrepreneurial families were in fact open to religion. In more than just a few such families, religion strongly influenced their habitus. Although they themselves would never have become involved in missionary work or supported their own offspring's choice of such a career, many donated money, or read mission publications in order to give themselves an air of piety. Religion and piety simply bolstered their sense of frugality, hard work and discipline. The Berlin Mission Society itself was, of course, connected organisationally to an aristocratic rather than a merchant milieu. But they had many supporters among that class for whom African conversion came to function as the visible success of spreading Christianity, virtue and other values abroad.

The conversion stories from among the Pedi carried messages about religion and virtue into the world of the intended readership back home in Germany. In order to underline this, Wangemann consciously confronted his audience with the contrast between the numbness of their own spiritual life and the vibrancy of African Christianity. The 'heathenism' of Wangemann's and his readers' home country stemmed from its perceived modernism, the reduction of a once all-encompassing religious feeling to a 'rationalist' belief and theology that dominated the established churches.[116] Like other mission directors of his time, Wangemann campaigned for a version of Christianity that came from and targeted the heart, albeit not in the Pietist conventicles and other forms of religious organisation that the state authorities found so suspect. Promoting the mission cause by depicting African conversion, Wangemann aspired to a particular version of middle-class respectability, along with the religious distinction attached to a minority within the middle classes. This was a project in which he, the mission adepts and a broader segment of mission supporters also struggled for self-respect and recognition, however. Hence the meaning of African conversion was not negotiated in African surroundings alone. It linked Germans with other European powers, and also distinguished them from the British, who had their own notions of civilisation and humanitarianism.[117] In the 1850s and 1860s, supporters of the mission in Berlin became entangled in

---

[116] Thomas Nipperdey, *Religion im Umbruch: Deutschland 1870–1918* (Munich: Beck, 1988); Franz Schnabel, *Deutsche Geschichte im 19. Jahrhundert*. Vol. 4: *Die religiösen Kräfte* (München: dtv, 1951 [Freiburg i. Br.: Herder, 1937]). In fact, most 'histories' of Christianity in nineteenth-century Germany focus more on church and religion and less on the institutionally separate setting of foreign missions, as they were written by scholars with no interest in the mission enterprise. For an example of the recent reinvigoration of the field, see Habermas and Hölzl, *Mission global*.

[117] Andrew Porter, *Religion Versus Empire: British Protestant Missionaries and Overseas Expansion 1700–1914* (Manchester: Manchester University Press, 2004).

a web of global connections – not as the citizens of a colonial power, but rather as observers of how the British Empire expanded and laid out structures to be followed in one's own ways.

To help his German constituency in their quest for respectability, Wangemann needed African conversions which, in his narrative, differed significantly from the modern conversions portrayed in this volume's chapter on Protestant conversion to Catholicism. There, we learned that conversion narratives by Catholic converts also engaged critically with the current dynamics of society, the church and religion in the nineteenth-century German territories. But converts and writers consciously claimed rationality, scholarship and education for themselves. Although in South Africa people understood conversion as a means of engaging with a world in motion and giving a new impetus to their societies, Wangemann portrayed African conversions as repetitions of old Christian developments in a world opened up by settler expansion and looming British colonialism. He reminded his constituency of Christianity's early expression and founding traditions in the hope of providing the nation, in both Germany and the Pedi Kingdom, with a religious legend. By describing distant worlds, Wangemann created a mirror with the aid of which readers in Germany could question and probe their own virtue and beliefs and the Berlin Mission Society could promote its own image. African conversions as rendered in the *Lebensbilder* collection legitimated ongoing mission activity and promised a kind of retreat from modernity and its implications. As long as mission supporters engaged with these surroundings, they would also be able to set themselves apart from the modernisation of the religious climate back home.[118]

Regular readers of the Berlin Mission's offerings could choose from among a range of publications, of which the portraits of African converts were but one. The main characters in the *Lebensbilder* had already featured in the monthly mission journal, the *Berliner Missionsberichte*, originally launched under the somewhat complicated title *Missions-Berichte der Gesellschaft zur Beförderung der evangelischen Missionen unter den Heiden*. The *Lebensbilder* collection now tried to attract new readers (and possibly donors) and was, as we have seen, intended to serve local pastors who supported the work of the mission as instructional material for the schools. The regular consumers of Berlin Mission publications may have been familiar with Wangemann's South African travel account, *Ein Reisejahr in Südafrika*, which had been published in 1868.[119] They

[118] Volk was also interested in the Australian settlers' religious development. They seemed to have provided him with a point of orientation, a foil against which he could reflect on and imagine his own conversion. It was most certainly not circumscribed by national borders. Wangemann and the constituency for which he wrote also needed this 'outside' in order to look back at the inner condition of religious life at home in Germany.

[119] Hermann Theodor Wangemann, *Ein Reise-Jahr in Süd-Afrika: Ausführliches Tagebuch über eine in den Jahren 1866 und 1867 ausgeführte Inspectionsreise durch die Missions-Gebiete*

may also have read *Maléo und Sekukúni*, a narrative of two African leaders, one of whom subscribed to the mission cause, the other one hostile to it, and published in 1869.[120] Only wealthy readers are likely to have purchased the early volumes of the first comprehensive mission history, which began to appear in 1872.[121] But it is naturally possible that readers of the Berlin Mission publications also consumed the products of other mission societies' engagement in the world, or those that dealt with explorations and discoveries beyond Europe. The array of mission publications was broad and, as popular reading matter, they targeted a wide audience.

Wangemann makes a crucial statement at the beginning of his text, dedicating the book to 'His Excellency the Privy Councilor and Vice President of the Royal-Imperial Supreme Court in Berlin Dr. jur. Heinrich Moritz von Rohr on the occasion of his ... fiftieth anniversary in office',[122] thus self-confidently asserting the Berlin Mission's connection to the bureaucratic elite.[123] This represents, of course, a claim to respectability. The connection to von Rohr embodies the claim that this religiously inclined segment of the (upper) middle classes associated with, or reached into, those segments of the bourgeoisie that were indeed politically influential, of lower aristocratic origin and probably wealthy.

A number of direct appeals to the audience turn the text into a communication of African conversion stories to German readers whom the author hoped would engage with, think about and reflect upon their own state of mind and outward conduct as Christians. Many of these interpellations are of a pedagogical nature and could be read as school assignments after the narration of a certain part of an African convert's life. Others, however, encouraged deeper reflection and could at times even be read as critiques of the religious and civilisatory state of society. Comparing the suffering of Mantladi with the martyrdom of the Smyrna Christian Polycarp, Wangemann shames the 'dear reader' and asks how he might feel 'if you compare the strength of your own faith with that of this man who, born and bred in heathendom, had been a heathen just four years previously?'[124]

der Berliner Missions-Gesellschaft (Berlin: Verlag des Missionhauses in Berlin, 1868).

120 Hermann Theodor Wangemann, *Maléo und Sekukuni: Ein Lebensbild aus Südafrika* (Berlin: Buchhandlung der Berliner evangelischen Missionsgesellschaft, 1868–69).

121 Hermann Theodor Wangemann, *Geschichte der Berliner Missiongesellschaft und ihrer Arbeiten in Südafrika*. 4 vols. (Berlin: Selbstverlag des ev. Missionshauses, 1872–1877).

122 Wangemann, *Lebensbilder*, between title page and preface. He had been a member of the Comité since 1844.

123 In fact, the Comité representatives were drawn from the respectable and often noble circles of Pietist and Berlin society, while rank and file missionaries were of much humbler origins. This was the rule for other mission societies as well; see, for example, Jon Miller, *The Social Control of Religious Zeal: A Study of Organizational Contradictions* (New Brunswick, NJ: Eerdmans, 1994).

124 Wangemann, *Lebensbilder*, 40.

The reader is also asked to compare himself to Sewúshan as a religious model, since he, who had once been a seer and a sorcerer (*Zauberer*), had turned into a staunch and unwavering believer who after his conversion preferred to face death rather than retreat from his newly acquired belief.[125] Clearly, this textual device, which Wangemann employs deliberately throughout the text, is woven into the narrative to remind readers of their own religious and cultural origins. Reading about Africans was like looking back at their own roots. It seemed as if the history of Christianity was repeating itself in the Pedi Kingdom, albeit in simplified form. For Christians attached to the Berlin Mission Society who despaired of the modern world, these episodes offered an escape from the complications they faced in their own social environment. It was like a new start. Rather than representing a belated entry, African converts embodied something innocent and noble that readers in Germany were on the brink of losing, or had already lost.

In a series of comparisons, Wangemann reminds his readers that the conversions he had witnessed were of a high moral standard, a standard seldom matched back in Germany.

> Alas, it is frequently no different among Christians. When someone is granted God's grace, his non-believing friends and relations raise a great lament and believe that the poor man has now been turned around, and they undertake diversions, presentations and pleadings in order to bring him back to the right path, to return him to the way of the flesh, the world and destruction. For just as the heathens feel that their countryman, who has converted, has been lost to their former community in recklessness and sin, and therefore regard every convert as lost to them, the same applies in this regard to the white worldlings of old Christendom.[126]

Of course, all this was very much in the mode of the noble savage.[127] But there was also a thread of admiration as well as admonition to decadent contemporaries in his own country. Wangemann also comments on the medieval legacy of the transfer of power, title and office at the death of a king. When he describes the succession dispute that had taken place between Sekwati and his three sons, he concludes for his German readers:

---

125 Ibid., 64.

126 Ibid., 17.

127 Patrick Brantlinger, 'Victorians and Africans: The Genealogy of the Myth of the Dark Continent', in *'Race', Writing, and Difference*, ed. Henry Louis Gates, Jr. (Chicago: Univ. of Chicago Press, 1985), 185–222.

> The fools who mock the term 'by divine right' know not what they do. For if we did not have hereditary kings by divine right, anointed by the Lord's mercy, we would experience more terrible atrocities and horrors in our lands, such as we have seen among the heathen. But who believes that?[128]

At first, Wangemann describes a disorderly succession process in Africa where nobody expected rules (and where missions and colonisers aspired to impose order). Towards the end of the story, however, he criticises secularisation and democratic tendencies, positing instead the rediscovery of the paradigm of the divine right of kings. The reference to a medieval institution, religious in its legitimation of power, represents a rhetorical device that appeared in German public discourse and the press more generally. People in mid-nineteenth-century Germany, a nation watching colonialism without colonies of its own, particularly liked to stress their medieval historical roots and used this consciousness to compensate for the lack of colonies.[129] Wangemann's point was a different one, however. He turned the argument of German or European civilisation upside down, stressing that if Germans had started out where the Africans were now, they would have fared still worse. This was a statement that promised that the Pedi, once incorporated into the realm of Christianity, and with the assistance of the Berlin Mission Society, would, perhaps, evolve even more favourably than Germans or Europeans. And perhaps more quickly.

Wangemann also lashes out at the 'faithless materialists' of his time, whom he confronts with the virtuous example of Makhoëtle:

> He never recalled having had any notion or concept of God or divine matters in his younger years. He was convinced that heaven and earth had always been there, and that man ceases to exist altogether once dead. Thus as a young man and a heathen he was already on the same level of cultivation as our highly learned, faithless materialists, in terms not of his reasoning but of the results of his investigations.[130]

In this statement he attacks those intellectuals who, in Wangemann's society, mocked religious people and looked down upon them with disdain. It is certainly no coincidence that these comparisons and reminders liken an emerging elite to prominent icons of early Christian history, and that the outstanding figures of Christianity among the Pedi are used to discredit a decadent elite in Germany. It must be conceded that, perhaps not surprisingly, a text such as Mampatshe's story lacks the textual devices that might have suggested direct linkages across

---

128 Wangemann, *Lebensbilder*, 131.

129 Fenske, 'Ungeduldige Zuschauer'.

130 Wangemann, *Lebensbilder*, 193–4.

continents and history. The direct comparisons link an emerging, thoroughly cultured yet religiously minor elite in South Africa with readers in the metropole who may have been cultured, but many of whom had moved away from the heartfelt Christianity that the mission was advocating. The virtuous grandmother was left to her own devices. Put another way, the comparisons connected an elite that had just been gifted with Christianity with a privileged population on the verge of losing it. Mampatshe's story, however, functions more immediately as a folk tale.

Conclusions

The spread of Christianity is often framed in terms of the multiplication of Christian churches and communities. And yet, particularly in the context of colonial and missionary encounters, it often makes sense to look at conversion and movement together, and to think of conversion and the conversation about it against the background of movement rather than in set frames. As this chapter has tried to emphasise, conversions often took place when established, and perhaps endangered, varieties of community came under threat. Only very gradually did they result in the making of new communities, congregations, in which rules and traditions could be identified as characteristic of these newly emerging Christian communities. The study of spreading Christianity and African conversion is also often linked to the frictions within, and over, Christian regimes in which, especially in the colonial context, Christians and converts from the colonised population were usually not accorded the same status and rank as Christians and missionaries (including their families) from the colonising societies. While it seems obvious that missionaries and their families represented links between the colony and the metropolitan setting 'in the colonising centre', this is far less clear for converts, even prominent ones. There has been a broad debate about their status as mediators, brokers and translators of Christianity. But scholars have not yet resolved the question of how these mediators and their activities were linked to the metropolitan centre.

This chapter ventures the suggestion that it was not only prominent Christians who were tied in some way or the other to the colonial metropole. It argues that African conversion more generally served as a resource through which the colonial centre underfed, remade and adjusted its middle-class self-conception and, in Berlin and the small towns and villages that supported the mission, fired the imagination of the colonial world. We would hardly go so far as to maintain that this connection was at the very heart of the evolution of nineteenth-century Germanness as Catherine Hall, for example, has argued for the Baptist mission in Jamaica and its impact in Birmingham and beyond.[131] Rather, the commitment of the Berlin Mission to its field of activity in South Africa reminded the emerging middle classes who read mission publications that there were other, competing, colonial empires reaching out to a world 'out there'. This chapter is also an effort to counterbalance Christopher Bayly's idea that the nineteenth century represented the emergence of 'empires of religion' in which the formal structures of theology were becoming more similar across the world.[132] In contrast, this chapter has focused on the men and women, families and polities that 'received' Christianity and developed attitudes and coping mechanisms in regard to this larger structure. For Africans, conversion represented a means of positioning themselves in their struggling, emerging or dissolving community – and hence in a world in motion.

Conceived against this background of movement and global connections, it was especially important for us to draw attention to the many ways in which women, especially married and elderly ones, committed themselves to, and engaged in, processes of conversion. It was they whose movement brought the balance of power between men and clan heads under stress. It was they who were considered to be the final link in achieving the lasting conversion of entire families. Thus this chapter has tried to argue for the importance of taking family networks as the units of analysis rather than concentrating on congregations and mission communities alone. Especially since 'families' represent an open concept, the story of religious change takes on a different quality when we focus on them than if, for instance, we look at how new religious groups took shape within churches or traditionally recognised religious institutions and structures. If we focus on families and kinship as the units of analysis, opportunities open up to see how converts and the people to whom they related moved geographically as well as in terms of social standing. At times, religion then served as a medium for achieving movement. At other times, religion itself became the framework within which notions of family, kinship and community were adjusted.

Converts, their families and kings recognised the power inherent to the new religion, of which they wished to command a share, provided they could reconcile it with their personal ambitions and the needs of their relations. A new power resided in Christianity, and hence, a promise in the act of conversion, to participate in knowledge and matters that came from afar and that, at the same time, reached back into some distant centre of colonial power that people in South Africa could hardly imagine in the 1850s and 1860s. Many of them were aware that adopting Christianity could be dangerous, as it undermined local power and knowledge. They found many ways to express that doubt – although not in

---

[131] Hall, *Civilising Subjects*.

[132] Christopher Alan Bayly, *The Birth of the Modern World 1780–1914: Global Connections and Comparisons* (Oxford: Blackwell, 2004), chap. 9.

learned theological treatises or within the context of resistance movements. More often they resorted to a language that referred to the vocabulary of medicine and other manipulative substances. It is up to us as historians to understand these expressions as peculiarly local and ethnographically informative details of the colonial encounter, or to discover in them reflections upon the tapestry of changing power and fortunes in more global terms.

Chapter 4
Reflections

Reflections in the Context of Thinking About Post-National and Post-Colonial Histories

Having taken our readers through three individual case studies, we would now like to use this chapter to explore more systematically and reflect in greater detail on some of the parallels, connections and contrasts between them. We maintain that this could only be done sensibly after taking the opportunity to explore the individual cases more deeply, since it was the details of those cases that opened our eyes for comparison and reflection. Hence in this chapter we will examine the individual cases and their areas of focus regarding conversion from the perspective of the studies that do not mainly treat that particular area of focus. More concretely, this will work as follows: proceeding from our specific regional and thematic specialisation, we will reflect on the connections between (written) portrayals of conversion, the meaning of gender and the actors' altered options for agency in a changing society, and in this way, beyond the parallel reading, further focus and condense certain aspects that particularly struck us. Moreover, we will subject certain excerpts from the main chapters to a new reading that only began to make sense to us *as a consequence* of our engagement with the other chapters.[1] It is not our intention to compare the settings in their totality, but rather to offer reflections – also comparative ones – on selected nodes of transformation that appeared to us particularly worthy of commentary following our reading of the individual, detailed studies.

After all, it was only then that the effects that underline the specific globality of our topic emerged: as an expanding religion, Christianity rooted itself in local settings, and the conversions that took place changed the face of Christianity. These processes of change, often initiated by conversion, had to be depicted in language – in our case in the shape of conversion narratives. Thus conversion and religious change were communicated to a wider imagined community. In colonial milieus, notions of the gender order, gender relations and gender

1 When we started writing the book, we initially thought that we could provide such comparisons immediately following each of the individual chapters. While writing the book, however, we realised that this did not suit our purpose as we would have had to artificially limit and fragment a more comprehensive argument we wished to develop. We would also have had to repeat ourselves as the book moved on with its successive chapters.

hierarchies came up against those societies' own practices and views on how gender shapes society. Precisely at the moment of the colonial encounter, European actors made broad and sometimes surprising movements towards indigenous social orders. Within the context of the settler societies explored here, however, these concessions were often scaled back once the colonial order had been established in order to conform more strongly to the initial concepts in the metropoles. In partially globalising scenarios of interdependency and repercussions, new options and scopes of action could emerge for local actors when they converted in the 1850s and 1860s. And these various transformations ran parallel to one another. They overlapped sometimes, but by no means always or necessarily.

The question that chiefly interests us here is what came of the differences and the at times unexpected parallels at the hinges and points of condensation and intersection we have identified here. It was our intention to suggest ways of thinking about writing post-national and post-colonial history – and thus about history itself – within the context of our experience of globalisation, which is interwoven and entangled in a sometimes contradictory manner that goes beyond local specifics. In this concluding chapter, we would like to specify, and in selected passages reflect upon, how our parallel readings open up new perspectives on the approaches and interpretations with which we began. We would also like to recall that the primary aim of our exercise was not to transfer our own points of view and approaches to other research fields. Rather, we wanted to 'take something back' from the process to our own respective fields, and quite generally to benefit from a situation in which we are working not with colleagues from our own research areas with whom we have been engaged in years of intense discussion, and with whom we share a historiography, but instead with colleagues who have varied areas of expertise in order to hone our viewpoints or shed new light on the unchallenged paradigms of our own research traditions. Now we hope to encounter readers willing to go along with this admittedly rather experimental approach, and develop it further for themselves using the impulses we have provided. We, at least, will be returning to our 'proper' fields of research enriched, and will view the research traditions and historiographies we continue to encounter there in a new light.

Upheaval, Change and Interdependencies in the 1850s and 1860s

Our studies concentrated mainly on the 1850s and 1860s, a time frequently referred to as an unspectacular period of transition. We have shown that a mix of conversion efforts and willingness to convert changed religious scenarios, and that this affected the gendered hierarchies of societies and also, at least to some extent, altered converts' courses and scopes of action. For that reason, we would like to ask how far this phase can be viewed as characteristic of transition, change and interdependencies. We ask how meaningful it is to read religious and social change parallel to one another within temporally parallel settings of conversion, and thus to correlate them with each other. It is our position that precisely as the nineteenth-century world was growing closer together, it becomes important to look at what was happening simultaneously. For quite clearly, and this is an initial finding of our parallel reading, simultaneousness does not mean that the same thing was happening everywhere. On the contrary: in the period we are interpreting, societies were quite obviously at different moments and cycles in their own respective transformations, which in turn fed into a more comprehensive transformation, one that in more recent global histories has generally been described from the viewpoint of political and economic change. That is why we have examined the commonalities and differences in the settings of conversion in this period, because we want to deduce particularities from them and at the same time identify parallels where at first glance we might expect something 'alien'. Yet can we go so far as to argue that an awareness of colonial encounters in 'distant' worlds was already dawning in Erfurt at this period? Volk at any rate showed an interest in events in the New World, and for example translated mission reports from the English. Wilhelm Knappe (1855–1910), who would later be a consul, was born just one generation after Volk in Erfurt. From 1886 he was stationed in the German colonial territories in the Pacific (e.g., the Marshall Islands and Samoa) and was involved in the Samoan crisis of 1889, among other events. The Pacific colonial world is very much present in Erfurt's museums today because of the South Seas collection.

And there are more questions. For example, were the (settler) colonial dynamics in which the mission participated intensified in both South Africa and among the Wotjobaluk? This question needs to be tested within the contexts of conversion, religious change and colonialism in relation to two groups of actors, the missionaries on the one hand, who served as the connection between the world of a Wilhelm Volk and his family and the colonial situation, and the converts on the other, who acquired knowledge about the power of this faraway world from the missionaries and appropriated it. Through conversion, and the acts that grew out of it, they sought, structurally and by individual example, to influence the missionaries and thereby also affected the metropoles.

The phase of the 1850s and 1860s in Europe may be interpreted as an under-researched time of transition, an in-between period that is generally read as one of standstill and consolidation after the Revolution of 1848/49. Despite the political reactions to the Revolution and the restoration of old circumstances, the demands posed during the Revolution remained very much alive. In addition, the great powers were also fighting to expand their (colonial) power. Thus, as we know, from 1850 Prussia rose to become the dominant great power in Germany. A decisive economic and industrial upswing became evident in Prussian customs policy and the German Customs Union formed by the German states in 1834. By the 1860s, Prussia had clearly outstripped the Habsburg Monarchy both economically and militarily. Liberal ideas helped to do away with the remnants of serfdom: while peasants and agricultural producers were incorporated into a more rationalised form of agriculture, many of them lost access to commons. Private property became a guiding principle of a post-revolutionary order in which bourgeois norms reigned supreme. Against the backdrop of these general changes, Volk took a critical view of Prussia's conquest of his home region (first in 1802–1806, and then, after the intermezzo of the French occupation, once and for all in 1815) and came to idealise a very distant past in response to this expansion of a great power that was reshaping his country. To what extent, however, the colonial situation studied in the second and third chapters of this book affected or intervened in Volk's own life circumstances can be determined only indirectly. At first glance, the German case study appears to bear little relationship to the others. Only breaking down the presumed repercussions for concrete historical areas such as writing about conversion and gender relations or exploring agency through conversion will offer further illumination in this respect. From the beginning, however, we were struck by one thing that the missionaries among the Wotjobaluk in Victoria, Australia, and among the Pedi in the South African Transvaal shared with the Catholic convert in Germany: these men were all critical of developments in the societies of their home countries. They not only wrote about and assessed conversions in the colonial context, but also criticised societal developments in their country of origin, whose inhabitants, they believed, were becoming increasingly estranged from 'true Christianity'. Thus aspects of the socio-political restoration in Germany entered into the colonial encounter on other continents, but they did so at their own pace. From the beginning, converts imbued the missionary's 'mission' with their own levels of meaning. In countless reports, the missionaries in turn used experiences from their encounters to hold up a mirror to their societies of origin.

From the 1850s, more generally, we have access to a sufficiently dense archival record for South Africa. The Pedi, whom we examined more closely in Chapter 3, found themselves in the midst of an as yet uncertain and therefore bewildering phase of transformation. Settlers were beginning to prospect and in some cases take possession of the land. They had also started to establish independent republics. State structures, however, remained extremely weak in the 1850s and 1860s. Further to the east, for instance in the colony of Natal, British colonialism was looming, but it was far from directly dominating the politics of an African kingdom that had just emerged from a troublesome period in the 1820s and 1830s and was now in the process of consolidating its territory and political might. In the course of this process, social and political hierarchies became increasingly differentiated. The capitalist penetration that would revolutionise the Witwatersrand some decades later was still unimaginable at this time, however. Thus missions in fact entered a highly ambiguous field of action in which power relations were anything but clear-cut. And, as a result, conversions and religious change always represented efforts to cope with situations of insecurity, transition and varying expectations. According to our interpretation, Wilhelm Volk was basically responding to a not dissimilar dynamic of transition and upheaval. He was disquieted and outraged by the Prussian takeover of Erfurt as well as by the Protestant state's increasingly strong influence over the city (while the influence of the Catholic Habsburgs in Germany waned), making a revival of the ancien régime ever less likely. The manner and degree of the felt threat may have differed, but the basic theme was a good deal more similar than we initially assumed.

Chapter 2 thus highlights the ways in which upheaval and change lent concrete local form to the oft-discussed 'global'. The interactions in which the Wotjobaluk people participated were most intimately framed by the connection, already noted in our introduction, between mission and empire. Long before the Berlin Mission in the Transvaal, for example, a church orientated towards mission and returning Christians to the faith had inscribed itself into a colonial situation. Because of its long activities as a transnational and global mission actor in a variety of colonial settings, it was well versed in the rules of colonial expansion. In fact, the Moravian Brethren positioned themselves far less than representatives of the Berlin Mission as the agents of a nationally framed confessional enterprise that was a latecomer to colonial affairs. After all, they had long since become ensconced in the Empire, which dominated Australia and thus also the Wotjobaluk. Nonetheless, the second chapter concludes, conversions in particular represented a strategy in this period for participating in the global, which came to the Wotjobaluk, as to so many other people, in a colonial guise. And yet Christianity was considered a universal religion, despite its implication in the colonial expansion of Europe. To that extent, there were naturally tensions between equality and hierarchy in the colonially influenced religious movement among the Wotjobaluk. After all, the promise of equality before God did not apply in the political reality or everyday lives of converts. The existing colonial penetration of society meant that the missions were quite successful in implementing their notions of hierarchy. Within the mission's politics of hierarchisation, the attempted intervention in gender orders ultimately represented a central measure for affirming change, which we shall address in more detail below. Efforts at ethnicisation, which were so relevant for the South African context – and still more so elsewhere in Africa, where so many 'tribes' were invented with the help of missionaries – were less central in Australia, however.

Overall, our attempts to explore the conceivable and demonstrable repercussions and interdependencies in our discussions left us with more questions than answers. We concluded that in order to answer the question of how to characterise the phase between the 1850s and the 1860s, we would need to leave the abstract level for a time in order to search for the answers in the concrete fields of transformation and interaction.

Textual Representations of Conversion and Religious Change

In all our cases and in all the narratives we subjected to a close reading there was an element of understanding and articulating conversion as a search for truth or true religion. This was most explicit in the case of Volk, whose conversion process lasted several years while he studied Catholic doctrine and compared it with the teachings of the Protestant church into which he was baptised. In his writings, Volk gives little credit to the Catholic priests who ultimately led the formal part of his conversion and administered the ritual of receiving him into the Roman Catholic Church. He does not cite these intellectual considerations as reasons for the conversion of his wife and daughter. In fact, they are completely absent from his account of these female conversions: his wife was gravely ill, and he as head of the family ordered his adolescent daughter to become a Catholic. Australian indigenous converts also voiced the New Testament notion of Christ as the path to truth. In her letter to another Aboriginal woman, Rebecca Pepper reminded her that 'Jesus saith I am the way to the truth and the life'. While the search for truth is not mentioned as the prime motivation for her conversion, this Bible quote in her letter suggests that it was a topic associated with religious change to Christianity. In the Pedi example, the search for 'truth' took on a variety of expressions. Searching for truth was implied in the 'virtue' that conversion and the adoption of Christianity instilled in people's ways of life, their 'right paths'. A convert such as Ruth Mampatshe 'searche[d] for the Lord'. But more poignantly, Wangemann used the conversion narratives to ask for the 'truth' and virtue of the lives and life paths of people back home in Germany.

Thus despite this common thread in all conversions, there were significant differences in the conversion styles in our case studies and, as we have shown, they took shape in vastly different contexts. This makes it imperative to discuss to what extent conversions from the indigenous religious beliefs of Australian Aborigines or the Pedi can be compared at all to the intra-Christian conversion of Europeans. Our parallel readings have shown that the power relations in colonial mission contexts were completely different to those in European conversion. While the perceived authenticity, and 'truth', of indigenous conversions was constantly being assessed by missionaries, the process by which an intra-Christian convert was pronounced qualified for the new faith was less clear. And yet in all three examples, the loyalty of the newcomers to their church was not taken as a given. The differences in actual conversion styles, from the Pietist mode of the Moravians with their emphasis on experience and the emotional performance of a 'changed heart' or the Lutherans with their emphasis on learning the catechism for Volk and his individual study of Catholic doctrine, naturally also influenced the conversion narratives. From a comparative perspective, these differences helped us to see the particular local conditions and contextual shape of each conversion even more clearly. However, as we have seen, these differences were not as absolute as one might expect. In the cases of the Australian conversions, the women's performances of the key Moravian tropes – awakening, weeping, remorse – were absent. And for Volk's wife and daughter no scripture study is mentioned. In the Pedi setting, royal wives and some 'grandmothers' went through particularly worthwhile conversion processes. They embodied power but not office in the church to come.

In the end, however, our interpretations of conversions and their meanings in an increasingly interdependent and entangled world characterised by ever more unequal power relations rest on the available documents, which are quite disparate for our respective areas of expertise. The discussion of the nature of these diverse sources (and archives) thus appears especially important to us in the framework of a post-national and post-colonial approach to history.

In Chapter 1, a convert from Erfurt writing under a pseudonym (and at times even anonymously), relates his conversion in several segments or parts. In addition, other authors also reported on his conversion, for example in the *Allgemeine Deutsche Biographie* (ADB) and other reference works and collections. These multiple layers are joined by a further one: to the degree that the author Wilhelm Volk published his narrative in partial segments and from partial perspectives, he made use of a variety of genres. He experimented with the genre of the *Entwicklungsroman*, disassociated himself from the theatre and drew upon the format of the scholarly treatise. All of this is illuminating to the extent that such complexity is also virtually constitutive of the conversion narratives we address 'for Africa' and 'in Australia' or in gender-specific terms. From the outset it was clear to us that conversions in colonial territories, while narrated by the converts, were generally recorded, translated, edited, published and disseminated by others – usually missionaries and the missionary writing machine behind them; much like Volk, missionaries proved extremely prolific writers.

The media they used varied, however. While Volk wrote for a – or perhaps even 'his' – educated reading public and did so in scholarly formats that were ultimately not widely read, the missionaries and above all their superiors back home preferred a popular narrative format. A minor peculiarity of missionaries may have been that they adopted prolific writing only in the course of their training (which generally occurred after their professional education and frequently also following a difficult scholastic socialisation). Had the mission not sent them to the colonies, they would have become the classic actors of

German-language history who, unlike Wilhelm Volk, left no written traces in the archives. But that was not to be their fate.

One of these groups of prolific writers was the Moravian missionaries, who gave written form to religious change and conversions among the Wotjobaluk. They guided, accompanied and judged the converts and their conversions according to strict standards over an extended period of time. The literature on colonial situations quite rightly pays particular attention to power relations at the intersections of translation and communication. In the framework of our parallel reading we found it especially striking that, although the missionaries on the ground frequently spoke with the converts and also mention this in their texts, their intended readership, while hoping for and expecting the conversion of the converts, preferred to attribute the *success* of conversions to their own initiative and material donations – thus devaluing the actual conversions and their protagonists, the converts. The conversions described the religious transformation of people who were supposed to become brothers and sisters, but who never completely became the 'equals' of the mission supporters.

Volk described this (parallel) transformation in the context of rival churches. In the process he stressed that there were clear regulations governing this conversion and that the aspiring convert in the presence of at least one priest and two witnesses had to abjure his errors, publicly profess allegiance to the Catholic Church and declare that he would practise the Catholic faith until his death. The priest then had to record the conversion in the church register, and the convert was presented with a certificate signed by himself, the witnesses and the priest. Volk's successful and permanent conversion was overseen not by missionaries but by the Protestant and Catholic public, which pronounced critically or approvingly on his publications, charitable endowments and other activities. As in the case of the Aborigines and the Pedi, what was at issue here was not just his individual qualifications to enter the church, but putting Volk to the test as a 'true member' of the new community (although perhaps, in Volk's environment this 'community' already existed, whereas in Australia and South Africa it was only just emerging and actually taking shape through individual people's conversions).

Consequently, the criteria for conversion and religious change are temporally shifted in the texts. Despite a religious awakening, conversion was never wholly unambiguous. It required constant supervision. Thus not only were many obstacles set up to admission to baptism; even after baptism or entry into the Christian community, when the process for converts such as Volk was considered complete, converts in colonial contexts still encountered suspicion. Volk faced doubts about his religious affiliation mainly *before* his conversion, but he was subject to public scrutiny *after* his conversion as well. The arguments for why Volk should be considered a failure or a success were, however, constructed differently from those applied to the failure of African or Australian converts.

If Volk failed or succeeded as a convert this was seen as an extension of his individual personality, and with regard to his capacity as an officeholder in the German administration. African or Australian converts failed because they were 'native' and considered to be of another 'race'. Equality was a promise. It was almost – but not completely – attainable. For converts in colonial situations, controls continued, ultimately for the rest of their lives. To be sure, colonial conversion narratives were structured as success stories, but their endings appear more open than in Volk's case.

But the complexity of the textual representations of conversion and religious change and the marked desire to retain control over converts were not the only remarkable aspects here. The multilingual nature of the Moravian publication organs and thus a certain decentralisation of the narrative direction are also striking. Conversions among the Wotjobaluk were not streamlined to meet the needs of a national reading public, but rather dispersed into an imagined and shared global world of supporters of the Moravian mission. The *Periodical Accounts* in particular contributed to the formation of a discourse in the guise of an 'information network', which in turn promoted an awareness of community building among Moravians scattered across the globe. The textual diversity of the Moravian mission texts is considerable, as suggested in Chapter 2: alongside letters by missionaries they mainly include mission diaries, letters by converts (including those from one mission station to another, e.g. between Ebenezer in colonial Australia and New Herrnhut in Greenland) and travel accounts. It is notable that there are scarcely any spiritual memoirs from Ebenezer, especially by converts, such as were still common among Moravians in the nineteenth century, although they were by no means as widespread as they had been a century earlier. Converts were not as well integrated into this community-building process as they should have been given their conversion efforts. On the one hand, the majority of converts have no written voice in the texts from colonial situations, since other people spoke *about* and assessed them instead. Moreover, the conversions of men and women were represented differently and according to different patterns, and thus generally pressed into a specific linguistic form, as we saw in Chapter 2. In the process, the conversions and conversion-related activities of female actors were in turn particularly marginalised, which means that the level of textual representation permits only highly limited views of a more complex and all-encompassing social reality.

In Chapter 3, which focuses on a selected region of southern Africa, the study of the textual representation of conversion and religious change shows changes in and repercussions for a readership located 'in Europe', in this case nationally in Germany and ideationally in the context of the Berlin Mission Society. The *Lebensbilder* represent an extraordinary text production on conversions, much as in the case of Volk (while the *Periodical Accounts* address the conversions as part of their regular reporting). Both Volk and Wangemann experimented with genres. Since Volk was writing in a setting that would be considered 'metropolitan' from the perspective of the 'colony' but urban, at best, from a European perspective, Wangemann operated with different genres from those chosen by authors who were writing in or about a colonial context.

When Hermann Theodor Wangemann published the *Lebensbilder*, German-language stories of converts in South Africa that he had collected in the decade before, in Berlin in 1871 his intention was not to offer an example for non-Christian Africans to emulate. Rather, he wanted to provide pastors in *Kaiserreich* Germany, and more specifically in the milieu of the Berlin Mission, with material for fundraising purposes and Sunday school instruction and to hold up a mirror to German society. With these biographical sketches depicting Christian converts in the Pedi Kingdom in South Africa, Wangemann criticised what he saw as a German society that did not sufficiently prize Christian values. At the same time, he portrayed a world in which the polarised gender order already being challenged in Europe did not apply. Given the fragile situation in which the Berlin Mission operated in the Pedi Kingdom, these structures could also not be enforced there. Wangemann did, however, try to show how society, especially that of 'ordinary people', was in some cases moving in that direction.

These individual portraits differ in many ways from other forms of writing about indigenous conversion, since the genealogy of converts' families would not usually have been mentioned. As a rule, it was ethnographic texts that constructed genealogies. Wangemann in fact experimented with the genre in creative ways. He not only referred to genealogies, the special area of expertise of ethnographers, but also described the landscapes and customs of various African groups, and interwove these descriptions with the genealogies. Thus he acknowledged, perhaps with some unease, that for many Africans conversion was an open concept and remained a flexible structure. In his text, the *Lebensbilder*, readers were also introduced to a genre that contained elements of the adventure story and aspired to imperial outreach. Wangemann's male associate, his guide, translator and informant Jacob Makhoëtle, who was himself a hunter, a convert and highly knowledgeable about the region where Wangemann travelled, is credited as a main source of information. The text claims further authenticity by emphasising that the author had acquired the information first-hand from the converts themselves.

Significantly, the panorama of converts portrayed here is arrayed around cannibal stories in the two middle chapters out of twelve. It would be worth looking more closely at how the inclusion of cannibal stories affected German readers' perceptions of the conversions. Were the cannibal stories related by Christian storytellers, and thus also by Jacob Makhoëtle, intended as a graphic means of contrasting the converts' former lives with their new Christian identities? That may have been Wangemann's intention, and it corresponded with oral styles used in the Pedi area to recount the horrors of war and upheaval experienced by many people, whose lives as 'ordinary' folk would never be captured individually as might the sufferings of kings, healers or other leaders, and perhaps even Christian converts. Wangemann of course did not speak personally with self-confessed cannibals. The genre only functioned because it was related through others who themselves had probably only heard about these things. In the end, however, the textual evidence that we as historians have to work with does not reflect on the audience or back onto the conversion stories. It would be fascinating to know to what extent the final product, which positions the conversion of Africans within such a specific literary trope of cannibalism, was perceived back home in the expanding centres of Christianity.

Reading the different forms of textual representation in conjunction does more than just draw our attention to the many similarities, some of which we did not expect, and the differences between them. Learning how conversions were represented in other historical settings helps us to identify elements that might resonate with local conventions of speaking about conversions in more than one setting. More particularly, however, it helps us to identify with greater precision which elements were specific to one local setting. Here we knew that those elements which we detected in only one of the three modes of textual representations certainly provided entry points for exploring, in our individual chapters, what may be considered unique to either the Wotjobaluk, converts to Catholicism in Erfurt or the Pedi setting.

As has been hinted at above, the texts proved fundamentally different to the extent that the conversion accounts produced in a colonial context include the category of race, whether implicitly or explicitly. 'Race' is not an issue in Wilhelm Gustav Werner Volk's works, for he divided people into Catholics and Protestants, educated and uneducated, men and women and even Germans and non-Germans. Although the *Lebensbilder* never address 'race' explicitly, it is always there in the background, not in references to skin colour or biology, but rather in discussions of religion. Among the Pedi there is sublime and largely unspoilt, not necessarily western, modern, let alone secularised, culture. After converting, Christians from this culture had a higher status than non-Christians (a fact that often angered South African settlers). For a mission-orientated readership, African converts served as examples worthy of emulation, who were contrasted with cannibals and cruel kings. In Wangemann's view, culture and religion put the Pedi in a position to become a nation. To what extent this 'nation' had its own specific 'race' is a subject upon which he remains silent. Racial hierarchies and the concept of whiteness were key social concepts in Australian colonial society as well, including the Christian missions. Notions of *difference* form part of the *Periodical Accounts*. Here, too, the definition of race is not biological but 'civilisational'. This is still clearer in other Moravian texts. As in the case of the Pedi, Christians are placed above non-Christians on the level of civilisation, and yet these Wotjobaluk Christians – brothers and sisters – are not treated as the equals of Europeans.

Readers will certainly have noticed that the discussion of the textual level of our topic focuses almost exclusively on authors, biographers and missionaries, and leaves aside converts such as the Wotjobaluk, the Pedi and Wilhelm Volk's family members. Conversion was a narrative. In fact, many people's conversions were a narrative of, and by, others, while – with the exception of Volk (but not of his wife and daughter) – the narrative itself was about the conversion of others. Particularly during the process of parallel reading, it proved quite difficult to discover anything about them, since the textual representations of conversion remained in the foreground. And we have come to the conclusion that in order to do this in a comparative manner that connects the case studies, we must in fact search for them in the remaining points of agency and gendered conversion.

Gendered Conversion in the Context of Changing Power Relations

It is no longer necessary to argue the point – as many of our predecessors had to do – that gender is a useful category of analysis. Its usefulness is abundantly clear and its legitimation no longer required, especially not when it comes to analysing conversion and religious change. In all three societies in which we studied religious change through the lens of religious conversion, gender was clearly a central category of social organisation. The emphasis on gender brought into particularly sharp focus the societal dynamics that arose from colonial influences, inner changes and the interplay between these two areas. Gender and age, in particular, and of course race, were cited as the central relational categories that dominated the mission initiative to procure conversions among Wotjobaluk society, just as they dominated the decisions among members of that society to affiliate with the new religion. Thus masculinities and femininities became characterised along altered lines. As settler society and colonialism were more firmly entrenched in Australia than in the South African Transvaal, for instance, missionaries had far greater scope to actually enforce an order they themselves considered useful and virtuous, regardless of the perfectly functional gender order that had accompanied the Wotjobaluk throughout their long history. Particularly in their neglect of the spiritual development and authority of Aboriginal women, Moravian mission sources clearly show that the missionaries recorded only what they considered noteworthy from the perspective of their own gender-hierarchical, locally influenced perspective. The challenge for them was that they encountered gender hierarchies and gender relations among the Wojtobaluk in Australia that were contextualised in a wholly different manner than in their society of origin. In Australia, notions of the gender order influenced by colonial settlers and the Moravians did not simply clash with notions of gender difference among the Wotjobaluk; the conflict ran far deeper. For gender orders and hierarchies *functioned* in a different way among the Wotjobaluk than the missionaries were accustomed to. Within this autonomously functioning gender order, the Moravians offered male and female converts different opportunities to join a new community – albeit always in subordination to the male missionaries, who wished to be placed at the very top of the new hierarchies. Especially in the first generation of converts, it was mainly young people whom the missionaries and their wives assigned power and influence that had previously been the privilege of senior Wotjobaluk men and women. Young men in particular were able to expand their sphere of influence because the Moravians officially also accorded them the right to preach (which was denied to women). Moreover, missionary matchmaking activities challenged the traditional prerogatives of Wotjobaluk elders.

This resonates to some extent with gender policies that intervened in the structure of German societies to create a particular social and political order. Just as the German middle class viewed the sexuality of young people, the lower classes or minorities as especially unbridled and threatening, the missionaries regarded it as their duty to discipline and control the sexuality of Wotjobaluk women in particular, and subsumed this under the dissemination of Christian values. The continuing mistrust with which they viewed Christian converts, and which they used as a pretext to infantilise and control Wotjobaluk Christians, resembled to some extent middle-class strategies in their society of origin of opposing the emancipation of women, young people and the lower classes while arguing in the same breath that they were neither politically mature nor educated enough for equality. A significant difference in the Australian context, however, was the inclusion of 'race' in these policies.

In the Moravians' wider society of origin, in Germany, a marked gender-hierarchical order existed in the nineteenth century, which proceeded from a polar model of the sexes and assigned different traits and spheres of action to men and women. The domestic arena was regarded as women's domain, while men were accorded responsibility for public affairs. These separate spheres were justified in terms of the differing nature of the sexes, which allegedly gave women more emotional and social competence and men more rationality and assertiveness. These gender differences generated a seemingly natural division of labour: women were to be primarily responsible for children and household, while men should support their families by practising their professions and seeing to the organisation of the state and its outward defence. In this logic, men represented the family to the outside world as heads of household, while leaving the running of the domestic establishment to women. This ideal-typical gender model, which evolved within the middle classes in the course of urbanisation and industrialisation, did not function naturally either in an agricultural setting or in the working-class milieu, where women always worked in the fields or the workshops and factories, and by no means limited their activities to the family household and childrearing. Perhaps it was for this very reason that this hierarchical gender model with its clear-cut distribution of tasks became so attractive for the lower classes: the idea that men could support their families without their wives and children having to work for money was considered the mark of a better way of life, and became an attractive model among the poor as well. When demands for better employment and educational opportunities for women emerged in the mid-nineteenth century they generally called into question not gender *differences* but the gender *hierarchy*.

Just as missionaries found the differently functioning gender order and hierarchies in Australia unsettling, in Germany, too, many people were disquieted by challenges to the gender hierarchy in the Revolution of 1848/49 and by the idea that the gender order needed to be changed. In his accounts, Volk himself inscribes the gender hierarchy into various passages and clearly distinguishes the way in which his wife arrived at her conversion from his own path: he describes his wife's conversion as an emotionally driven process, while portraying his own as a rational process grounded in scholarship. The patriarchal violence that Volk exerts in his interpretation of the conversions of his wife and daughter exhibits certain parallels to the power claims of missionaries, which they sought to extend beyond their own families to the mission.

In the light of the second chapter, on the Wotjobaluk, the gender aspects of Pedi conversions, as portrayed in the third chapter, can also be highlighted in a new way. Here, too, men and women had different experiences and their conversions were described and valued differently by Wangemann and by the Pedi themselves. The *Lebensbilder* clearly show that gendered differences were further complicated by social hierarchies within Pedi society – which the missionaries were more than happy to note as it was the ambition of many missions and colonial powers more generally to create hierarchies (which the colonial powers tended to describe using the introduced notion of 'the tribe' still employed today). In Pedi society, the conversions of royal wives as well as chiefs of high rank were treated differently to those of female or male commoners. They were also represented differently in missionaries' textual representations of conversions.

Pedi kinship and authority structures assigned specific powers to women in positions of seniority (e.g., grandmothers, aunts of the king), and they were assured respect from male members of the younger generations (e.g., grandsons, nephews). At the same time, younger women of marriageable age were often prevented from converting by their fathers (and perhaps their mothers as well?), since conversions diminished their value on the marriage market. As the mission actively discouraged the marriage of converted women to unconverted men, it limited the social authority of local elders and of African families in this respect. The conversion of the upper ranks of society, as celebrated in some of the conversion narratives, bears some parallels to conversions among the aristocracy in early modern Europe. In many instances, women were prominent converts (e.g., Queen Christina of Sweden), but their actual behaviour after conversion was not policed to the same extent as other women's. Conversion, or public association with a mission, could work in the interest of dynastic politics by building political alliances in a world where political associations were in flux. In such cases, king's wives converted in order to support the political ambitions of their husbands and/or their own lineages and families of origin.

As senior aristocratic women were important for genealogies and the authentication of power by descent in Pedi society, this was transferred directly to the process of legitimising the new Christian community. Ruth Mampatshe was one of the king's aunts (a cousin of his mother), and as an acknowledged 'mother of the king' she was needed to legitimise the new Christian community. The success of the Christian congregation was directly dependent on this legitimisation process within African society. Only after she moved to the new Christian community, and this legitimised the group, was she baptised, despite her weak Christian beliefs, in an act of recognition by the missionaries. Baptism, one could argue, was granted to 'prominent' converts such as Ruth Mampatshe (whom the missionaries never classified as such) for political rather than religious reasons, a fact the missionaries would never have conceded. Similarly, the common missionary trope of women's resistance to Christianity is absent from this particular narrative. Instead, the conversion narrative focuses on the lasting establishment of a Christian congregation based on family ties and happy submission to the patriarchal patronage of male missionaries, which entailed converts distancing themselves from their former allegiance to the 'heathenish' king. This was certainly a result of the fragile status of the mission among the Pedi, where they had not yet succeeded in establishing full-fledged mission station households. Once women converted we hear nothing about their spiritual leadership – but we are warned about young men's independent Bible-study groups. The missionaries' masculine gendered power depended on successfully controlling younger men, and exercising spiritual authority over them. While male homosocial groupings and activities were part of the mission setup, independent spiritual interpretation and leadership by local men were not. If young men were sent out to evangelise, which was deemed highly desirable, the message they disseminated to others needed to be controlled.

Female converts from the upper ranks of society were subject to little or no mission patronage (in fact, this began only in the context of the second encounter between the mission and the Pedi in the 1880s). They continued to conduct their affairs as before, without having to learn how to sew dresses, free of constant surveillance of their sexual behaviour and living away from the mission. Those who permanently moved to mission sites were not royal wives, although some of them did flee the kingdom when the mission decided to withdraw.

Women converts from the upper ranks were not subject to the same inventions of gender practices as other converted women in Africa and Australia – at least not at this transitional period of evangelisation in the Pedi Kingdom. As we saw, they were neither required to learn sewing from the missionary's wife nor were they reprimanded for their sexual conduct or participation in religious ceremonies. It would be interesting to know in more detail how different this prominent visibility of women in the *Lebensbilder* is from the contemporary mission reports sent home at the time and published in the monthly mission journal, the *Berliner Missionsberichte*. The Pedi mission was certainly a pet project of the Berlin Mission, if not the absolute favourite. This might account for the many deviations from the more usual modes of representing conversions by African men and, more particularly, women of high social standing.

It remains to be noted that gender appears to structure society all over the world. 'Female' and 'male' may be defined and connoted differently, but along with other factors such as age, social status, religious and ritual affiliation, gender reveals a central function in the differentiation of society and the place of religion within it.

Conversion and Agency

Under the impression of great societal transformations that were either looming, already felt, or apparently interrupted for a moment, people reacted to uncertainty and upheaval, the loss of affiliation as well as the possibility of locating themselves anew by converting. The converts in our three studies dealt quite differently, however, with the option of using conversion to explore new spheres of agency.

In most African societies, conversion rates remained quite low in the nineteenth century. Nevertheless, even before mass conversions, Christianity offered societies the opportunity to deal with innovations and to clarify personal as well as communal relationships to the new developments. Especially where people succeeded in coping with crises, and those on the ground therefore had reason to recognise the great power of the newly acquired god, the missionaries succeeded in gaining a foothold for the new religion in the region. Wherever colonial administration was already established it essentially supported the missionary presence, even if the missionaries and the colonial authorities did not always share the same interests. For converts, this meant that in a gradually emerging power structure, they could use their access to the mission or the colonial administration to better enforce their own interests and those of their families and communities. In the process they created room for manoeuvre within the changes that they themselves could usually influence only indirectly.

The conversion of the Pedi in a world in motion captures, in a series of portraits of converts, key social issues implicated in colonial conversions more generally. Indigenous conversions, which missionaries deemed successful as long as the people were baptised and maintained an approved, ongoing association with the mission, were defined by many other factors that lay outside the immediate borders and concerns of the missions. As all our cases show, conversions took place as a family dynamic. Considerations of religious change were determined by a series of Pedi concerns about power and kinship, and their political strategies of repositioning themselves in a colonial world in motion. For instance, while the Pedi used Christianity to their own ends and especially to reposition themselves in a changing world, they sought to compensate for their loss of power to colonial office holders. They also tried to respond to a loosening of social ties by (re)-acknowledging social hierarchies and by processes of realignment within Pedi society that were largely impervious to missionary interference. In both fields of agency, the nature of Pedi conversion was shaped by an outspoken sense of social stratification among both the Pedi and the missionaries who reported on their conversions. Finally, preaching was an important field in which male converts and evangelists could attain prestige and power. The large number of chapters in the *Lebensbilder* devoted to the life stories of preaching converts reminds us of this.

As to the realm of family and kinship, it is worth noting that conversions always occurred in a context in which family and kin relations mattered greatly. Conversions took place in a society in which the strong ties and dependencies within the family, kin networks and lineages did not permit isolated individual decisions to convert. People who converted without the consent and support of their families were isolated, weakened and not well served by Christianity, as the example of the grandmother Hanna in the *Lebensbilder* shows. Josef Kathedi's father even accused his son of having destroyed him by converting. The new male elite thus considered it more than appropriate to imagine new, fictitious genealogies, which not only incorporated the missionaries but also made reference to a high secular ruler in Prussia.

The Wotjobaluk were drawn into the hierarchising tendencies of the mission and the colonial administration by the missionaries' efforts to convert and 'civilise' them. Gendered hierarchies, as we have seen, were part of the mission regime and male converts could acquire some degree of agency as evangelists by preaching and as translators. Outside of the mission, in the wider colonial society, both men and women who had attended the mission school could use their literacy skills in English to intervene in colonial life. Aboriginal men, some of them converts and others not, used their writing skills to demand land from the government on which they could settle, for example. As we have seen, Philip Pepper was among the men who wrote to the Victoria government in this regard in 1859. These men also tried to use their social connections and enlist missionaries to intervene on their behalf. Similarly, Aboriginal women used their literacy skills to write letters to the colonial government and the Aboriginal Protection Board to complain about unjust treatment and request support for their families and communities. Literacy skills, communication networks and contacts acquired through mission connections, more than simply Christian conversion, could provide indigenous people with a new set of skills with which to negotiate colonial society.

But association with a Christian mission did not offer only advantages for converts' social agency. Indigenous people who converted to Christianity and who continued to live at the mission faced missionaries' interventions in their marriage arrangements, one of the key social networks in indigenous societies. The missionaries betrothed Nathanel Pepper to an Aboriginal woman from Western Australia, several thousand kilometres from Victoria. 'Wrong' Aboriginal marriages, that is, matches arranged with Christian partners that did not observe the appropriate kin affiliations, would have caused some upheaval in indigenous society, and Aboriginal elders often opposed them. Conflicts with family members because of association with a mission were reported, but in many cases family ties persisted whether people converted or not. Finally, indigenous Australians undermined the scope of social agency, i.e., they exercised a good deal more agency than we would normally anticipate or than the mission records were willing to reveal, as evident in the examples of Jenny's patronage of the mission.

The convert Volk in Erfurt, who had to give up his professional career because of his conversion, had a quite different scope of action. After converting, he was able to devote far more time to his activities as a writer than he could before his conversion, or could have, had he never converted. To that extent he was able to reposition himself vis-à-vis society as a person, a thinker and a man of scholarly ambition. As far as we know, after his conversion, his dismissal from his post and the entry of his daughter into a convent, the widowed Volk concentrated wholly on his charitable, literary and missionary activities and moved mainly in Catholic circles. He was stylised in eulogies and biographical publications as a 'homo catholicus' who had dedicated his life to the Catholic cause. An important factor for Germany, in contrast to Australia and South Africa, was that power relations between the confessions had largely been fixed since the seventeenth century. When people converted or left the church altogether in the nineteenth century it did not essentially challenge this situation. Although confessional conflicts remained influential in the regions studied here, the conversions that had been common since the sixteenth century no longer possessed the explosive force to threaten the overall social order. On the level of the family, however, conversions could prove very explosive indeed and their effects were lasting. Families in which some, but not all, members converted, as was the instance with Volk, sometimes broke off contact with one another.

Outlook

During our joint reflections we gained the impression that additional spheres of activity also deserve closer analysis. The mobility of converts is one such area where we might use parallel reading to expand our exploration of the intensive links between conversions in a variety of cases. Conversion frequently appears to take place at liminal sites outside the converts' usual spheres of activity. Conversions are causally connected with migrant labour and population mobility in the context of the founding of states and nations. In order to elaborate such a theme we would like to expand on the interpretations we undertook here, and we intend to do so in a later publication.

In closing, we would like instead to return once again to what it means for three authors to write a book jointly, and not as an anthology. The idea for this book was born within the research group 'Self-Narratives in Transcultural Perspective', in which the method of 'decentred comparison' developed. The research group successfully questioned the tight interconnections between individuality and written self-fashioning. We further developed this method as 'parallel reading' with a thematic focus, taking the temporal dimension very seriously by concentrating on the 1850s and 1860s in all three case studies.

Each chapter has both a thematic and a specific geographical focus. We were particularly struck by the different states of the literature on conversion in our respective regional areas of study, and especially by the different historiographies and terminologies that have developed around the topic of conversion in the German/European context or the post-colonial histories of Australia and South Africa. For that reason, each chapter briefly addresses the specific historiography not just on the theme (narrative, gender, social change), but also the region. A chapter containing our reflections seemed to us an important (and experimental) extension of our interpretation in which we could once again address certain overlaps between our examples in the form of a conversation with one another.

We would like to close by revisiting the term 'conversion' one last time. While used here in the broader sense, the notion of conversion nevertheless proves (as one would expect, especially after the comparative discussion), to be quite Eurocentric and closely tied to the Christian tradition. Following our regionally- and actor-specific studies, we suggest that the comparative study of conversions should adopt a new, open concept of change of religion, which would apply to Europe as well, and inquire into rituals of changeover and appropriation that are not orientated towards the rules of religious conversion defined by constitutional and ecclesiastical law in the land of the Reformation. In European history too, the subject of a 'change of religion' must also be given back its openness, in order to prevent the old notions of conversion studies from narrowing our focus. Despite the difficulties that the terminology and the disparate state of the sources and research bring with them for such parallel readings, we are convinced that our results confirm that the most fascinating topics for the new historiography are often to be found at the intersection of global processes and their local manifestations. Moreover, we are persuaded that they can be described and analysed productively where, proceeding from these intersections, they take us back to the kind of specific, local societal dynamics generally deemed to have been only indirectly affected by the global integration of the time.

Archival Sources and Bibliography

Archival Sources

Chapter 1

The records contained in the following archives of the Erfurt Diocese and the Prussian State constitute the main sources for Chapter 1, in addition to the published conversion accounts of Wilhelm Gustav Volk (see Bibliography).

Bistumsarchiv Erfurt

Die Volk'sche Anstalt. gen. Angefangen 1856, geschlossen 1882, No 1.

Acta des Bischöfl. Geistlichen Gerichts zu Erfurt, betr. die von dem Herrn Geheimen Regierungsrath Volk zu Erfurt errichtete Erziehungs-Anstalt für verwahrloste katholische Kinder, 1856 [–1932].

Acta betreffend den Bau einer katholischen Kirche zu Ranis, vol. II.

Bischöfliches Generalvikariat Paderborn: Pfarrstellen u.ä., Behörden, Einrichtungen, Stiftungen etc. im Bereich des heutigen Bistums Erfurt, Acta Specialia betreffend die Mission zu Ranis. Bischöfliches General-Vicariat zu Paderborn, 1862–1930.

Geheimes Staatsarchiv Preußischer Kulturbesitz (=GStA PK) Berlin

I. HA Rep. 77, Ministerium des Innern, Tit. 185 a, Nr. 21 Bd. 3, Acta betr. die Conduiten-Listen von den Beamten der Regierung zu Erfurt, 1848–1866.

I. HA Rep. 77, Ministerium des Innern, Tit. 397, Nr. 4 Bd. 8 Acta betr. die Anstellung der Räthe zu Assessoren bei der Regierung zu Erfurt 1849–1862 [unpaginated].

Chapter 2

The Unitätsarchiv Herrnhut holds the most substantial archival collections pertaining to the Moravian Church, including correspondence with individual mission stations. For the Moravian missions in Australia these include diaries and letters by individual missionaries. The State Library of Victoria in Melbourne holds some letters by Aboriginal women who were sent from Western Australia to the Moravian mission in Victoria as well as the Howitt papers.

Unitätsarchiv Herrnhut,Germany (= UA)
Rubrik 15 V I a 8/9 Zeitungsausschnitte und Drucksachen 1852–1902
R 15 A 63.33 and 38 2 Briefe Gouveneur Australians an La Trobe zur Gründung einer Missionsarbeit in Australien
R 15 A 55 Kopierbücher F.W. Kuehn 1866–1887
R 15 A 56 Kopierbücher W. Bechler 1881–1886
R 15 A 56 Kopierbücher L.Th. Reichel 1873–1878
R 15 V I a 4. 1 Spieseke Diarium Boga-See 1855–August 1856
R 15 V I a 5. 4 Meissels Tagebuch 1864–68
R 15 V I b 1 Tagebuch Ebenezer a) 1858–62; b)1863–68 c) 1869–88
R 15 V I b 2 Berichte Ebenezer 1865, 1875–77
R 15 V I 6 Briefwechsel mit Ebenezer
R 15 V II a 1 Briefe und Berichte von Hagenauer 1885–1891

State Library of Victoria, Melbourne, La Trobe Collection
Bessy Flower letters to Anne Camfield, MS 12117
Schooling, C.W. (ed.) extracts from 'Periodical Accounts relating to the Mission of the Church of the United Brethren established among the heathen' MS 9896.
Howitt papers MS 9356
Papers of Friedrich Augustus Hagenauer, 1829–1909, including the Visitors' Book of Ramahyuck Aboriginal Mission, 1870s–1900, MS 9556, shelf 9/6c, MCFB 4.
Visitors' Book, Lake Tyers, MS 11934

Chapter 3

Reference is made to selected material drawn from the archives of two mission societies. These archives hold the voluminous correspondence between the mission headquarters and their mission stations in the field. They also contain data on the personal affairs of missionaries and various other official papers. Some time ago, the archival holdings of the Berlin Mission Society were transferred to the Landeskirchliches Archivzentrum in Berlin and hence to the auspices of the Territorial Church of Berlin-Brandenburg. The archive of the Evangelisch-Lutherisches Missionswerk is still accessible in Hermannsburg. In both archives the referencing systems are currently being changed. Users may be obliged to check between old and new references.

Archive of the Berlin Mission Society, Berlin (now part of the Landeskirchliches Archivzentrum in Berlin)
Die Inspektionsreise des Herrn Direktors Wangemann in Süd-Afrika betreffend, 1866, bmw 1/ 796 (old reference: I.5.16a).

Acta die Inspectionsreise des Herrn Director Wangemann in Süd-Afrika betreffend, 1867, Dok.134, not dated, bmw 1/798 (old reference: I.5.16a).

Archive of the Evangelisch-Lutherisches Missionswerk, Hermannsburg (ELM)
A: S. A. 42–2 a Berseba
A: S. A. 42–26 a Cuane/ Mosetla

Bibliography

Adreßbuch oder vollständiger Wohnungs-Anzeiger für die Stadt Erfurt. Herausgegeben von Trütschler von Falkenstein, Köngl. Polizei-Lieutnant. Erfurt: Hennings und Hopf, 1855.

Adreßbuch oder vollständiger Wohnungs-Anzeiger für die Stadt Erfurt. Herausgegeben von Wilhelm Eduard Schubotz, Polizei-Secretair. Erfurt: printed by the editor, 1862.

Adreßbuch oder vollständiger Wohnungs-Anzeiger für die Stadt Erfurt. Herausgegeben von Wilhelm Eduard Schubotz, Polizei-Secretair. Erfurt: printed by the editor, 1865.

Adreßbuch oder vollständiger Wohnungs-Anzeiger für die Stadt Erfurt. Herausgegeben von Wilhelm Eduard Schubotz, Polizei-Secretair und Königlicher Polizei-Anwalt. Erfurt: printed by the editor, 1868.

Aland, Kurt. *Über den Glaubenswechsel in der Geschichte des Christentums.* Berlin: Alfred Töpelmann, 1961.

Allen, Margaret. '"That's the Modern Girl": Missionary Women and Modernity in Kolkata, 1907–1940'. *Itinerario* 34, 3 (2010): 83–96.

Allen, Margaret. '"A Breach of Confidence by Their Greatly Beloved Principal": A Furore at Women's Christian College, Chennai, India, 1940'. In *Women's Activism: Global Perspectives from the 1890s to the Present,* edited by Francisca de Haan, Margaret Allen, June Purvis, and Krassimira Daskalova, 168–82. London: Routledge, 2013.

Allitt, Patrick. *Catholic Converts: British and American Intellectuals Turn to Rome.* Ithaca, and London: Cornell University Press, 1997.

Attwood, Bain. 'Off the Mission Stations: Aborigines in Gippsland, 1860–1890'. *Aboriginal History* 10, 2 (1986): 131–51.

Austin-Broos, Diana. '"Right Way t'il I Die": Christianity and Kin on Country at Hermannsburg'. In *Religious Change, Conversion and Culture,* edited by L. Olsen, 226–53. Sydney: Sydney Association for Studies in Society and Culture, 1996.

Barry, Amanda, Joanna Cruickshank, Andrew Brown-May and Patricia Grimshaw (eds). *Evangelists of Empire? Missionaries in Colonial History.*

Melbourne: eScholarship Research Centre in collaboration with the School of Historical Studies, 2008.

Barwick, Diane E. *Rebellion at Coranderrk.* Canberra: Aboriginal History, 1998.

Bayly, Christopher A. *The Birth of the Modern World, 1780–1914: Global Connections and Comparisons.* Oxford: Blackwell, 2004.

Belich, James. *Replenishing the Earth: The Settler Revolution and the Rise of the Anglo-World, 1783–1939.* Oxford: Oxford University Press, 2009.

Bell, Diane. *Ngarrindjeri Wuruwarrin: A World That Is, Was, and Will Be.* North Melbourne: Spinifex Press, 1998.

Bell, Diane. *Daughters of the Dreaming.* 3rd edn. North Melbourne: Spinifex Press, 2002.

Bendikowski, Tillmann. '"Eine Fackel der Zwietracht": Katholisch-protestantische Mischehen im 19. und 20. Jahrhundert'. In *Konfessionen im Konflikt: Deutschland zwischen 1800 und 1870: Ein zweites konfessionelles Zeitalter*, edited by Olaf Blaschke, 215–41. Göttingen: Vandenhoeck & Ruprecht, 2002.

Berliner Missionsberichte [alias: *Missions-Berichte der Gesellschaft zur Beförderung der evangelischen Missionen unter den Heiden*].

Beyreuther, Erich. 'Lostheorie und Lospraxis'. In *Studien zur Theologie Zinzendorfs: Gesammelte Aufsätze*, 109–35. Neukirchen: Olms, 1962.

Bilbe, Mark C. *Wupperthal: The Formation of a Community in South Africa, 1830–1965.* Köln: Rüdiger Köppe, 2009.

Bischoff, Eva. *Kannibale-Werden: Eine postkoloniale Geschichte deutscher Männlichkeit um 1900.* Bielefeld: Transcript, 2011.

Blaha, Walter. 'Erfurt unter dem Einfluß der Französischen Bürgerlichen Revolution 1789–1814'. In *Geschichte der Stadt Erfurt: Hrsg. im Auftrag des Rates der Stadt Erfurt von Willibald Gutsche*, edited by Willibald Gutsche, 180–213. Weimar: Hermann Böhlaus, 1986.

Blaschke, Olaf (ed.). *Konfessionen im Konflikt: Deutschland zwischen 1800 und 1970: Ein zweites konfessionelles Zeitalter.* Göttingen: Vandenhoeck & Ruprecht, 2002.

Bley, Helmut. 'Südafrikanische Welt'. In *Enzyklopädie der Neuzeit.* Vol. 13, edited by Friedrich Jäger, 19–27. Stuttgart: Metzler, 2011.

Brantlinger, Patrick. 'Victorians and Africans: The Genealogy of the Myth of the Dark Continent'. In *'Race', Writing, and Difference*, edited by Henry Louis Gates, Jr. 185–222. Chicago: University of Chicago Press, 1985.

Bredekamp, Henry, and Robert Ross (eds). *Missions and Christianity in South African History.* Johannesburg: Witwatersrand University Press, 1995.

Brierley, Jean, and Thomas Spear. 'Mutesa, the Missionaries and Christian Conversion in Buganda'. *International Journal of African Historical Studies* 21, 4 (1988): 601–18.

Brock, Peggy (ed.). *Indigenous Peoples and Religious Change.* Leiden: Brill, 2005.

Brock, Peggy. 'Nakedness and Clothing in Early Encounters between Aboriginal People of Central Australia, Missionaries and Anthropologists'. *Journal of Colonialism and Colonial History* 8, 1 (2007). http://muse.jhu.edu.ezproxy.library.uwa.edu.au/journals/journal_of_colonialism_and_colonial_history/v008/8.1brock.html

Brock, Peggy. *The Many Voyages of Arthur Wellington Clah: A Tsimshian Man on the Pacific Northwest Coast.* Vancouver: UBC Press, 2011.

Brock, Peggy, and Jacqueline Van Gent. 'Generational Religious Change Among the Arrernte at Hermannsburg, Central Australia'. *Australian Historical Studies* 120 (2002): 303–18.

Broome, Richard. *Aboriginal Victorians: A History since 1800.* Crows Nest, NSW: Allen and Unwin, 2005.

Broome, Richard. *Aboriginal Australians: A History since 1788.* 4th edn. Crows Nest: Allen and Unwin, 2010.

Broomhall, Susan, and Jacqueline Van Gent (eds). *Governing Masculinities in the Early Modern Period: Regulating Selves and Others.* Surrey, UK: Ashgate Publishing, 2011.

Burbank, Jane, and Frederick Cooper. *Empires in World History: Power and the Politics of Difference.* Princeton: Princeton University Press, 2010.

Burton, Antoinette. *Burdens of History: British Feminists, Indian Women, and Imperial Culture, 1865–1915.* Chapel Hill: University of North Carolina Press, 1994.

Carl, Gesine, and Angelika Schaser. 'Konversionsberichte des 17. bis 19. Jahrhunderts als Selbstzeugnisse gelesen: Ergebnisse und Forschungsperspektiven'. *Digitale Quellenedition Konversionserzählungen*, 2013. http://www.geschkult.fu-berlin.de/e/konversionen/ergebnisse/beitraege/Konversionsberichte_als_Selbstzeugnisse_gelesen.pdf?1369918255.

Carlebach, Elisheva. *Divided Souls: The Convert Critique and the Culture of Ashkenaz, 1750–1800.* New York: Leo Baeck Institute, 2003.

Chakrabarty, Dipesh. *Provincializing Europe: Postcolonial Thought and Historical Difference.* Princeton: Princeton University Press, 2000.

Chant, Barry. 'Hetherington, Isabella (1870–1946)'. In *Australian Dictionary of Biography.* National Centre of Biography, Australian National University. Accessed December 19, 2011. http://adb.anu.edu.au/biography/hetherington-isabella-12980/text23459.

Charlesworth, Max, Howard Morphy, Diane Bell, and Kenneth Maddock (eds). *Religion in Aboriginal Australia: An Anthology.* 3rd edn. St. Lucia: University of Queensland Press, 1992.

Chidester, David. *Savage Systems: Colonialism and Comparative Religion in Southern Africa.* Charlottesville: University of Virginia Press, 1996.

Clark, Christopher M. 'The Politics of Revival: Pietists, Aristocrats, and the State Church in Early Nineteenth-Century Prussia'. In *Between Reform, Reaction, and Resistance. Studies in the History of German Conservatism from 1789 to 1945*, edited by Larry E. Jones, and James Retallack, 31–60. Providence: Berg, 1993.

Clarus, Ludwig [Wilhelm Gustav Volk]. *Simeon: Wanderungen und Heimkehr eines christlichen Forschers.* Vol. 3. Schaffhausen: Fr. Hurter'sche Buchhandlung, 1862–1863.

Clarus, Ludwig [Wilhelm Gustav Volk]. *Die Zusammenkunft gläubiger Protestanten und Katholiken zu Erfurt im Herbste 1860 und deren Verlauf: Eine auf eigene Theilnahme und sämmtliche bekannt gewordene Quellen gegründete Darstellung und Mahnung zur Fortsetzung des Werkes.* Paderborn: Druck und Verlag der Junkermann'schen Buchhandlung, 1867.

Comaroff, John, and Jean Comaroff. *Of Revelation and Revolution.* Vol. 1, *Christianity, Colonialism and Consciousness in South Africa.* Chicago, and London: University of Chicago Press, 1991.

Comaroff, John, and Jean Comaroff. *Of Revelation and Revolution.* Vol. 2, *The Dialectics of Modernity on a South African Frontier*. Chicago, and London: University of Chicago Press, 1997.

Conrad, Sebastian. *Globalgeschichte: Eine Einführung*. Munich: C.H. Beck, 2013.

Couzens, Tim. *Murder at Morija: Faith, Mystery, and Tragedy on an African Mission*. Johannesburg: Random House; Charlottesville: Univ. of Virginia Press, 2003.

Crais, Clifton. *White Supremacy and Black Resistance in Pre-Industrial South Africa: The Making of the Colonial Order in the Eastern Cape, 1770–1865.* Cambridge: Cambridge University Press, 1992.

Cruickshank, Joanna. '"A Most Lowering Thing for a Lady": Aspiring to Respectable Whiteness on Ramahyuck Mission, 1885–1900'. In *Creating White Australia*, edited by Jane Carey, and Claire McLisky, 85–102. Sydney: Sydney University Press, 2009.

Cruickshank, Joanna. 'Race, Time and Modernity: Australian Faith Missions in the Early Twentieth Century'. Paper presented at the Australian Historians Association conference, Perth, July 2010.

Curthoys, Ann, and Marilyn Lake (eds). *Connected Worlds: History in Transnational Perspective.* Canberra: ANU E-Press, 2006.

Curtis-Wendland, Lisa. '(Re)constructing Missionary Wives: Frieda Strehlow and German Lutheran Women in Central Australia, 1892–1922'. PhD diss. Monash University, Melbourne, 2009.

Curtis-Wendland, Lisa. 'Corporal Punishment and Moral Reform at Hermannsburg Mission'. *History Australia* 7, 1 (2010): 7.1–7.17.

Curtis-Wendland, Lisa. 'Missionary Wives and the Sexual Narratives of German Lutheran Missions to Australia'. *Journal of the History of Sexuality* 20, 3 (2011): 498–519.

Darwin, John. *After Tamerlane: The Rise and Fall of Global Empires, 1400–2000*. London: Penguin Books, 2008.

Davis, Natalie Z. *Women on the Margins: Three Seventeenth-century Lives*. Cambridge, and London: Harvard University Press, 1995.

Deacon, Desley, Penny Russell, and Angela Woollacott (eds). *Transnational Ties: Australian Lives in the World*. Canberra: ANU E-Press, 2008.

Deacon, Desley, Penny Russell, and Angela Woollacott (eds). *Transnational Lives: Biographies of Global Modernity, 1700–Present*. Basingstoke: Palgrave Macmillan, 2010.

Dedering, Tilman. *Hate the Old and Follow the New: Khoekhoe and Missionaries in Early Nineteenth-Century Namibia*. Stuttgart: Franz Steiner Verlag, 1997.

Delius, Peter. *The Conversion*. Johannesburg: Ravan Press, 1984.

Delius, Peter. *The Land Belongs to Us: The Pedi Polity, the Boers and the British in the Nineteenth-century Transvaal*. London: Heinemann, 1984.

Delius, Peter. 'Witches and Missionaries in Nineteenth-Century Transvaal'. *Journal of Southern African Studies* 27, 3 (2001): 429–43.

Delius, Peter. 'Recapturing Captives and Conversations with 'Cannibals': In Pursuit of a Neglected Stratum in South African History'. *Journal of Southern African Studies* 36, 1 (2010): 7–23.

Der alte Fritz, was er ist und was er will. Probeblatt, Erfurt, 20. Dezember 1851.

Dowe, Christopher. *Auch Bildungsbürger: Katholische Studierende und Akademiker im Kaiserreich*. Göttingen: Vandenhoeck & Ruprecht, 2006.

Dursteler, Eric R. *Renegade Women: Gender, Identity and Boundaries in the Early Modern Mediterranean*. Baltimore: Johns Hopkins University Press, 2011.

Dussart, Françoise. *Warlpiri Women's Yawulyu Ceremonies: A Form of Socialization and Innovation*. Canberra: Australian National University, 1988.

Dussart, Françoise. *The Politics of Ritual in an Aboriginal Settlement: Kinship, Gender and the Currency of Knowledge*. Washington, DC, and London: Smithsonian Institute Press, 2000.

Elbourne, Elizabeth. *Blood Ground: Colonialism, Missions, and the Contest for Christianity in the Cape Colony and in Britain, 1799–1853*. Montreal: McGill-Queens University Press, 2002.

Elbourne, Elizabeth. 'Mother's Milk: Gender, Power and Anxiety on a South African Mission Station, 1839–1840'. In *Missionaries, Indigenous Peoples and Cultural Exchange*, edited by Patricia Grimshaw, and Andrew May, 10–23. Brighton, Portland, and Toronto: Sussex Academic Press, 2010.

Elbourne, Elizabeth. 'Christian Soldiers, Christian Allies: Coercion and Conversion in Southern Africa and Northeastern America at the Turn of the Nineteenth Century'. In *Beyond Conversion and Syncretism:*

Indigenous Encounters with Missionary Christianity, 1800–2000, edited by David Lindenfeld, and Miles Richardson, 79–114. New York: Berghahn Books, 2012.

Elbourne, Elizabeth. 'The Bannisters and Their Colonial World: Family Networks and Colonialism in the Early Nineteenth Century'. In *Within and Without the Nation: Canadian History as Transnational History*, edited by Karen Dubinsky, Adele Perry and Henry Yu. Toronto: University of Toronto Press, forthcoming.

Ellis, David. 'Erweckungsbewegung und Rationalismus im vormärzlichen Brandenburg und Pommern'. In *Wunderwelten: Religiöse Ekstase und Magie in der Moderne*, edited by Nils Freytag, and Diethard Sawicki, 53–82. Munich: Fink, 2006.

Elphick, Richard. *The Equality of Believers: Protestant Missionaries and the Racial Politics of South Africa*. Charlottesville: University of Virginia Press, 2012.

Elphick, Richard, and Rodney Davenport (eds). *Christianity in South Africa: A Political, Social and Cultural History*. Berkeley: University of California Press, 1997.

Etherington, Norman. *Preachers, Peasants and Politics in Southeast Africa, 1835–1880: African Christian Communities in Natal, Pondoland and Zululand*. London: Royal Historical Society, 1978.

Etherington, Norman (ed.). *Missions and Empire*. Oxford: Oxford University Press, 2005.

Faull, Katherine. '"Girls Talk" – das "Sprechen" von Kindern: Herrnhutische Seelsorge an den grossen Mädchen im 18. Jahrhundert'. *Unitas Fratrum* 57/58 (2006): 37–56.

Faull, Katherine M. (ed.). *Moravian Women's Memoirs: Their Related Lives 1750–1820*. Syracuse: Syracuse University Press, 1997.

Fenske, Hans. 'Ungeduldige Zuschauer: Die Deutschen und die europäische Expansion 1815–1880'. In *Imperialistisiche Kontinuität und nationale Ungeduld im 19. Jahrhundert*, edited by Wolfgang Reinhard, 87–123. Frankfurt am Main: Fischer Verlag, 1991.

Fleischer, Manfred. *Katholische und lutherische Ireniker: Unter Berücksichtigung des 19. Jahrhunderts*. Göttingen, Frankfurt am Main, and Zürich: Musterschmidt, 1968.

Fleischer, Manfred. 'Lutheran and Catholic Reunionists in the Age of Bismarck'. *Church History* 38 (1969): 43–66.

Fränkel, Ludwig Julius. 'Volk, Wilhelm'. *Allgemeine Deutsche Biographie*. Vol. 40, herausgegeben von der Historischen Kommission bei der Bayerischen Akademie der Wissenschaften, 227–30. 1896. http://de.wikisource.org/wiki/ADB:Volk,_Wilhelm.

Graf, Friedrich Wilhelm. 'Die Spaltung des Protestantismus: Zum Verhältnis von evangelischer Kirche, Staat und Gesellschaft im frühen 19. Jahrhundert'.

In *Religion und Gesellschaft im 19. Jahrhundert*, edited by Wolfgang Schieder, 157–90. Stuttgart: Klett-Cotta, 1993.

Griffiths, Gareth. 'Popular Imperial Adventure and the Discourse of Missionary Texts'. In *Mixed Messages: Materiality, Textuality, Missions,* edited by Jamie S. Scott and Gareth Griffiths, 51–66. New York: Palgrave Macmillan, 2005.

Griffiths, Gareth. '"Trained to Tell the Truth": Missionaries, Converts, and Narration'. In *Mission and Empire*, edited by Norman Etherington, 153–72. Oxford History of the British Empire, Companion Series. Oxford: Oxford University Press, 2005.

Grimshaw, Patricia. 'Faith, Missionary Life, and the Family'. In *Gender and Empire*, edited by Philippa Levine, 260–80. Oxford: Oxford University Press, 2004.

Grimshaw, Patricia. 'Reappraisals of Mission History: An Introduction'. In *Missionaries, Indigenous Peoples and Cultural Exchange*, edited by Patricia Grimshaw and Andrew May, 1–9. Eastbourne and Portland: Sussex Academic Press, 2010.

Grimshaw, Patricia, Elizabeth Nelson and Sandra Smith (eds). *Letters from Aboriginal Women in Victoria, 1867–1926.* Melbourne: Melbourne University, History Department, 2002.

Grimshaw, Patricia, and Andrew May (eds). *Missionaries, Indigenous Peoples and Cultural Exchange.* Brighton, Portland, and Toronto: Sussex Academic Press, 2010.

Gross, Michael B. 'The Catholic Missionary Crusade and the Protestant Revival in Nineteenth-Century Germany'. In *Protestant, Catholics and Jews in Germany*, edited by Helmut Walser Smith, 245–65. Oxford: Berg, 2001.

Günther, Dagmar. *Das nationale Ich? Autobiographische Sinnkonstruktionen deutscher Bildungsbürger des Kaiserreichs.* Tübingen: Niemeyer, 2004.

Gugelot, Frédéric. *La conversion des intellectuels au catholicisme en France 1885–1935.* Paris: CNRS éditions, 1998.

Guy, Jeff. *The Heretic: A Study of the Life of John William Colenso, 1814–1883.* Johannesburg, and Pietermaritzburg: University of Natal Press, 1983.

Guy, Jeff. *The View Across the River: Harriette Colenso and the Zulu Struggle Against Imperialism.* Cape Town: David Philip, 2001.

Habermas, Rebekka, and Richard Hölzl (eds). *Mission global: Eine Verflechtungsgeschichte seit dem 19. Jahrhundert.* Cologne: Böhlau, 2014.

Hagenauer, F.A. *Further Facts Relating to the Moravian Mission.* Melbourne: Fergusson and Moore, 1861–1867.

Hagenauer, F.A. *Mission Work Among the Aborigines of Victoria.* Melbourne: Diocesan Book Society, 1880.

Haggis, Jane, and Margaret Allen. 'Imperial Emotions: Affective Communities of Mission in British Protestant Women's Missionary Publications, 1880–1920'. *Journal of Social History* 41, 3 (2008): 692–716.

Hahn-Hahn, Ida von. *Von Babylon nach Jerusalem*. Mainz: Kirchheim und Schott, 1851.

Hall, Catherine (ed.). *Cultures of Empire: A Reader; Colonizers in Britain and the Empire in the Nineteenth and Twentieth Centuries*. New York: Routledge, 2000.

Hall, Catherine. *Civilising Subjects: Metropole and Colony in the English Imagination, 1830–1867*. Chicago: University of Chicago Press, and Cambridge: Polity Press, 2002.

Hamilton, Carolyn (ed.). *The Mfecane Aftermath: Reconstructive Debates in Southern African History*. Johannesburg: Witwatersrand University Press, 1995.

Harran, Marilyn J. *Luther on Conversion: The Early Years*. Ithaca: Cornell University Press, 1983.

Harries, Patrick. 'Exclusion, Classification and Internal Colonialism: The Emergence of Ethnicity Among the Tsonga-Speakers of South Africa'. In *The Creation of Tribalism in Southern Africa*, edited by Leroy Vail, 82–117. London: Currey; Berkeley: Univ. of California Press, 1989.

Harries, Patrick, and David Maxwell (eds). *The Spiritual in the Secular: Missionaries and Knowledge about Africa*. Grand Rapids, Michigan, and Cambridge: Eerdmans, 2012.

Harris, John. *One Blood: 200 Years of Aboriginal Encounter with Christianity; A Story of Hope*. Sutherland, NSW: Albatross Books, 1990.

Hastings, Adrian. *The Church in Africa, 1450–1950*. Oxford: Clarendon Press, 1995.

Haupt, Heinz-Gerhard. 'Politische Konversion in historischer Perspektive: Methodische und empirische Überlegungen'. In *Zeitperspektiven: Studien zu Kultur und Gesellschaft; Beiträge aus der Geschichte, Soziologie, Philosophie und Literaturwissenschaft*, edited by Uta Gerhardt, 267–304. Wiesbaden: Franz Steiner, 2003.

Heindl, Waltraud. *Gehorsame Rebellen: Bürokratie und Beamte in Österreich 1780 bis 1848*. Vienna, Cologne and Graz: Böhlau, 1991.

Herder, Gwendolin. *Entwicklungslinien volksbildnerischer Verlagsarbeit zwischen Kölner Ereignis und Märzrevolution (1837–1848): Der christliche Buchhandel am Beispiel des Verlages Herder in Freiburg im Breisgau*. Bonn: Herder, 1989.

Heß, Ulrich. 'Bürgerlich-demokratische Revolution, Durchsetzung der kapitalistischen Gesellschaftsordnung und Gründung der Sozialdemokratischen Arbeiterpartei (1848–1870)'. In *Geschichte der Stadt Erfurt*, hrsg. im Auftrag des Rates der Stadt Erfurt von Willibald Gutsche, 243–80. Weimar: Hermann Böhlaus, 1986.

Heß, Ulrich. 'Weitere Entfaltung des Kapitalismus am Vorabend der Bürgerlich-demokratischen Revolution (1815–1847)'. In *Geschichte der Stadt Erfurt*, hrsg. im Auftrag des Rates der Stadt Erfurt von Willibald, 215–42. Weimar: Hermann Böhlaus, 1986.

Hölscher, Lucian (ed.). *Datenatlas zur religiösen Geographie im protestantischen Deutschland: Von der Mitte des 19. Jahrhunderts bis zum Zweiten Weltkrieg.* 4 Vols. [Vol. 1, *Norden*, Vol. 2, *Osten*, Vol. 3, *Westen*, Vol. 4, *Süden*]. Berlin, and New York: Walter de Gruyter, 2001.

Hoffmann, C. *Vom Kraal zur Kanzel: Lebensgeschichte des Eingeborenenpastors Timotheus Sello.* Berlin: Buchhandlung der Berliner evangelischen Missionsgesellschaft, 1914.

Hofmeyr, Isabel. *'We Spend Our Years As A Tale That Is Told': Oral Historical Narrative in a South African Chiefdom.* Portsmouth: Heinemann, Johannesburg: Witwatersrand University Press, and London: Currey, 1994.

Hofmeyr, Isabel. '"Wailing For Purity": Oral Studies in Southern African Studies'. *African Studies* 54, 2 (1995): 16–31.

Hofmeyr, Isabel. *The Portable Bunyan: A Transnational History of the Pilgrim's Progress.* Princeton: Princeton University Press, 2003.

Horn, Wilhelm. *Erfurts Stadtverfassung und Stadtwirtschaft in ihrer Entwicklung bis zur Gegenwart: Ein Beispiel zur Verfassungsgeschichte und Sozialpolitik der deutschen Städte.* Jena: G. Fischer, 1904.

Horton, David (ed.). *The Encyclopaedia of Aboriginal Australia.* Vol. 2. Canberra: Aboriginal Studies Press, 1994.

Horton, Robin. 'African Conversion'. *Africa* 41, 2 (1971): 85–108.

Huggins, Jackie. 'White Aprons, Black Hands: Aboriginal Women Domestic Servants in Queensland'. *Labour History* 69 (1995): 188–95.

Hurter, Friedrich. 'Vorrede'. In *Geburt und Wiedergeburt. Erinnerungen aus meinem Leben und Blicke auf die Kirche.* Vol. 1, III–XIV. Schaffhausen: Verlag der Hurter'schen Buchhandlung.

Hutton, Joseph Edmund. *A History of Moravian Missions.* London: Moravian Publication Office, 1922.

Jensz, Felicity. 'Three Peculiarities of the Southern Australian Moravian Mission Field'. *Journal of Moravian History* 7 (2009): 7–30.

Jensz, Felicity. 'Controlling Marriages: Friedrich Hagenauer and the Betrothal of Indigenous Western Australian Women in Colonial Victoria'. *Aboriginal History* 34, 1 (2010): 34–54.

Jensz, Felicity. *German Moravian Missionaries in the British Colony of Victoria, Australia, 1848–1908.* Leiden: Brill, 2011.

Jolly, Margaret, and Martha Macintyre (eds). *Family and Gender in the Pacific: Domestic Contradictions and Colonial Impact.* Cambridge: Cambridge University Press, 1989.

Jolly, Margaret. '"To Save the Girls for Brighter and Better Lives": Presbyterian Missions and Women in the South of Vanuatu, 1848–1870'. *The Journal of Pacific History* 26, 1 (1991): 27–48.

Kaufmann, Georg Heinrich. 'Reichensperger, August'. In *Allgemeine Deutsche Biographie*. Vol. 53, edited by Historische Kommission bei der Bayerischen Akademie der Wissenschaften, 276–81. 1907. http://de.wikisource.org/wiki/ADB:Reichensperger,_August

Kehrein, Joseph. *Biographischliterarisches Lexikon der katholischen deutschen Dichter, Volks- und Jugendschriftsteller.* Vol. 2. Würzburg: Leo Woerl'sche Buch-, Kunst-, und Verlagsbuchhandlung, 1871.

Kendall, Calvin B., Oliver Nicholson, William D. Phillips Jr., and Marguerite Ragnow (eds). *Conversion to Christianity from Late Antiquity to the Modern Age: Considering the Process in Europe, Asia, and the Americas.* Minneapolis: CEMH, 2009.

Kenny, Robert. *The Lamb Enters the Dreaming: Nathanael Pepper and the Ruptured World.* Melbourne: Scribe, 2007.

Klippstein, Peter-Jürgen. 'Die Inschriften der Grabsteine auf dem Brühler Friedhof in Erfurt, aufgezeichnet von Wilhelm Lorenz'. *Jahrbuch für Erfurter Geschichte* 4 (2009): 225–55.

Koschorke, Klaus (ed.). *'Christen und Gewürze': Konfrontation und Interaktion kolonialer und indigener Christentumsvarianten.* StAECG 1. Göttingen: Vandenhoeck & Ruprecht, 1998.

Kriel, Lize. *The Malaboch Books: Kgaluši in the 'Civilization of the Written Word'.* Stuttgart: Franz Steiner, 2009.

Kriel, Lize, and Alan Kirkaldy. '"Praying is the Work of Men, Not the Work of Women": The Response of Bahananwa and Vhavenda Women to Conversion in Late-Nineteenth-Century Lutheran Missionary Territories'. *South African Historical Journal* 61, 2 (2009): 316–35.

Krstić, Tijana. 'Illuminated by the Light of Islam and the Glory of the Ottoman Sultanate: Self-Narratives of Conversion to Islam in the Age of Confessionalization'. *Comparative Studies in Society and History* 51 (2009): 35–63.

Krstić, Tijana. *Contested Conversions to Islam: Narratives of Religious Change in the Early Modern Ottoman Empire.* Stanford: Stanford University Press, 2011.

Lake, Marilyn, and Henry Reynolds. *Drawing the Global Colour Line: White Men's Countries and the Challenge of Racial Equality.* Cambridge: Cambridge University Press, 2008.

Lake, Meredith. 'Salvation and Civilisation: First Missionary Encounter at Sydney Cove'. In *Evangelists of Empire? Missionaries in Colonial History,* edited by Amanda Barry, Joanna Cruickshank, Andrew Brown-May, and Patricia Grimshaw, 87–103. Melbourne: eScholarship Research Centre in collaboration with the School of Historical Studies, 2008.

Landau, Paul S. *The Realm of the Word: Language, Gender and Christianity in a Southern African Kingdom*. London: James Currey, and Cape Town: David Philip, 1995.

Lazar, Lance Gabriel. 'Negotiating Conversions: Catechumens and the Family in Early Modern Italy'. In *Piety and Family in Early Modern Europe*, edited by Marc R. Forster, and Benjamin J. Kaplan, 152–77. Aldershot: Ashgate, 2005.

Leeb, Rudolf, and Kurt Aland. 'Über den Glaubenswechsel in der Geschichte des Christentums'. *wiener zeitschrift zur geschichte der neuzeit* 7 (2007): 123–33.

Leonhard, Jörn, and Ulrike von Hirschhausen. *Empires und Nationalstaaten im 19. Jahrhundert.* 2nd edn. Göttingen: Vandenhoeck & Ruprecht, 2011.

Lessing, Hanns et al. (eds). *Deutsche evangelische Kirche im kolonialen südlichen Afrika: Die Rolle der Auslandsarbeit von den Anfängen bis in die 1920er Jahre [The German Protestant Church in Colonial Southern Africa: the Impact of Overseas Work from the Beginnings until the 1920s].* Wiesbaden: Harrassowitz, 2011/2012.

Lester, Alan. *Imperial Networks: Creating Identities in Nineteenth Century South Africa and Britain.* London, and New York: Routledge, 2001.

Lester, Alan, and David Lambert (eds). *Colonial Lives across the British Empire: Imperial Careering in the Long Nineteenth Century.* Cambridge: Cambridge University Press, 2006

Levine, Philippa (ed.). *Gender and Empire.* Oxford: Oxford University Press, 2004.

Lienemann, Wolfgang. 'Einführung' to *Religiöse Grenzüberschreitungen. Studien zu Bekehrung, Konfessions- und Religionswechsel.* Studien zur Außeneuropäischen Christentumsgeschichte. Vol. 20, edited by Christine Lienemann-Perrin, and Wolfgang Lienemann, 3–37. Wiesbaden: Harrassowitz, 2012.

Lienemann-Perrin, Christine, and Wolfgang Lienemann (eds). *Religiöse Grenzüberschreitungen: Studien zur Bekehrung, Konfessions- und Religionswechsel* [Crossing Religious Borders. Studies on Conversion and Religious Belonging]. Wiesbaden: Harrassowitz, 2012.

Lindenfeld, David, and Miles Richardson (eds). B*eyond Conversion and Syncretism: Indigenous Encounters with Missionary Christianity, 1800–2000.* New York and Oxford: Berghahn, 2012.

Lost, Christine. *Das Leben als Lehrtext: Lebensläufe aus der Herrnhuter Brüdergemeine* (= Beiheft of *Unitas Fratrum*, 14. Herrnhut: Herrnhuter Verlag, 2007.

Lotz-Heumann, Ute, Jan-Friedrich Missfelder, and Matthias Pohlig (eds). *Konversion und Konfession in der Frühen Neuzeit.* Gütersloh: Gütersloher Verlagshaus, 2008.

Lozar, Angelika, and Angelika Schaser. 'Die Rückkehr zum "wahren Glauben": Konversionen im 17. Jahrhundert'. *Frühneuzeit-Info* 13 (2002): 65–74.

Lydon, Jane. 'The Experimental 1860s: Charles Walter's Images of Coranderrk Aboriginal Station, Victoria'. *Aboriginal History* 26 (2002): 78–130.

Lydon, Jane. *Fantastic Dreaming: The Archaeology of an Aboriginal Mission.* Lanham: AltaMira Press, 2009.

Martin, Phyllis M. 'Life and Death, Power and Vulnerability: Everyday Contradictions at the Loango Mission, 1883–1904'. *Journal of African Cultural Studies* 15, 1 (2002): 61–78.

Mason, John C.S. *The Moravian Church and the Missionary Awakening in England, 1760–1800.* Woodbridge, Suffolk, UK: Royal Historical Society, and Rochester: Boydell Press, 2001.

Maynes, Mary Jo, Jennifer L. Pierce and Barbara Laslett. *Telling Stories: The Use of Personal Narratives in the Social Sciences and History.* Ithaca and London: Cornell University Press, 2008.

Meissner, Jochen, Ulrich Mücke and Klaus Weber. *Schwarzes Amerika: Eine Geschichte der Sklaverei.* Munich: C.H. Beck, 2008.

Merlan, Francesca. 'Gender in Aboriginal Social Life: A Review'. In *Social Anthropology and Australian Aboriginal Studies*, edited by Ronald M. Berndt, and Robert Tonkinson, 15–76. Canberra: Aboriginal Studies Press, 1988.

Mettele, Gisela. *Weltbürgertum, oder Gottesreich: Die Herrnhuter Brüdergemeine als globale Gemeinschaft, 1727–1857.* Göttingen: Vandenhoeck & Ruprecht, 2009.

Meyer, Birgit. *Translating the Devil: Religion and Modernity Among the Ewe in Ghana.* Edinburgh: Edinburgh University Press, 1999.

Miller, Jon. *The Social Control of Religious Zeal: A Study of Organizational Contradictions.* New Brunswick: Eerdmans, 1994.

Mills, Kenneth, and Anthony Grafton (eds). *Old Worlds and New.* Rochester: University of Rochester Press, 2003.

Missions-Blatt aus der Brüdergemeine. Zum Besten der Heiden-Missionen, 1837–1941.

Minkenberg, Michael and Ulrich Willems. 'Politik und Religion im Übergang: Tendenzen und Forschungsfragen am Beginn des 21. Jahrhunderts'. Edited by Michael Minkenberg and Ulrich Willems. *Politik und Religion*, Politische Vierteljahresschrift Sonderheft 33 (2002): 13–41. Wiesbaden: Verlag für Sozialwissenschaften, 2003.

Morton, John. 'Aboriginal Religion Today'. In *The Oxford Companion to Aboriginal Art and Culture*, edited by Sylvia Kleinert and Margo Neile, 9–16. Melbourne: Oxford University Press, 2000.

Muldoon, James (ed.). *Varieties of Religious Conversion in the Middle Ages.* Gainesville: University Press of Florida, 1997.

Nachrichten aus der Bruedergemeine, 1819–1894.

Nielssen, Hilde, Inger Marie Okkenhaug and Karina Hestad Skeie (eds). *Protestant Missions and Local Encounters in the Nineteenth and Twentieth Centuries*. Leiden: Brill, 2011.

Nipperdey, Thomas. *Deutsche Geschichte, 1800–1866: Bürgerwelt und starker Staat.* Munich: C.H. Beck, 1983. English: *Germany from Napoleon to Bismarck, 1800–1866*, trans. Daniel Nolan (Princeton: Princeton University Press, 1996).

Nipperdey, Thomas. *Religion im Umbruch: Deutschland, 1870–1918.* Munich: C. H. Beck, 1988.

Nipperdey, Thomas. 'Religion und Gesellschaft: Deutschland um 1900'. *Historische Zeitschrift* 246 (1988): 591–615.

Nippold, Friedrich. *Welche Wege führen nach Rom? Geschichtliche Beleuchtung der römischen Illusion über die Erfolge der Propaganda.* Heidelberg: Verlagsbuchhandlung von Fr. Bassermann, 1869.

Olupona, Jacob K. *African Religions: A Very Short Introduction.* Oxford: OUP, 2014.

Osterhammel, Jürgen. 'Transnationale Gesellschaftsgeschichte: Erweiterung oder Alternative?' *Geschichte und Gesellschaft* 27 (2001): 464–79.

Osterhammel, Jürgen. *Die Verwandlung der Welt: Eine Geschichte des 19. Jahrhunderts.* Munich: C. H. Beck, 2009.

Osterhammel, Jürgen, and Niels P. Petersson. *Globalization: A Short History.* Princeton, and Oxford: Princeton University Press, 2005.

Paletschek, Sylvia. *Frauen und Dissens: Frauen im Deutschkatholizismus und in den freien Gemeinden, 1841–1852.* Göttingen: Vandenhoeck & Ruprecht, 1990.

Peel, John D.Y. *Religious Encounter and the Making of the Yoruba.* Bloomington: Indiana University Press, 2003.

Peinhardt, Helmut. *Erfurt im 19. Jahrhundert: Bilderchronik; Aus Archivalien des Stadtarchivs Erfurt* [anläßlich der 1250-Jahrfeier der Stadt Erfurt]. Erfurt: Verlags-Haus Thüringen, 1992.

Peires, Jeff. *The Dead Will Arise: Nongqawuse and the Great Xhosa Cattle-Killing Movement of 1856–7.* London: James Currey, 1989.

Peper, Ines. *Konversionen im Umkreis des Wiener Hofes um 1700.* Cologne, Weimar, and Vienna: Böhlau, 2010.

Pepper, Phillip, and Tess De Araugo. *The Kurnai of Gippsland.* Melbourne: Hyland House, 1985.

Pepper, Phillip, and Tess De Araugo. *You Are What You Make Yourself to Be.* Melbourne: Hyland House, 1989.

Periodical Accounts relating to the Missions of the Church of the United Brethren established among the Heathen, London: Printed for the Brethren's Society for the Furtherance of the Gospel, 1790– 1889.

Perkins, Rachel, and Marcia Langton (eds). *First Australians: An Illustrated History*. Victoria: The Miegunyah Press, 2008.

Petrich, Hermann. *Hermann Theodor Wangemann: Sein Leben und Wirken für Gottes Reich und für das Missionswerk insonderheit.* Berlin: Buchhandlung der Berliner evangelischen Missionsgesellschaft, 1895.

Pitassi, Maria-Cristina, and Daniela Solfaroli Camillocci (eds). *Les Modes de la conversion confessionelle à l'Epoque moderne: Autobiographie, altérité et construction des identités religieuses.* Firenze: Leo S. Olschki, 2010.

Pomeranz, Kenneth. *The Great Divergence: China, Europe and the Making of the Modern World Economy*. Princeton: Princeton University Press, 2000.

Portelli, Alessandro. 'Oral History as Genre'. In *Narrative and Genre*, edited by Mary Chamberlain, and Paul Thompson, 23–45. London: Transaction Publishers, 1998.

Porter, Andrew. '"Cultural Imperialism" and Protestant Missionary Enterprise, 1780–1914'. *Journal of Imperial and Commonwealth History* 25, 3 (1997): 367–91.

Porter, Andrew. *Religion Versus Empire? British Protestant Missionaries and Overseas Expansion, 1700–1914*. Manchester: Manchester University Press, 2004.

Portmann-Tinguely, Albert. 'Volk, Wilhelm Gustav Werner'. In *Biographisch-Bibliographisches Kirchenlexikon*. Vol. XIX (2001): columns 1499–1506.

Prevost, Elizabeth E. 'Assessing Women, Gender, and Empire in Britain's Nineteenth-Century Protestant Missionary Movement'. *History Compass* 7, 3 (2009): 765–99.

Prevost, Elizabeth E. 'Contested Conversions: Missionary Women's Religious Encounters in Early Colonial Uganda'. In *Missionaries, Indigenous Peoples and Cultural Exchange*, edited by Patricia Grimshaw, and Andrew May. Eastbourne, and Portland: Sussex Academic Press, 2010.

Rambo, Lewis R. *Understanding Religious Conversion.* New Haven: Yale University, 1993.

Ranger, Terence. *Are We Not Also Men? The Samkange Family & African Politics in Zimbabwe, 1920–64*. Harare: Baobab, 1995.

Riesebrodt, Martin. *Cultus und Heilsversprechen: Eine Theorie der Religionen.* Munich: C.H. Beck, 2007.

Robertson, Susan. *The Bell Sounds Pleasantly: Ebenezer Mission Station.* Doncaster, VIC: Luther Rose Publications, 1992.

Robinson, Shirleene. '"We Don't Want One That Is Too Old": Aboriginal Child Domestic Servants in Late 19th and early 20th-century Queensland'. *Aboriginal History* 27 (2003): 162–82.

Rosenthal, David August. *Convertitenbilder aus dem neunzehnten Jahrhundert: Erster Band: Deutschland.* Schaffhausen: Hurter'sche Buchhandlung, 1866.

Rosenthal, David August. *Convertitenbilder aus dem neunzehnten Jahrhundert. Erster Band: Deutschland*, 3rd edn. Schaffhausen: Hurter'sche Buchhandlung 1889.

Rowe, John. 'Mutesa and the Missionaries: Church and State in Pre-Colonial Buganda'. In *Christian Missionaries and the State in the Third World*, edited by Holger Bernt, and Michael Twaddle, 52–65. Oxford: OUP, 2002.

Rüther, Kirsten. *The Power Beyond: Mission Strategies, African Conversion, and the Development of a Christian Culture in the Transvaal*. Münster: Lit, 2001.

Rüther, Kirsten. '"Sekukuni, Listen!, *Banna*!, and to the Children of Frederick the Great and Our Kaiser Wilhelm": Documents in the Social and Religious History of the Transvaal, 1860–1890'. *Journal of Religion in Africa* 34, 3 (2004): 207–34.

Rüther, Kirsten. 'Christianisierung'. In *Enzyklopädie der Neuzeit*. Vol. 2, edited by Friedrich Jäger, 741–57. Stuttgart: Metzler, 2005.

Rüther, Kirsten. 'Through the Eyes of Missionaries and the Archives They Created: The Interwoven Histories of Power and Authority in the Nineteenth-Century Transvaal'. *Journal of Southern African Studies* 38, 2 (2012): 369–84.

Rüther, Kirsten. 'Imminent Colonialism: Violence on Lutheran Mission Stations and the Ending of the Pre-Colonial Zulu State'. In *Development, Modernism and Modernity in Africa*, edited by Augustine Agwuele, 278–93. London: Routledge, 2012.

Rüther, Kirsten. 'Der Streit um Englisch als Unterrichtsfach in lutherischen Missionsschulen Südafrikas, ca. 1895–1910: Impulse für eine Geschichte der Resonanzen'. In *Mission global: Eine Verflechtungsgeschichte seit dem 19. Jahrhundert*, edited by Rebekka Habermas, and Richard Hölzl, 91–110. Cologne: Böhlau, 2014.

Rutherdale, Myra. '"It is not Soft Job to be Performed": Missionaries and Imperial Manhood in Canada, 1880–1920'. In *Missionaries, Indigenous People and Cultural Change*, edited by Patricia Grimshaw, and Andrew May, 52–66. Eastbourne: Sussex Academic Press, 2010.

Saurer, Edith. 'Romantische KonvertitInnen. Religion und Identität in der Wiener Romantik'. In *Paradoxien der Romantik. Gesellschaft, Kultur und Wissenschaft in Wien im frühen 19. Jahrhundert*, edited by Christian Aspalter et al., 229–55. Vienna: Facultas, 2006.

Schapera, Isaac. *Tribal Innovators: Tswana Chiefs and Social Change, 1795–1940*. London: Athlone Press, 1970.

Schaser, Angelika. '"Zurück zur heiligen Kirche": Konversionen zum Katholizismus im säkularisierten Zeitalter'. *Historische Anthropologie* 15 (2007): 1–23.

Schaser, Angelika. 'Inclusion et exclusion : La recherche sur les conversions religieuses en Allemagne à l'époque moderne'. In *Religion ou confession: Un bilan franco-allemand sur l'époque moderne (XVIe–XVIIIe siècles)*, edited by Philippe Buttgen, and Christophe Duhamelle, 577–94. Paris: Édition de la Maison des Sciences de l'Homme, 2010.

Schaser, Angelika. 'Schreiben um dazuzugehören: Konversionserzählungen im 19. Jahrhundert'. In *Selbstzeugnis und Person: Transkulturelle Perspektiven*, edited by Claudia Ulbrich, Hans Medick, and Angelika Schaser, 381–98. Cologne, Weimar and Vienna: Böhlau, 2012.

Schatz, Klaus. *Zwischen Säkularisation und Zweitem Vatikanum: Der Weg des deutschen Katholizismus im 19. und 20. Jahrhundert*. Frankfurt am Main: Knecht, 1986.

Schmid, Pia. 'Die Kindererweckung in Herrnhut am 17. August 1727'. In *Neue Aspekte der Zinzendorfforschung*, edited by Martin Brecht, and Paul Peucker, 114–33. Göttingen: Vandenhoeck & Ruprecht, 2006.

Schnabel, Franz. *Deutsche Geschichte im 19. Jahrhundert*. Vol. 4, *Die religiösen Kräfte*. Munich: dtv, 1951 [Freiburg i. Br.: Herder, 1937].

Scott, Jamie S., and Gareth Griffiths (eds). *Mixed Messages: Materiality, Textuality, Missions*. New York: Palgrave Macmillan, 2005.

Semple, Rhonda Anne. *Missionary Women: Gender, Professionalism and the Victorian Idea of Christian Mission*. Woodbridge, Suffolk; Rochester: Boydell Press, 2003.

Semple, Rhonda. 'Missionary Manhood: Professionalism, Belief and Masculinity in the Nineteenth-Century Imperial Field'. *Journal of Imperial and Commonwealth History* 36, 3 (2008): 397–415.

Sheringham, Michael. 'Conversion and Turning Points'. In *Encyclopedia of Life Writing*. Vol. 1, edited by Margaretta Jolly, 233–4. London: Fitzroy Dearborn, 2001.

Sidenvall, Erik. *The Making of Manhood Among Swedish Missionaries in China and Mongolia, 1890–1914*. Leiden: Brill, 2009.

Simensen, Jarle (ed.). *Norwegian Missions in African History*. Vol. 1, *South Africa, 1845–1906*. Oslo: Norwegian University Press, 1986.

Simensen, Jarle. 'Religious Change as Transaction: The Norwegian Mission to Zululand, South Africa, 1850–1906'. *Journal of Religion in Africa* 16 (1986): 82–100.

Sinha, Mrinalini. *Colonial Masculinity: The 'Manly Englishman' and the 'Effeminate Bengali' in the Late Nineteenth Century*. Manchester: Manchester University Press, 1995.

Smaby, B. Prior. *Transformation of Moravian Bethlehem: From Communal Mission to Family Economy*. Philadelphia: University of Pennsylvania Press, 1988.

Smaby, B. Prior. 'Female Piety Among Eighteenth-Century Moravians'. *Pennsylvania History* 64 (1997): 151–67.

Smaby, B. Prior. 'No One Should Lust for Power ... Women Least'. In *Pious Pursuits: German Moravians in the Atlantic World*, edited by Michelle Gillespie, and Robert Beachy, 159–73. New York, and Oxford: Berghahn Books, 2007.

Smyth, Robert Brough. *The Aborigines of Victoria*. Melbourne: J. Ferres, 1876.

Sommer, Elisabeth W. *Serving Two Masters: Moravian Brethren in Germany and North Carolina, 1727–1801*. Lexington: University Press of Kentucky, 2000.

Sonntag, C. *Anna Moschabelo*. Berlin: Buchhandlung der Berliner evangelischen Missionsgesellschaft, 1914.

Spitzer, Leo. *Lives in Between: Assimilation and Marginality in Austria, Brazil, West Africa 1780–1945*. Cambridge: Cambridge University Press, 1989.

Stapleton, Timothy J. 'Reluctant Slaughter: Rethinking Maqoma's Role in the Xhosa Cattle-Killing, (1853–1857)'. *International Journal of African Historical Studies* 26, 2 (1993): 345–69.

Steinmetz, George. *The Devil's Handwriting: Precoloniality and the German Colonial State in Qingdao, Samoa, and Southwest Africa*. Chicago: University of Chicago Press, 2007.

Stewart, Pamela J. and Andrew Strathern. 'Reinforcing Comparative Dimensions'. In *Religious and Ritual Change: Cosmologies and Histories*, edited by Pamela J. Stewart and Andrew Strathern, 329–52. Durham: Carolina Academic Press, 2009.

Stoler, Ann Laura and Frederick Cooper. 'Between Metropole and Colony: Rethinking a Research Agenda'. In *Tensions of Empire: Colonial Cultures in a Bourgeois World*, edited by Ann Laura Stoler, and Frederick Cooper, 1–56. Berkeley: University of California Press, 1997.

Stoler, Ann Laura, and Frederick Cooper. *Tensions of Empire: Colonial Cultures in a Bourgeois World*. Berkeley: University of California Press, 1997.

Subrahmanyam, Sanjay. *Explorations in Connected History: From the Tagus to the Ganges*. Oxford: Oxford University Press, 2005.

Taylor, Charles. *A Secular Age*. Cambridge: Belknap Press of Harvard University Press, 2007.

Teter, Magdalena. 'Jewish Conversions to Catholicism in the Polish-Lithuania Commonwealth of the Seventeenth and Eighteenth Centuries'. *Jewish History* 17, 3 (2003): 257–83.

Thadden, Rudolf von. *Trieglaff: Eine pommersche Lebenswelt zwischen Kirche und Politik, 1807–1948*. Göttingen: Wallstein Verlag, 2010.

Tjelle, Kristin Fjelde. *Missionary Masculinity: The Case of Norwegian Lutheran Missions to the Zulus, 1870–1930*. Oslo: Oslo University Press, 2012.

Trapido, Stanley. 'The South African Republic: Class Formation and the State, 1850–1900'. *Collected Seminar Papers on the Societies of Southern Africa in the 19th and 20th Centuries* 3 (1971/72): 53–65.

[Trippe, Karl Friedrich]. *Denkmal auf Volk's (Ludwig Clarus) Grab, gesetzt von jüngster Freundeshand (Erlös für Volk's Stiftungen)*. Erfurt, 1869.

Trobe, B. La. *The Moravian Missions: A Glance at 164 Years of Unbroken Missionary Labours*. London: G. Norman and Sons, 1896.

Tyrell, Hartmann. '"Organisierte Mission": Protestantische Missionsgesellschaften des langen 19. Jahrhunderts' ['"Organized Missions": Protestant Missionary Societies in the Long Nineteenth Century']. In *Etappen der Globalisierung in christentumsgeschichtlicher Perspektive* [Phases of Globalization in the History of Christianity]. StAECG 19, edited by Klaus Koschorke, 255–72. Wiesbaden: Harrassowitz, 2012.

Ulbrich, Claudia, Hans Medick, and Angelika Schaser (eds). *Selbstzeugnis und Person: Transkulturelle Perspektiven*. Cologne, Weimar and Vienna: Böhlau, 2012.

Ulmer, Bernd. 'Die autobiographische Plausibilität von Konversionserzählungen'. In *Wer schreibt meine Lebensgeschichte? Biographie, Autobiographie, Hagiographie und ihre Entstehungszusammenhänge*, edited by Walter Sparn, 287–95. Gütersloh: Mohn, 1990.

Van Gent, Jacqueline. '*Blickwechsel*: Arrernte Encounters with Lutheran Missionaries in Central Australia'. In *Luther zwischen den Kulturen*, edited by Hans Medick, and Peer Schmidt, 396–420. Göttingen: Vandenhoeck & Ruprecht, 2004.

Van Gent, Jacqueline. 'Changing Concepts of Embodiment and Illness among the Western Arrernte at Hermannsburg Mission'. In *Indigenous Peoples, Christianity and Religious Change*, edited by Peggy Brock, 227–48. Leiden: Brill, 2005.

Van Gent, Jacqueline. 'Side-wounds, Sex and Savages: Moravian Masculinities and Early Modern Protestant Missions'. In *Governing Masculinities in the Early Modern Period: Regulating Selves and Others*, edited by Susan Broomhall, and Jacqueline Van Gent, 189–208. Aldershot: Ashgate, 2011.

Van Gent, Jacqueline. 'The Lives of Others: Moravian Indigenous Converts' Writings and the Politics of Colonial Autobiographies'. In *Selbstzeugnis und Person: Transkulturelle Perspektiven*, edited by Claudia Ulbrich, Hans Medick, and Angelika Schaser, 87–102. Cologne, Weimar and Vienna: Böhlau, 2012.

Viljoen, Russel. *Jan Paerl, A Khoikhoi in Cape Colonial Society, 1761–1851*. Leiden: Brill, 2006.

[Volk, Wilhelm Gustav Werner]. 'Katholische Mission in Australien'. *Historisch-Politische Blätter* 4 (1839): 437–45, 454–64, 530–39.

[Volk, Wilhelm Gustav Werner]. 'Briefliche Mittheilungen aus Preußen über das Ehescheidungsgesetz: Von einem Protestanten'. *Historisch-Politische Blätter für das katholische Deutschland* 11 (1843): 49–56.

[Volk, Wilhelm Gustav Werner]. *Die Berliner Gewerbeausstellung und die Ausstellung des heiligen Rockes in Trier mit besonderer Bezugnahme auf den Rongeschen Brief: Ein Brief aus Berlin von einem Protestanten*. Münster: Druck und Verlag von Friedrich Regensberg, 1845.

[Volk, Wilhelm Gustav Werner]. *Geständnisse eines im Protestantismus aufgewachsenen Christen über religiöse Erziehung und Bildung*. Mainz: Kirchheim, Schott und Thielmann, 1846.

[Volk, Wilhelm Gustav Werner]. *Glaubenslehrjahre eines im Protestantismus erzogenen Christen*. Regensburg: Druck und Verlag von Friedrich Regensberg, 1852.

[Volk, Wilhelm Gustav Werner]. *Aus dem Leben einer Convertitin: Mitgetheilt von Ludwig Clarus* [Wilhelm Gustav Werner Volk]. Schaffhausen: Verlag der Fr. Hurter'schen Buchhandlung, 1859.

'Volk, Wilhelm Gustav Werner'. In *Deutsche Biographische Enzyklopädie*. Vol. 10. Munich: De Gruyter, 1999, 243–4.

Volz, Stephen. 'Them Who Kill the Body: Christian Ideals and Political Realities in the Interior of Southern Africa during the 1850s'. *Journal of Southern African Studies* 36, 1 (2010): 41–56.

Wagner, Roger. 'Zoutpansberg: The Dynamics of a Hunting Frontier, 1848–67'. In *Economy and Society in Pre-industrial South Africa*, edited by Shula Marks, and Anthony Atmore, 313–49. London: Longman, 1980.

Wangemann, Hermann Theodor. *Ein Reise-Jahr in Süd-Afrika: Ausführliches Tagebuch über eine in den Jahren 1866 und 1867 ausgeführte Inspectionsreise durch die Missions-Gebiete der Berliner Missions-Gesellschaft*. Berlin: Verlag des Missionshauses in Berlin, 1868.

Wangemann, Hermann Theodor. *Maléo und Sekukuni: Ein Lebensbild aus Südafrika*. Berlin: Buchhandlung der Berliner evangelischen Missionsgesellschaft, 1868–1869.

Wangemann, Hermann Theodor. *Geschichte der Berliner Missionsgesellschaft und ihrer Arbeiten in Südafrika*. 4 vols. Berlin: Selbstverlag Ev. Mission, 1872–1877.

Wangemann, Hermann Theodor. *Lebensbilder aus Südafrika: Ein Beitrag zur Kirchen- und Culturgeschichte des neunzehnten Jahrhunderts*, 3rd edn. Berlin: Verlag des Missionshauses in Berlin, 1876.

Wangemann, Hans. *D. Dr. Wangemann, Missionsdirektor: Ein Lebensbild*. Berlin: Wiegandt und Grieben, 1899.

Warneck, Gustav. 'Einleitung' to *Johann Friedrich Riedel, ein Lebensbild aus der Minahassa auf Celebes*, edited by R. Grundemann, 5–23. Gütersloh: Bertelsmann, 1873.

Wehler, Hans-Ulrich. *Deutsche Gesellschaftsgeschichte*. Vol. 3, *Von der 'Deutschen Doppelrevolution' bis zum Beginn des Ersten Weltkrieges 1849–1914*. Munich: C.H. Beck, 1995.

Weiner, Annette B. *Inalienable Possessions: The Paradox of Keeping While Giving.* Berkeley: University of California Press, 1992.

Weir, Todd. 'Between Colonial Violence and Socialist Worldview: The Conversions of Ernst Däumig'. *German History* 28 (2010): 143–66.

Werner, Yvonna Maria (ed.). *Christian Masculinity: Men and Religion in Northern Europe in the 19th and 20th Centuries.* Leuven: Leuven University Press, 2011.

Wilde, Charles. 'Acts of Faith: Muscular Christianity and Masculinity among the Gogodala of Papua New Guinea'. *Oceania* 75, 1 (September 2004): 32–48.

Wilson, Kathleen. *The Island Race: Englishness, Empire and Gender in the Eighteenth Century.* London: Routledge, 2003.

Wilson, Kathleen (ed.). *A New Imperial History: Culture, Identity and Modernity in Britain and the Empire, 1660–1840.* Cambridge: Cambridge University Press, 2004.

White, Christopher. 'A Measured Faith: Edwin Starbuck, William James, and the Scientific Reform of Religious Experience'. *The Harvard Theological Review* 101, 3/4 (2008): 431–50.

Wohlrab-Sahr, Monika. 'Conversion to Islam between Syncretism and Symbolic Battle'. *Social Compass* 46 (1999): 351–62.

Wohlrab-Sahr, Monika. *Konversionen zum Islam in Deutschland und den USA.* Frankfurt am Main, and New York: Campus, 1999.

Wohlrab-Sahr, Monika, Volkhard Krech and Hubert Knoblauch. 'Religiöse Bekehrung in soziologischer Perspektive: Themen, Schwerpunkte und Fragestellungen der gegenwärtigen religionssoziologischen Konversionsforschung'. In *Religiöse Konversion. Systematische und fallorientierte Studien in soziologischer Perspektive,* edited by Hubert Knoblauch, Volkhard Krech, and Monika Wohlrab-Sahr, 7–35. Konstanz: Universitätsverlag Konstanz, 1998.

Woollacott, Angela. *Gender and Empire.* Basingstoke: Palgrave Macmillan, 2006.

Worden, Nigel. *The Making of Modern South Africa,* 2nd edn. Oxford: Blackwell, 1995.

Index

Entries in bold type refer to illustrations